MEDIEVAL & ENGLISH & THEATRE

VOLUME FORTY-THREE (2021)

MEDIEVAL & ENGLISH & THEATRE

VOLUME FORTY-THREE (2021)

Executive Editor: Meg Twycross
General Editors: Sarah Carpenter, Elisabeth Dutton, & Gordon Kipling

D. S. BREWER

Medieval English Theatre is an international refereed journal publishing articles on medieval and early Tudor theatre and pageantry in all its aspects (not confined to England), together with articles and records of modern survivals or equivalents. Most issues are illustrated. Contributions to be considered for future volumes are welcomed: see end of this volume and website for further information:
<www.medievalenglishtheatre.co.uk>.

© *Medieval English Theatre* and contributors (2022)

All Rights Reserved. Except as permitted under current legislation, no part of this work may be photocopied, stored in a retrieval system, published, performed in public, adapted, broadcast, transmitted, recorded or reproduced in any form or by any means, without the prior permission of the copyright owner

First published 2022
D. S. Brewer, Cambridge

ISBN 978 1 84384 630 7
ISSN 0143-3784

D. S. Brewer is an imprint of Boydell & Brewer Ltd
PO Box 9, Woodbridge, Suffolk IP12 3DF, UK
and of Boydell & Brewer Inc.
668 Mt Hope Avenue, Rochester, NY 14620-2731
website: www.boydellandbrewer.com

A catalogue record for this title is available from the British Library

The publisher has no responsibility for the continued existence or accuracy of URLs for external or third-party internet websites referred to in this book, and does not guarantee that any content on such websites is, or will remain, accurate or appropriate

MEDIEVAL & ENGLISH & THEATRE

VOLUME FORTY-THREE (2021)

CONTENTS

List of Illustrations	vi
Note on Cover image and Online Links	vii
List of Common Abbreviations	viii
Editorial	1

Meg Twycross
　　The Prince of Peace and the Mummers: Richard II and the
　　Londoners' Visit of 1376/1377 … 3

Sarah Carpenter
　　Chivalric Entertainment at the Court of Henry IV: The
　　Jousting Letters of 1401 … 39

　　Appendix (*Meg Twycross and Philip Bennett*):
　　Transcription and Translation of BL MS Cotton Nero D II
　　fols 260^v–262^r … 80

Michael Pearce
　　'Maskerye claythis' for James VI and Anna of Denmark … 108

James H. Forse
　　Peers and Performers in the Reign of Henry VI … 124

Philip Butterworth
　　'That Gam Me Thoght Was Good!': Structuring Games into
　　Medieval English Plays … 191

Elisabeth Dutton
　　Feminism, Theatre, and Historical Fiction: Anna of Cleves in 2021 … 224

Editorial Board	237
Submission of Articles	238

ILLUSTRATIONS

Sarah Carpenter 'Chivalric Entertainment at the Court of Henry IV'

FIG. 1	The Meeting of Henry IV and Manuel II Palaeologus in 1400. *St Albans Chronicle.* Lambeth Palace Library MS 6 fol. 240^r.	53
FIG. 2	Sketch of the arms of Sir William Bardolf, Norfolk and Suffolk Roll. London: College of Arms, MS Vincent 164 fol.87^r.	60
FIG. 3	Two crests representing fire-breathing dragons. Wapenboek Gelre, Brussels: KBR MS 15652–56 pages 112 and 122, details.	66
FIG. 4	Design for a palfrey with a fantastic harness. Album Bellini Jacopo fol. 47^r. Paris: Louvre, Cabinet des Dessins.	69
FIG. 5	London: British Library Additional MS 74236, page 216.	79

Philip Butterworth 'That Gam Me Thoght Was Good!'

FIG. 1	'Dick Coming Up Full Bounce'. *Boy's Own Annual* 22 (1899–1900) 656.	203
FIG. 2	*Abobbed* played by young men. *The Romance of Alexander*, Oxford: Bodleian Library MS Bodley 264 fol. 130^r, detail.	206
FIG. 3	*Abobbed* played by young women. *The Romance of Alexander*, Oxford: Bodleian Library MS Bodley 264 fol. 130^v, detail.	206
FIG. 4	'Cock-Fighting' as played by school boys. From an unidentified boys' magazine c.1908.	216
FIG. 5	'A Trussed Fowl'. Dorothy Canfield and Others *What Shall We Do Now? Over Five Hundred Games and Pastimes* (New York: Stokes, 1907) 37.	217
FIG. 6	'Water Sports – The Seaside Regatta'. *The Boy's Own Paper* 31 (London: Boy's Own Paper Office, 1908–9) 649.	218

Full credit details are provided in the captions to the images in the text. The editors, contributors and publisher are grateful to all the institutions and persons for permission to reproduce the materials in which they hold copyright. Every effort has been made to trace the copyright holders; apologies are offered for any omission, and the publisher will be pleased to add any necessary acknowledgement in subsequent editions.

COVER IMAGE

The cover image is a detail from Paris: BNF MS français 2646, the *Chroniques* of Jean Froissart, fol. 92^v. This is the last of a four-volume set made in Bruges in the 1470s for Louis de Gruuthuse. It purports to be an illustration of the 1390 jousts held at Smithfield by Richard II: see Sarah Carpenter, 'Chivalric Entertainment at the Court of Henry IV' page 63 in this volume. The whole image combines the episode of the procession to the tournament (in the foreground) with a jousting scene before ladies in a stand (in the background). Each lady leads her knight by a coloured cord. The armour and the dress are in the style of the 1470s, not the 1390s.

This image can be found online at
<https://gallica.bnf.fr/ark:/12148/btv1b8438607b/f190.item>
and is used in compliance with the copyright rules of the Bibliothèque nationale de France.

ONLINE LINKS

An active list of all the URLs referred to in the current volume is posted on the METh website at <www.medievalenglishtheatre.co.uk/urlsvol43.html>. This enables the reader to view coloured images and link to video, besides giving access where possible to online texts and articles.

COMMON ABBREVIATIONS

AND	*Anglo-Norman Dictionary Online* edited William Rothwell, David Trotter, Geert De Wilde, and others, Aberystwyth University, 2005–ongoing <https://anglo-norman.net>.
CSPS	*Calendar of the State Papers Relating to Scotland and Mary, Queen of Scots, 1547–1603* edited Joseph Bain, 13 vols (Edinburgh: HM General Register House, 1898–1969).
DMLBS	*A Dictionary of Medieval Latin from British Sources* edited R.E. Latham, D.R. Howlett, and R.K. Ashdowne (British Academy: Oxford, 1975–2013); available online via subscribing libraries or from <http://logeion.uchicago.edu> (search by headword).
DOST	*A Dictionary of the Older Scottish Tongue* edited W. Craigie, A.J. Aitken, J.A.C. Stevenson, and M.G. Dareau, 12 vols (London: Oxford UP, [1937]–2002); online under *Dictionaries of the Scots Language* at <www.dsl.ac.uk>, ongoing.
EETS	*Early English Text Society*:
	OS Original Series
	ES Extra Series
	SS Special Series.
HMC	Historical Manuscripts Commission.
MED	*Middle English Dictionary*: online version © 2001, the Regents of the University of Michigan <https://quod-lib-umich-edu> available via subscribing libraries.
NRS	National Records of Scotland.
ODNB	*Oxford Dictionary of National Biography*: online version (Oxford UP, 2004–ongoing) at <www.oxforddnb.com/> available via subscribing libraries.
OED	*Oxford English Dictionary*: online version © 2019 Oxford UP <www.oed.com> available via subscribing libraries.
REED	*Records of Early English Drama*.
STS	*Scottish Text Society*.
TNA	The National Archives, Kew.

EDITORIAL

For its forty-third meeting, in 2021, the Medieval English Theatre Conference returned to its traditional spring slot, but was once again online as COVID continued to restrict travel. The event was hosted with efficiency and aplomb by Clare Egan at Lancaster University; the university's Northern Premodern Seminar also kindly sponsored the meeting. The day began with tributes from John McGavin and Elsa Strietman to Peter Happé, eminent scholar of early theatre and METh stalwart, whose loss is keenly felt by many of us. The papers that followed interpreted the Conference theme of 'Environments' in various ways: in a session on Biblical environments, Daisy Black considered who was 'the bigger ram' in relation to Towneley's masculinities, and Gillian Redfern discussed Chester's Mrs Noah; the international environments of Anna of Cleves were explored by Nadia van Pelt and Elisabeth Dutton; consideration of the natural environment was focused on snails, the appearance of which in *Thersites* (c.1537, attributed to Nicholas Udall) was discussed by Liz Oakley-Brown.

The digital environment, which we have all occupied for some time now, was exploited and explored in the afternoon sessions: complete with snail, *Thersites* was staged by the Beyond Shakespeare Company as a digital interlude, to great applause; then papers on medieval theatre in virtual spaces were presented by Jenna McKellips, director of an innovative Zoom adaptation of the Digby *Mary Magdalen*, and Beyond Shakespeare's Robert Crighton. As we cautiously but delightedly return to live theatre venues, it seems likely that we will also continue to take advantage of what virtual theatre, as developed by skilled practitioners, has to offer – including collaboration by actors across continents, recordings that can be used for research and teaching, and the capacity to reach new audiences. For METh, too, online meetings have allowed friends and colleagues from across the world to join our gatherings.

Some essays in the next issue of *Medieval English Theatre* will reflect in more depth on virtual performance environments; the essays in this present volume tend more towards the ludic and the royal. Four essays here consider medieval royal and noble patronage, and performance for or by kings and queens. Meg Twycross discusses the first descriptive record of a ceremonial mumming, in 1377 – an elaborate procession through London culminating in a disguised visit to present gifts to the young Prince

EDITORIAL

Richard, embedded in a game of dice. Sarah Carpenter explores chivalric entertainment at the court of Henry IV, focusing on the jousting letters of 1401 that proposed combats as part of the Christmas entertainment offered by the King to the visiting Emperor of Byzantium; Michael Pearce describes the *maskerie* of James VI and his wife Anna of Denmark, at the Scottish court; James Forse's analysis of archival data reveals a striking increase in payments to travelling performers sponsored by the nobility in the troubled reign of Henry VI. All four of these articles attend to the precise historical contexts of performance, and show the political work that royal and noble entertainments were designed to do. Dice appear again in Philip Butterworth's article, which explores the incorporation of ostensibly non-theatrical 'games' into theatrical 'plays': the games are given new meaning in their new contexts, just as jousts and dances are in royal entertainments. Finally, Elisabeth Dutton discusses the portrayal of Anna of Cleves in the 2017 hit musical *SIX*, in which the ludic and the royal come together as the wives of Henry VIII present their lives in a song contest: the musical and several modern novels draw on eye-witness accounts of Anna's first meeting with Henry VIII, a highly dramatic historical moment that obfuscates the roles of performer and spectator.

Two weeks after the 2021 METh meeting, the death of Prince Philip moved many for whom, regardless of their view of the monarchy, his sheer longevity had made him a familiar figure who would be missed; at the funeral the Queen, masked and solitary, was seen by some commentators to represent the nation in a new way, and the constraints imposed by the COVID pandemic on the funeral invited reflection on the modern performance of royalty. The essays presented here are not, of course, a response to these events; they are, however, narratives of historical spectacle and theatrical display for strategic royal purpose, and they draw attention to the importance of interpreting royal performance with careful attention to the nuances of historical context.

THE PRINCE OF PEACE AND THE MUMMERS:
Richard II and the Londoners' Visit of 1376/1377

Meg Twycross

This is an expansion of material which Sarah Carpenter and I treated briefly in *Masks and Masking*.[1] It shows how a folk custom can be adapted, overtly as a mini-drama, and covertly as a means of political negotiation. It also shows how context, expectations, and costume can between them create a message, a message the more powerful because, according to the 'rules' of the game, it is delivered in complete silence. Besides this, it raises salutary caveats about our modern expectations: that the ostensible message will be the same as the underlying one.

The story has been told several times by historians of folk custom, of London, and of Richard II.[2] Each group has their agenda and consequently their slant on what they see in it. As far as I know, no-one has attempted to put it in its wider context of the liturgical/festive season and its imaginative baggage, which provided the theme for another major performance piece in the same week, the Chancellor's speech at the Opening of Parliament – though this also has been treated separately.[3] The sequence and dating of these liturgical feasts and how they provided the setting for both the Parliament and the mumming, is an important part of the following discussion.

This is how it was reported. On the evening of Sunday 1 February 1377, a torch-lit cavalcade passed through the City of London via Cheapside, and crossed the river over London Bridge, making towards Kennington. There were 130 riders, *dégisement arrayés* ('dressed in costume'):

---

1   Meg Twycross and Sarah Carpenter *Masks and Masking in Medieval and Early Tudor England* (Aldershot: Ashgate, 2002) 151–8; see also chapters on 'Mumming' and 'Amorous Masking'.

2   In most detail by Anne Lancashire *London Civic Theatre* (Cambridge UP, 2002) 41–3, who also treats of the later mummings. Also Nigel Saul *Richard II* (New Haven and London: Yale UP, 1997) 21–2, who points briefly to the political message.

3   Saul *Richard II* 18–19; May McKisack *The Fourteenth Century* (Oxford: Clarendon Press, 1959) 395–6; Michael Bennett *Richard II and the Revolution of 1399* (Stroud: Sutton, 1999) 16–17 (both episodes).

Et en le premer comencement chivacherent xlviii come esquiers ount este, deux et deux ensemble, vestuz en cotes et cloches rouge de saye ou de sendelle et lour faces covertes od visers bien et avenablement faitz; et apres ces esquiers veindrent xlviii come chivalers ount este, bien arraiez en mesme la maner; et apres les chivalers vient une excellentment arraye et bien mounte come empereur ust este, et apres luy, par lespace de c pees vient une noblement arraie come une pape; et apres luy viendrent xxiiii come cardinalles / arraiez et apres les cardinalles viendrent viii ou x arraiez ode visers nayrs come deblers nyent amyables, apparauntz come legates ...[4]

And in the vanguard rode 48 as if they had been squires, two by two, dressed in tunics and cloaks of red say or sendal, and their faces covered with masks well and suitably made; and after these squires came 48 as if they were knights, well costumed in the same fashion; and after the knights came one person, excellently costumed and well mounted as if he had been an Emperor, and after him, at a distance of about 100 paces, came one person splendidly costumed as a Pope; and after him came 24 costumed like cardinals; and after the cardinals came 8 or 10 costumed with black masks like devils, distinctly unpleasant, seemingly as legates ...

This procession, which attracted a large audience, was accompanied *od graunt noys*[5] *de ministralcie, de trumpers et de nakers, des cormus et de chalmus et graunte plente des torches de cire illuminez* ('with a great sound of minstrelsy, of trumpeters and kettledrums, of bagpipes and shawms, and a great number of wax torches burning'). They were making for the Manor of Kennington, a residence of the recently deceased Black Prince, eldest son of King Edward III, where his widow Joan of Kent was staying with her ten-year-old son Richard, now the heir apparent. This is a journey of nearly three miles taking them, after they left the suburb of Southwark, through country roads in the January dark.

---

4 *The Anonimalle Chronicle 1333 to 1381 written at St Mary's Abbey, York* edited V.H. Galbraith (Manchester UP, 1970) 102–3. On the significance of the dating, see below pages 19–20.

5 A *noise* did not necessarily imply cacophony: *OED* sv *noise* †3. a. 'A pleasant or melodious sound. Obsolete', (b) 'A company of band of musicians'; *MED* sv *noise* 1 (f) 'the sound of a musical instrument'.

THE PRINCE OF PEACE AND THE MUMMERS

Kennington Manor was completely demolished in 1531 by Henry VIII and the materials used in the construction of Whitehall. However, it was excavated in 1965–8, so we can see the ghosts of the buildings in which the mumming was played out. The Black Prince had built a Great Hall roughly 88' long by 53' wide, raised about 6' above ground level. The nearest in size is John of Gaunt's 1390s Great Hall at Kenilworth, the remains of which still exist, and give some idea of the scale and magnificence.[6] At right angles to the Hall at the east was a building two or three storeys high and about 87' long by 34' wide, assumed to be the Great or Prince's Chamber of the records, a set of private rooms into which the nobility could retire, and from which the Prince, his mother, and their guests came into the Hall to meet the mummers.[7]

Visiting the Princess Joan and her son that night were her brother-in-law John of Gaunt, Duke of Lancaster, now the eldest surviving son of Edward III, 'and ye earles of Cambridge, Hertford, Warwick, and Suffolck, and many other lordes'.[8]

> *et quaunt ils furount venuz deinz le manoir, descenderent au pee et entrerent en la sale. Et tost apres le prince ovesqe sa meir et les autres seignours viendrent hors de la chaumbre en la sale et les ditz mummers les saluerent, monstrauntz une payre des dys sur une table pur iuer ovesqe le prince, le queux diz furount subtilement faitz issint qe come le prince ietast il deveroit gayner; et les ditz iuers et mummers metterount al prince troys iuels chescune apres autre, une pelit dor, une cupe dor et une anel dor; les queux le dit prince gayna a troys iettes come fust ordine; et apres ils metterount a la princes sa meir et al duk de Loncastre et as autres countz, a chescune de eux ane*

---

6 <www.heritagegateway.org.uk/Gateway/>. Enter 'Kenilworth The Great Hall and Strong Tower'; grid ref is: SP2779972270. For images, see <www.english-heritage.org.uk/visit/places/kenilworth-castle/history-and-stories/history/>.

7 For the excavation report with ground plans, see Dr Graham Dawson *The Black Prince's Palace at Kennington, Surrey* (Oxford: British Archaeological Reports 26, 1976). For a more general account, see H.M. Colvin, R. Allen Brown, and A.J. Taylor *The History of the King's Works Volume 2: the Middle Ages* (London: HMSO, 1963) 967–9; Anthony Emery *Greater Medieval Houses* 3 vols (Cambridge University Press, 2006) 3: 245–6, 247.

8 The slightly inaccurate translation is possibly by the sixteenth-century antiquarian John Stowe, possibly by Francis Thynne; London: British Library MS Harley 247 fol. 172ᵛ, quoted from Paul Reyher *Les Masques anglais* (Paris: Hachette, 1909) 499.

anelle dore et la meir et les seignours les gayneront. Et puis le prince fist porter le vine et beverount od graunt leeste, comaundauntz a les ministralles defair lour ministralcie; et comencerount de trumper et de naker et piper et le prince et les seignours daunceront dun part et les mummers dautre part par longe temps et puis beverount et pristrent conge et departirent devers Loundres.[9]

And when they [that is, the cavalcade] had come into the manor, they dismounted and entered into the hall; and immediately afterwards, the Prince with his mother and the other lords came out of the chamber into the hall, and the said mummers saluted them, showing a pair of dice upon a table to play with the Prince, which dice were subtly made, so that when the Prince cast, he would win. And the said players and mummers laid before the Prince three jewels, one after the other, the first a ball of gold, then a cup of gold, then a gold ring, which the said Prince won at three throws, as had been arranged beforehand; and after that they set before the Princess his mother, the Duke of Lancaster, and the other Earls, every one a gold ring, and the mother and the lords won them; and then the Prince caused wine to be brought, and they drank with great joy, commanding the minstrels to play; and the trumpets began to sound and other instruments to pipe, etc., and the Prince and the lords danced on the one side, and the mummers on the other a great while. And then they drank and took their leave, and so departed toward London.

The mysterious visitors were 'the commons of London', and their expedition was *pur moummere ledit prince* ('in order to mum the said Prince').[10]

Mumming

This was what late medieval England called a 'mumming', if a very elaborate one. It was not a 'Mummers' Play': the 'Here come I, St George' playlet is a rural confection of the eighteenth century at the earliest.[11] Mumming was a

---

9 *Anonimalle Chronicle* 102–3.

10 The punctuation in Galbraith's edition is misleading: *hommes degisement arrayes et bien mountez a chivalle pur moummere; le dit prince*; *Anonimalle Chronicle* 102.

11 See Thomas Pettitt '"This Man is Pyramus": A Pre-history of the English Mummers' Plays' *Medieval English Theatre* 22 (2000) 70–99.

midwinter folk custom, and largely an urban one. Essentially it was a house-visit custom of a type the British do not really have any more. Halloween trick-or-treaters, and the Scottish guisers, and possibly Christmas carollers are the nearest thing, but we tend to keep them on the doorstep, though they are (normally) let into the more public quasi-domestic spaces of pubs and hospitals. By tradition, in a house visit, the householder is obliged to give the visitors free access to his house, even if he does not know who they are. He must provide them with refreshment and some form of reward. In return for this they must provide entertainment, and leave, eventually, in good order – though the licence of the Christmas season may suggest a relaxed concept of what this entails.[12]

Mumming had a further distinctive and potentially dangerous ingredient:

> ... *ne nul voise pur mummer ne nul autre jeu jeuer oue visure ne en nulle autre estrange gise par quelle il ne poet estre connue sur peine denprisonement.*[13]

> ... nor shall anyone go around mumming or playing any other game with a mask or in any other strange fashion *by which he cannot be recognised* on pain of imprisonment.

It is a game where the player conceals his identity. This is done in a variety of ways: unfamiliar and/or shape-concealing costume; the abolition of the face, either with soot, flour, shoe-blacking, or a full-face mask; and the abolition of the voice, either by keeping complete silence, or by distorting it in such a way as to be unrecognizable. The word *mum* has been given a variety of etymologies, but in the fourteenth and fifteenth centuries English speakers connected it with *mum* meaning '(to be) silent', as in 'keep mum'.[14] The derivative *mumble* suggests a variant, the low-voiced muttering of someone in a full face-mask.

---

12   Twycross and Carpenter *Masks and Masking* chapter 4.
13   Guildhall Letter Book H, fol. 224[r]. All items from the manuscripts are summarized in *Calendar of Letter-Books Preserved among the Archives of the Corporation of the City of London at the Guildhall* edited Reginald Sharpe, 11 vols (London: J.E. Francis, 1899–1912), this one on 322. These quotations are from the original manuscript.
14   *Promptorium parvulorum* edited A.L. Mayhew *EETS ES 102* (1908) 296.

This might suggest that the original point of the game was to guess who the mummer really was. But in fourteenth-century London this did not seem to be the main point. Instead, it was focused on another, traditional, Christmas game. A much earlier London proclamation, of 14 December 1334, though it does not use the word *mum*, shows what this was:

> ... *nul homme ne aille en ceste feste de Noel oue compaignies desgisees ou fauvisages ou en autre maner as hostels des bons gentz de la citee pur juwer as dees mes chascun se face bien a ese en son hostel demeyne.*[15]

> ... no man shall go at this feast of Christmas with groups of people dressed up in false faces or in any other fashion to the houses of the good folks of the city in order to play at dice; but let everyone make himself at ease in his own home.

Despite many similar proclamations[16] and even in 1511 an Act of Parliament specifically forbidding the practice,[17] it was still lively enough for 'Mumming' to appear as a character 'with a Visor' and 'his boxe and his Dice' in Ben Jonson's 1616 *Masque of Christmas*. Here all Christmas's entourage are London apprentices, which suggests that it was a custom with staying power.[18] In England at the time, dice was a 'Christmas game' in the sense that at other times of the year it was in theory illegal, at least to apprentices and servants. The nobility continued to lose large sums at it all the year round.[19]

15 Guildhall Letter Book E, fol. 2ʳ.

16 Proclamations are recorded in the Guildhall Letter Books in London in 1352, 1372, 1376, 1380, 1383, 1404, 1405, 1417, 1418, 1437, and 1451 (when they mysteriously peter out). Also e.g. *The Maire of Bristowe is Kalendar* edited Lucy Toulmin Smith (Camden Society NS 5; London: 1872) 80–5; *REED: Newcastle upon Tyne* edited J.J. Anderson (Toronto UP, 1982) 24–6; *REED: Chester* edited Laurence Clopper, 2 vols (Toronto UP, 1979) *1* 56. See Ian Lancashire *Dramatic Texts and Records of Britain: a Chronological Topography to 1558* (Cambridge UP, 1984) #888, 890, 894, 897, 900, 903, 904, 909, 913, 915, 921, 922, 935, and 939.

17 *The Statutes of the Realm ... from original records (1101–1713)* edited by A. Luders and others, 10 vols (London: Dawsons of Pall Mall, 1810–28) *3* 30.

18 Ben Jonson *Christmas his Masque* in *Works* edited C.H. Herford, P. and E. Simpson, 11 vols (Oxford: Clarendon Press, 1925–52) 7 218–21, lines 56–8.

19 Specifically by a statute of 1461: 'And also that noo lorde, nor other persone of lower astate, condicion or degree, whatsoever he be, suffre any dicyng or pleiyng at the

There is no room here to go into all the ramifications of the custom, but it will be plain that it could potentially slide over the edge from being exciting and tantalizing to being very threatening. The householder had to let into his private space a group of people of whom he knew nothing. They tended to be young men, moving as a gang. They had drunk quite a lot of alcohol along the way. It was dark outside and candlelit inside. They were masked, and, unlike in other identity-concealing games, did not unmask. They demanded money, though under the pretence of a game of chance: it was generally understood that the dice would be weighted in their favour. House-visit customs have generally been *quêtes*: 'And we won't go until we've got it.' And this particular encounter-custom upset the normal balance between householder and visitor. Instead of playing by the host's rules, the mummers force the household to play by theirs. The rules of the game keep them in an uneasy equilibrium, but it is a power play, with an unspoken edge of aggression.

The authorities felt themselves justified in treating such customs with suspicion as a possible cloak for terrorism. The fact that the visitors were masked made this unnervingly possible, and later chroniclers claim at least two genuine attempts. In 1400 a group of Ricardian nobles 'purposed to falle on the kyng [*Henry IV*] sodeynly at Wyndesore undir the colour of mummeres in Cristmasse tyme',[20] and in 1415, Lollards were accused of

---

cardes within his hous, or elles where he may let it, of any of his servauntes or other, oute of the .xij. dayes of Cristmasse'; 'Edward IV: November 1461' in *Parliament Rolls of Medieval England* edited Chris Given-Wilson and others (Woodbridge: The Boydell Press, 2005) at <www.british-history.ac.uk/no-series/parliament-rolls-medieval/november-1461>. The view of it as a Christmas game was reinforced by the Statute of 1495: 'noon apprentice ne servaunt of husbondry, laborer ner servaunt artificer pley at the tables from the .x.th day of January next commyng ... ner at the tenys, closshe, dise, cardes, bowles ner any other unlaufull game in no wise out of Cristmas, and in Cristmas to pley oonly in the dwelling house of his maister or where the maister of any the seid servauntes is present'; <www.british-history.ac.uk/no-series/parliament-rolls-medieval/october-1495>. Earlier Acts (e.g. 1410) objected to these *jeues importunes* ('useless games') as a distraction from the statutory archery practice. For an entertaining introduction to 'Medieval Gambling' (with copious footnotes), see <www.susanhigginbotham.com/posts/medieval-gambling/>.

20 *John Capgrave's Abbreuiacion of Cronicles* edited Peter J. Lucas *EETS OS 285* (1983) 216. This however seems to be a later interpretation: Capgrave is using Walsingham, who merely says *sub simulatione ludorum natalitiorum* ('under the cover of Christmas games'); Thomas Walsingham *Historia anglicana* edited H.J. Riley *Rolls Series 28A* (1863) *2* 243. Froissart however says they had arranged a (Christmas) joust *at Oxford*,

planning 'a mommynge at Eltham, and undyr coloure of the mommynge to have dystryte [*destroyed*] the kyng [*Henry V*] and Hooly Chyrche'.²¹

So why did the 'commons of London' use this potentially threatening format to pay a late-Christmas visit to the young Prince Richard? 'Commons' here of course refers to the Mayor, Aldermen, and more influential businessmen rather than to the general mass of Londoners.

Ceremonial Mummings

With hindsight, we can see that this is the first recorded (not necessarily the chronological first) of many stylizations of the traditional mumming, a folk-custom which was turned into an art-form. The City of London seems to have taken it up, possibly because it was associated with the City rather than with the court, and used it as a format for ceremonial visits and gift-exchange between city guilds, and between city and court.²² Even later, they were adapted by the court itself for its own Christmas

---

but that the king, who was at Windsor, was warned and did not come; *Les chroniques de Sire Jean Froissart Tome 3* edited J.A.C. Buchon (Paris: Wattelier, 1867) 363–4; Book 4 ch. 80. Hall likewise says that this cover was not a mumming but a 'solempne iustes'; *Hall's Chronicle* (London: Johnson, 1809, reprint New York: AMS Press, 1965) 16; while Holinshed reports both Hall's version (the joust) and Walsingham's 'maske or mummerie'; Raphael Holinshed *Chronicles: Richard II 1398–1400, Henry IV and Henry V* (Oxford: Clarendon Press, 1923) *Henry IV* 17–21.

21 *Gregory's Chronicle* in *The Historical Collections of a Citizen of London in the Fifteenth Century* edited James Gairdner (Camden Society Series 2: 17; London: 1876) 108. This was the Acton conspiracy. There is no mention in the earlier chronicles of a disguise, or even that the assassination attempt took place at court, merely that the King was to celebrate Epiphany at Eltham. The conspirators, however, gathered in London: *Gesta Henrici Quinti* edited F. Taylor and J.S. Roskell (Oxford: Clarendon Press, 1975) 6–7, and Gregory seems to have assumed that the Twelfth Night festivities were to be the occasion.

The attempted assassination of king or duke under cover of a masquerade later becomes a common motif in Elizabethan and Jacobean revenge tragedy: see Inga-Stina Ewbank '"Those Pretty Devices": A Study of Masques in Plays' in *A Book of Masques in Honour of Allaryce Nicoll* edited T.B. Spencer and Stanley Wells (Cambridge UP, 1967) 437–47. Supervacuo in *The Revenger's Tragedy* declares 'A masque is treason's licence ... 'Tis murder's best face when a vizard's on' (Act 5 scene 1 lines 196–7).

22 See e.g. Meg Twycross and Elisabeth Dutton 'Lydgate's *Mumming for the Mercers of London*' in *The Medieval Merchant* edited Caroline Barron and Anne F. Sutton (Harlaxton Medieval Studies 24; Donington: Shaun Tyas, 2014) 310–49.

entertainments, as with Henry VIII's famous mumming to Cardinal Wolsey in the late 1520s.[23]

In the visit to Prince Richard we have all the traditional ingredients of the folk-custom mumming, but with a twist. It takes place at night in the Christmas season: not in the Twelve Days of Christmas, but the extended forty-day period which went up to 2 February, the Feast of the Purification.[24] The mummers are costumed – *degisement arrayés* – and masked. It is a house visit which summons down the master of the household with his guests from the private apartments to meet the visitors. The ten-year-old Richard must still have been feeling his way into the role of master, even with the benevolent supporting shadow of his mother behind him, after the death of his father the Black Prince the previous summer. Or perhaps by this time – six months is a long time in a ten-year-old's life – he was perfectly happy with it. The mummers challenge him to a game of dice; but this time the dice are weighted in the householder's favour 'so that when ye prince shold cast he shold winne'.[25] It is a graceful way of giving a New Year's present, implying that the boy-prince is the favourite of Fortune. The gift-giving is repeated to the other influential members of the court: 'the Princess his mother, the Duke of Lancaster, and the other Earls', each of whom 'wins' a gold ring. The Prince fulfils the obligations of hospitality by calling for wine, 'and they dronck with great ioye'. The mummers have brought other entertainment with them, the musicians, and they play, 'and ye prince and ye lordes danced on ye one side, and ye mummers on ye other a great while', in divided harmony, before a final toast, after which the mummers 'tooke their leaue, and so departed toward London'.

So what was going on, and why did the anonymous chronicler think it sufficiently important to record in his work?

It was clearly more than just a random house visit. The *Chronicle* describes it at the beginning as *une graunte desporte et solempnite*. It must have been heralded in advance: the other house guests at Kennington were not just casual guests of the Prince and his mother, but *furount illeoqes ovesqe luy pour vere la solempnite* ('were there with him to see the

---

23 Twycross and Carpenter *Masks and Masking* 166–8.
24 Lydgate's 'Mumming for the Goldsmiths' also took place on 2 February at night: Twycross and Dutton 'Lydgate's Mumming' 318; John Lydgate *Minor Poems Part II: Secular Poems* edited H.N. MacCracken EETS OS 192 (1934) 698.
25 Reyher *Les Masques anglais* 499.

entertainment', almost 'the ceremonial').[26] And the Londoners did not think that it came under their own blanket prohibition against mumming, which had been issued again for Christmas that year.[27] The scale alone, a cavalcade of 130 mummers, made it an official public event, which attracted many people out into Cheapside to see it.[28]

There were other costumed processions with which the Londoners had become familiar, and which were both themed and, interestingly, masked: Edward III's tournament cavalcades through London.[29] On Sunday 16 June 1331 (Edward was eighteen), for the *hastiludium* at Stepney, twenty-five knights were dressed in red and green with mantles embroidered with gold arrows. Their squires, over fifty of them, wore white with one green sleeve, the sleeves also embroidered with gold arrows. All were masked. They rode in procession to St Paul's, where the knights made offerings. Later that year, on 22 September, in Cheapside, the cavalcade of knights and squires was gorgeously costumed and wearing masks like Tartars. Each knight had on his right a lady who led him by a silver chain.[30] Other accounts of *hastiludia* imply that the contestants were disguised, but do not specifically link this to the processions, though this seems likely: in 1343, the home team apparently

---

26 *Anonimalle Chronicle* 102.

27 Letter Book H fol. liv: *Proclamacio q' nul voise ove visure ne faux visage* (undated), but for Christmas 1376; *Calendar of Letter-Books: H, 1375–1399* 54, online at <www.british-history.ac.uk/london-letter-books/volh/pp49–63>.

28 *Anonimalle Chronicle* 102: *parmy Chepe ove plusours gents le virent*.

29 We know most about them because they are recorded by the chroniclers. Civic processions may equally have been themed, but apart from the Fishmongers' parades of 1298 and 1313, we have no written evidence of them; for 1298, John Stow *A Survey of London. Reprinted From the Text of 1603* edited C.L. Kingsford, 2 vols (Oxford: Clarendon Press, 1908) *1* 95–6; for 1313, 'Annales Londonienses' in *Chronicles of the reigns of Edward I and Edward II* edited William Stubbs, 2 vols (Rolls Series 76; London: HMSO, 1882) *1* 220–1. The 1298 event had a fishy theme, with gilt sturgeons and salmons, and 64 horses disguised as luces (pikes); the 1313 procession featured a pageant ship. It is possible that there were others of the same kind: however, recorded mayoral and company events, together with the Midsummer Watch, seem to have concentrated visually on matching livery to give a sense of corporate solidarity.

30 'Annales Paulini de tempore Edwardi Secundi' in *Chronicles of the Reigns of Edward I and Edward II* 1 353–5.

fought as the Pope and twelve cardinals;[31] in 1359, celebrating the marriage of John of Gaunt and Blanche of Lancaster, the King, his four sons, and other nobles, jousted as the Mayor and twenty-four aldermen; in 1362, possibly to celebrate the marriage of the Black Prince and Joan of Kent, the defenders were the Seven Deadly Sins.[32]

Why exactly this last theme was chosen we shall never know; various suggestions have been made.[33] It is noticeable that the chroniclers never explain the significance of the impersonations; they merely describe the costumes. The audience were clearly expected to guess from their knowledge of Arthurian romance, love allegory, or current events. The previous Pope-and-cardinals motif, in 1343, is mentioned by the chronicler Adam Murimuth immediately after he copies a stiff series of royal letters to the newly elected (and French) Clement VI about the evils of papal nominations to English benefices; but again, the reader is left to make the connection, if any. It is not clear, either, why the home team decided to impersonate the current popular target of dislike, any more than why they should have decided to do the same for the Seven Deadly Sins.

The 1377 mumming procession is clearly in the same mode as the tournament ridings, even to the insistence on the number of knights and squires in matching red costumes. Would it evoke the same sense of riding to an encounter? And how does this fit in with the mumming format? The masks and the disguises belong to both, and the focus could easily be switched. Have we in fact got a game of two halves?

The characters of the procession appear to be making a political comment, which will become plain as we look at the agenda in Parliament. But it is clear that, once they arrive at their destination, this was not to

---

31 Adam Murimuth *Continuatio chronicarum* edited Edward Maunde Thompson (Rolls Series 93: London, HMSO, 1889) 146.

32 *Chronica Johannis de Reading et Anonymi Cantuariensis* edited James Tait (Manchester UP, 1914) 131, 151.

33 Sarah Carpenter suggests it was a wry joke at 'the pulpit commonplace that tournaments were a hotbed of all seven', *Masks and Masking* 116; Anthony Goodman that it was a provocative comment on the reactions to the marriage of the Black Prince and Joan of Kent; *Joan, the Fair Maid of Kent* (Woodbridge: The Boydell Press, 2017) 71; John of Reading does not interpret it, but the entry follows immediately after a discussion of the effects of the plague on morals as women became desperate at the loss of their men and even married their own brothers to safeguard inheritance; *Chronica* 130.

be the main point of the exercise. It looks as if we have a double-layered message, or rather two messages; not so much a 'hidden transcript'[34] as a change of direction. We need to look at both in turn.

The Political Context

Any major public theatrical event of this kind carried a political cargo, if only because it was one group of society drawing attention to itself and its values. A themed and costumed procession provided the opportunity to make a more pointed statement, though obliquely, and possibly less dangerously; it could always be claimed that the interpretation was in the mind of the beholder.

The ostensible message delivered by the characters and costumes in the procession is fairly easy to decipher. Parliament had just been assembled for the usual pressing reason; fund-raising. It was being asked to grant a poll tax (the first ever) in support of the expected resumption of hostilities with France. The reasons given for this explains something about the curious cast list of the Londoners' mumming. In his opening speech the Chancellor states that the King, by special request of the Pope, had condescended to a truce with France, under cover of which the French (treacherous as usual) had been arming for a resumption of hostilities. The implication is that the current Pope, Gregory XI né Pierre Roger de Beaufort, a Frenchman himself, had engineered the truce specifically to this end.

As we have seen, Parliament had other longstanding grievances against the Pope.[35] As nowadays, though with a different target, those grievances were centred on foreigners siphoning money out of the kingdom for

---

34 For the 'hidden transcript', see J.C. Scott *Domination and the Arts of Resistance: Hidden Transcripts* (New Haven and London: Yale University Press, 1990) for the concept. This has been applied to folk-drama by Max Harris in his work on Latin-American adoptions and adaptations of Spanish folk-customs: see Max Harris *Festivals of Aztecs, Moors, and Christians: Dramatisations of Reconquest in Spain and Mexico* (Austin: University of Texas Press, 2000).

35 Especially, as in 1343, to do with the papal monopoly on the appointment to benefices (papal provisions). These topics were introduced immediately after the Chancellor's speech by the King's Chamberlain, because they 'ought not to be put in the mouth of a prelate in this case because they concern our holy father the pope'; *Parliament Rolls* <www.british-history.ac.uk/no-series/parliament-rolls-medieval/january-1377> #13. See McKisack *Fourteenth Century* 272–95 for a succinct account of the problems.

what was seen as the enrichment of a rapacious alien bureaucracy. The Londoners, in common with the rest of the country, were decidedly anti-papal. It seems highly likely that the cortège was making a political statement. However, it would not be fitting to lampoon the Pope himself too obviously, so the satire is saved for the papal legates, Machiavellian brokers of a fake peace, caricatured by the diabolical black masks.[36]

Apart from this dig at papal diplomacy, the mumming on the surface of it is a purely complimentary fiction: the two highest-ranking figures in Christendom ride to pay homage to the young child whom circumstances have suddenly made a key figure. They are carefully described generically as *an* Emperor, *a* Pope. The flock of devilish legates are unsettling – the two scenarios, the satirical and the complimentary, do not map comfortably on each other – but the mock Emperor seems to be a wholly benign figure. There seems no particular reason to identify him with the current incumbent, Charles IV of Luxembourg (died 1378). Richard was to marry his daughter Anne in January 1382, but when the marriage was first proposed in 1377, it was rejected by his advisors.[37] The Emperor seems to have been drifting away from France, and after the Schism he supported the Italian Urban VI,[38] but at this time there does not appear to have been anything that would mark him out as a particular opponent of the French.

It does not therefore seem particularly pointed as a political message. The citizens express the current popular views about the untrustworthiness of Popes in general, and of this one in particular, given the nation from which he comes. The costumed figures seem to be no more nor less appropriate to the riding than the satirical caricature giants are to the Nice Festival of Flowers. They do not seem to have had particularly meaningful roles once they were in the Hall and the mumming proper was under way. Emperor and Pope may have thrown the dice, they may not; in either case, the chronicler does not mention them.

---

36 The Great Schism had not yet taken place. Gregory XI had moved from Avignon to Rome the previous week. The majority of cardinals, like the Pope, were French, and thus seen as potentially in league with the enemy.

37 Saul *Richard II* 83–4.

38 Saul *Richard II* 86–8. The marriage with Anne of Bohemia was not initially popular, however, and Richard was generally thought to have been able to do better for himself.

Once the disguised company has dismounted and been admitted into the hall, the game enters a new phase. The costumed procession is a display for its audience to observe. When the mummers meet the householders, the dynamic changes. It is now an encounter that engages both parties. The game of dice pushes the audience into becoming actors. A relationship, however strange and edgy, is being set up. Emotions – excitement, tension, competition – are stirred. But the predatory side of the traditional mumming is played down when it becomes clear that they are there to give rather than to grab. These mummers are conciliatory, friendly, even generous. This is a different kind of political statement from the standard satire of the procession. It suggests negotiation.

Richard, Gaunt and the Londoners

To understand what was involved, we have to look at the events of the preceding year, and how they affected everyone who was present at the mumming: Richard, his mother, his uncle John of Gaunt, and the Londoners themselves.

The year 1376/7 was the end and the beginning of an era. It was King Edward III's Jubilee year, the end of fifty years on the throne.[39] But his reign, once so golden, was disintegrating in uncertainty, suspicion, and political upheaval. He was clearly entering his last illness. His household was corrupt; his mistress, Alice Perrers, and her adherents were said to be feathering their nests while they could. A Parliament summoned for the end of April 1376,[40] and known popularly as 'the Good Parliament', refused the King further subsidies for the war with France until he removed her and her faction. Then, on 8 June 1376, Edward's eldest son and heir apparent, the Black Prince, died, and the agenda of the current Parliament collapsed.[41] Moreover, the succession came into question: Richard of Bordeaux, the Prince's son and Edward's grandson, was only nine years old. At best the country was looking forward to a long minority, and as the Wise Mouse says

---

39   He had succeeded his deposed father on 25 January 1326/7 at the age of 14. His coronation was on 1 February 1327, 50 years to the day to the probable date of the mumming.

40   28 April–6 July 1376.

41   According to Thomas Walsingham, *extincto Principe, extinctus est cum eo profecto Parliamenti præsentis effectus* – the death of the Prince also meant the death of the agenda of the current Parliament; *Historia anglicana 2* 231.

THE PRINCE OF PEACE AND THE MUMMERS

in *Piers Plowman*,[42] 'þere þe catte is a kitoun þe courte is ful elyng' – *Ve terre vbi puer rex est* (Ecclesiastes 10:18). The effective ruler of the kingdom was now John of Gaunt,[43] the King's oldest surviving son.

As for the Londoners, the events of 1376 had left them feeling edgy. Several prominent City magnates had been impeached for fraud in the Good Parliament. An internal power struggle had just forced through a major reorganization of the local electoral system. London was a quasi-independent entity, with jealously guarded chartered rights of self-determination. Relations with central government were tense. They were haunted by the fear that the King, or his deputy Gaunt, might make an excuse of internal dissension or disorder to remove these rights and 'take the City into his hand'.[44]

The City's nervousness focused on Gaunt. He was not a conciliatory character and tended to react violently if he thought the honour and prerogatives of the royal family, and of himself as its representative, were being called into question. London and he frequently fell out. Ugly rumours began to circulate round the city. Gaunt was planning to poison Prince Richard and take the crown for himself.[45] He was not in any case of royal

42   William Langland *Piers Plowman: The Prologue and Passus I–VII of the B.Text* edited J.A.W. Bennett (Oxford: Clarendon Press, 1972) Prologue line 190. It is suggested that this scene is directly about the events of this year and the Commons' attempts to bell the cat, or neutralize John of Gaunt's influence. The Wise Mouse is often identified with Peter de la Mare, the anti-corruption Speaker of the House of Commons in the 'Good Parliament' of summer 1376, who was had up before the Council in November 1376 and imprisoned in Nottingham Castle. He was still there at the time of the mumming. See *ODNB* sv *Mare, Sir Peter de la*. For a discussion of the Langland passage and its various interpretations, see Gwilym Dodd 'A Parliament full of rats? *Piers Plowman* and the Good Parliament of 1376' *Historical Research 79 #203* (February 2006) 21–49; online at <https://onlinelibrary.wiley.com/doi/full/10.1111/j.1468-2281.2005.00237.x>.

43   Walsingham *Historia anglicana* 322; ... *qui usque ad obitum Regis stetit regni gubernator et rector* ('who remained the governor and ruler of the realm up to the death of the King'). For some time it had seemed that he would be the legitimate heir, as the Black Prince was clearly ill, and his son too young to govern.

44   Ruth Bird *The Turbulent London of Richard II* (London: Longmans, Green, 1949) 23–6.

45   *Chronicon Angliae 1328–1388* edited E.M. Thompson *Rolls Series 64* (1874) 92. The *Chronicon Angliae* is deeply prejudiced against Gaunt and repeats all the slanders against him with gusto. These rumours came to a head after the date of the mumming, when Gaunt threatened the Bishop of London for his part in the trial of John Wycliffe.

blood, but the baby son of a Ghent butcher substituted by Queen Philippa when the real prince was overlain by his nurse, 'and that was why he favoured the Flemings two hundred times more than Englishmen'.[46] Strong pressure was brought to bear on the King to declare Richard Prince of Wales and heir apparent in his father's place. Eventually this was done in November 1376.[47]

Gaunt set about to neutralize both the work of the previous Parliament and the rumours of his disloyalty. A reactionary parliament (the 'Bad Parliament') was summoned for the New Year, to open on Tuesday 27 January 1376/7.[48] The Prince of Wales, now ten, presided from the throne as the King's deputy, and Gaunt went out of his way to demonstrate conspicuous loyalty to his brother's son:

> *Dux vero dominum principem plus aliis visus est honorare. Collocavit ergo eum in regia sede honorifice, et posuit verba sua in ore ejus.*[49]

> The Duke was seen to honour the Lord Prince more than anyone. For he placed him ceremoniously in the royal throne and placed his own [Gaunt's] words in his [Richard's] mouth.

For once he had scored a public relations coup. The chroniclers record immense popular enthusiasm for the golden boy who was soon to bring a fresh start to the kingdom.[50]

---

46   *Anonimalle Chronicle* 104–5.
47   Saul *Richard II* 17.
48   'Edward III: January 1377' in *Parliament Rolls* <www.british-history.ac.uk/no-series/parliament-rolls-medieval/january-1377>.
49   *Chronicon Angliae* 111. Gaunt himself had presided over the Good Parliament *vice* his ailing father and elder brother.
50   Later that year, everyone in the coronation parade was dressed in white, to emphasize Richard's innocence:
     > *Fuit igitur dies ille jocunditatis et laetitiae ... dies diu expectatus renovationis pacis et legum patriae, quae jam diu exulaverant, desidia Regis senis et avaritia obsecundantium sibi servorum ejus*
     > For that was the day of rejoicing and happiness ... the long-awaited day of the renewal of peace and the laws of the land, which the inertia of the aged King and the avarice of his parasitic servants had banished for so long.
     >   Walsingham *Historia Anglicana* 2 331.

The Opening of Parliament

This Parliament officially assembled on Tuesday 27 January, though the actual opening was prorogued until the following day as not all the delegates had arrived.[51] The Londoners' mumming was four days later, on Sunday 1 February. Previous discussions have followed Galbraith's edition in placing it a week earlier, on 25 January, but the *Anonimale Chronicle* says that it was *le dymaigne proschein avaunt la Purificacion de Nostre Dame a sayre et deinz noet* ('the next Sunday before the Purification of our Lady in the evening and at night'), Sexagesima Sunday.[52] That year, 2 February was a Monday, and *proschien avaunt* suggests 'immediately before'. The *Chronicle* situates the event generally *en celle temps*, after reporting the decisions on the poll tax, which suggests (but does not prove) that it was after the Opening of Parliament; the next item is on 11 February, when the King (Edward III) went on his last journey by barge through London to Sheen. The exact date does not seriously affect my argument, though the Londoners' visit seems more apt if it followed the opening ceremony which emphasized the role of the child Prince as his grandfather's successor in an unmistakably decisive way.

The speech opening Parliament by the Chancellor, Adam Houghton, Bishop of St David's,[53] reflects the prevailing mood, and may cast some light on the unspoken agenda of the mumming. It is a performance piece in its own right, though in a completely different mode from the silent masked dicing. In a way it is its obverse: verbal, explicit, hortatory. As a piece of image building it was superb, and it must have made a lasting and possibly disastrous psychological impression on the ten-year-old boy who was its subject.

This table shows the sequence of events, and adds one more crucial feature: Epiphany and its fortuitous importance to Richard himself.

---

51 *Parliament Rolls* <www.british-history.ac.uk/no-series/parliament-rolls-medieval/january-1377> #3.

52 *Anonimalle Chronicle* 102; C.R. Cheney *A Handbook of Dates* revised Michael Jones (Cambridge UP, 2000) 170. Galbraith gives 'January 25' in a footnote, and the previous version of this paper used that date, but 1 February seems more plausible.

53 The speech is reported in full in 'Edward III: January 1377' *Parliament Rolls* <www.british-history.ac.uk/no-series/parliament-rolls-medieval/january-1377>. It was in French, which was probably Richard's first language: he would have understood what it was saying.

TABLE 1: Sequence of Events

Tuesday 6 January: EPIPHANY	Birthday of Richard of Bordeaux
Sunday 25 January: Conversion of St Paul	51st regnal year of Edward III – Jubilee
Tuesday 27 January	Official Opening of Parliament
Wednesday 28 January	Actual Opening of Parliament: the Chancellor's speech
Sunday 1 February	Londoners' Mumming at Kennington
Monday 2 February: Purification of the Blessed Virgin Mary	Last day of festive season, Parliament in session

The Chancellor's address is a tour de force of its kind, contriving to interweave royal compliment and Parliamentary fund-raising with scriptural and liturgical exegesis. After an opening lamenting the absence of the King because of his serious illness, explained as *Quos diligo castigo* ('those whom I love, I chastise'),[54] and the over-optimistic reassurance that he has almost recovered, the Chancellor proceeds through a proof that God indeed loves the King, because, like the just man of Psalm 127,[55] he is surrounded by his sons and his sons' sons – *Et regardez, seignurs, si unqes nul roy Cristien ou autre seignur al monde eust si noble et graciouse dame a femme ou tielles filz come nostre seignur le roy ad euz, princes, ducs et autres.* ('And behold, Lords, if ever any Christian King or other Lord had so noble

---

54 Presented as if it were a biblical quotation. The nearest are Hebrews 12:6: *Quem enim diligit Dominus castigat: flagellat autem omnem filium quem recipit.* ('For whom the Lord loveth, he chastiseth; and he scourgeth every son whom he receiveth'; Douai-Rheims translation), and Revelation 3:19: *Ego quos amo arguo et castigo* ('Such as I love, I rebuke and chastise'); but the form suggests that Houghton is remembering a version from commentators, possibly Tertullian *De Patientia* ch. 11: *Ego, inquit, quos diligo, castigo;* <urn:cts:latinLit:stoa0275.stoa023.opp-lat1:11>.

55 Vulgate Psalm 127:3–4, 6 (AV 128):

3. Uxor tua sicut vitis abundans in lateribus domus tuae. Filii tui sicut novella olivarum in circuitu mensae tuae 4. ecce sic benedicetur homo qui timet Dominum ... 6. et videas filios filiorum tuorum. Pax super Israhel.
3. Thy wife as a fruitful vine, on the sides of thy house. Thy children as olive plants, round about thy table. 4. Behold, thus shall the man be blessed that feareth the Lord ... 6. And mayst thou see thy children's children, peace upon Israel.

Abundance of children was still being quoted on memorial tablets in the sixteenth century as a sign of God's especial favour.

and gracious a lady as his wife, or such sons as your Lord the King has had, Princes, Dukes, and others') – to the current manifestation of this: *Et nostre seignur le roi, Dieu graces, poet ore veer ycy le filz de son filz* ('And our Lord King, thanks be to God, can now here see the son of his son'). As the Psalm says (verse 6), *et videas filios filiorum tuorum. Pax super Israhel* ('And mayst thou see thy children's children, peace upon Israel'). Edward is thus doubly a just man and loved by God; and as a result the succession, it is implied, is secure. And now as witness to this, and a guarantee of 'peace upon Israel', Edward has sent his son's son to preside over them in Parliament.

Epiphanies

There is no room to go into the detail of what follows, but in the manner of a medieval sermon the speech interlaced several motifs. The liturgical season throughout January and just into the beginning of February is rich in feasts which can be worked into a common theme, and which would be vivid in the recent memory of everyone assembled for the parliament. Besides this, by a truly felicitous coincidence, Richard's recent birthday was on 6 January, the Feast of the Epiphany.[56] It had already attracted an aura of legend. The story is told that three kings, of Majorca, Armenia, and Castile, were present at the time in Bordeaux, where Richard was born, and gave him gifts.[57] It was the feast particularly devoted to kings, and Richard during his reign made the annual offering at the Mass of gold, frankincense, and myrrh,[58] a custom started by his grandfather and still followed today, though the

---

56   For Richard's attachment to the Feast of the Epiphany, see Shelagh Mitchell 'Richard II: Kingship and the Cult of Saints' in *The Regal Image of Richard II in the Wilton Diptych* edited Dillian Gordon, Lisa Monnas, and Caroline Elam (Studies in Medieval and Early Renaissance Art History 21; Coventry: Harvey Miller 1997) 115–24 at 122–4.

57   Saul *Richard II* 12. See on the likelihood of this tradition Michael Jones 'The Baptism of Richard of Bordeaux' at <https://m.facebook.com/TheGorgeousHistoryGeeks/posts/the-baptism-of-richard-of-bordeaux-the-future-richard-ii-and-the-three-magi-a-gu/1646486475449011/>. The *Chronica* of William Thorne of Canterbury gives the more impressive line-up of *iij. magi, scilicet rex Ispaniæ, rex Naverniæ, & rex Portugaliæ, qui quidem reges dederunt puero munera preciosa* ('three Magi, that is, the King of Spain, the King of Navarre, and the King of Portugal, which Kings gave the boy precious gifts'); *Historiæ anglicanæ scriptores X ... ex vetustis manuscriptis nunc primùm in lucem editi* edited Roger Twysden (London: Cornelius Bee, 1652) col. 2142.

58   Mitchell 'Kingship and the Cult of Saints' 123 and 314 notes 78–80.

Queen now does it by proxy.[59] The Parliament itself is associated in the chronicles with the Feast of the Purification, 2 February, which was on the following Monday.[60] The Chancellor links the two, and then draws in other references from the liturgical season, to focus on the theme of Epiphany: the early manifestations of Christ.

As is well known, the liturgical year had created its own selective narrative from the Bible in the sequence of Gospel readings from week to week and feast day to feast day. Moreover, in the Proper of the Mass and the Breviary, readings, psalms, chants, and prayers created a web of allusion and metaphor around the theme of that particular feast. The Chancellor's opening address is, as one would expect from a bishop, firmly in that tradition.

Epiphany means 'manifestation'. Originally in the East the feast on 6 January was held in honour of the Baptism of Christ, when

> 16 ... the heavens were opened to him: and he saw the spirit of God descending as a dove and coming upon him
>
> 17 And behold a voice from heaven, saying, This is my beloved Son, in whom I am well pleased.
>
> Matthew 3:16–17

But in the West, this was replaced by the celebration of the first manifestation of Christ to the Gentiles, that is, the Magi. The original connection with the Baptism (renamed the *Theophany*, the appearance of God) was displaced into the liturgy of the following Sunday, and of the Octave.

This seems to have set off a chain of epiphanies: on the next Sunday after the Octave, the Gospel tells of the twelve-year-old Christ in the Temple; and on the next Sunday, the Marriage at Cana, known as the *Bethphany*, or 'manifestation in the house'.

---

59 The Court Circular for 6 January 2021 reads 'Today being the Feast of the Epiphany, a Eucharist was held in the Chapel Royal, St. James's Palace, when the customary offerings of Gold, Frankincense and Myrrh were made on behalf of The Queen by the Reverend Canon Paul Wright (Sub-Dean of Her Majesty's Chapels Royal)'; <www.royal.uk/court-circular>. The Queen is usually now at Sandringham on that date.

60 Walsingham *Historia Anglicana* 2 323. Houghton's somewhat backhanded references to Edward III in relation to the Feast of the Conversion of St Paul (25 January, the day of the mumming) are not so relevant here.

TABLE 2: Gospels

Adoration of the Magi	Epiphany	Matthew 2:1–12
Baptism	Sunday within Octave and Octave of Epiphany	John 1:29–34
Christ & the Doctors	Sunday after Octave of Epiphany	Luke 2:42–52
The Marriage at Cana	Second Sunday after Epiphany	John 2:1–11

It was even believed by biblical commentators that three of these were anniversaries:

> Þe þrotteneth (*thirteenth*) day aftur hys burth, he wes schewod by þe offryng of þre kynges; and þat same day, nyne and twenty ȝer and þryttene dayes aftur, he was folwod (*baptized*) in þe watur of flom [*the river*] Iordan; and þat same day, twelmoneþ aftur, he turned watur into wyn at a weddyng in þe Cane of Galylee.[61]

The Feast of the Purification on 2 February was also in its way an epiphany: when Simeon recognized the Christ child as 'A light to lighten the Gentiles and the glory of thy people Israel' (Luke 2:32).

TABLE 3: Epiphanies in 1377

Adoration of the Magi	Epiphany [Richard's birthday]	6 January
Baptism	Sunday within Octave and Octave of Epiphany	11 & 13 January
Christ & the Doctors	Sunday after Octave of Epiphany	18 January
[Chancellor's speech]	[Richard presides over the Opening of Parliament]	[28 January]
Presentation of Christ in the Temple	Purification (Gospel: Luke 2:22–32)	2 February

The theme that emerges must have seemed almost miraculously relevant to the opening of this Parliament: the revelation of a wonder child, and his first active public appearance at the age of twelve (slightly anticipated

---

61 *John Mirk's Festial* edited Susan Powell, 2 vols *EETS OS 334* and *335* (2009 and 2011) 1 47; *De epiphania domini*.

here). Even the layout of the usual iconography of Christ and the Doctors must have seemed echoed in the Painted Chamber where Richard presided over Parliament, under the painted eye of Edward the Confessor.

It was certainly wonderful material for an opening address. Richard is presented as no less than a youthful Christ figure, sent by the King,

> *pur vous y conforter et joier de lui, par meisme la manere come l'escripture y parole, 'Hic est filius meus dilectus, hic est desideratus cunctis gentibus'.*

> so that you may take comfort from this and rejoice in him, in the same fashion as Scripture speaks about it: 'This is My beloved Son; this is He that is desired of all nations'.[62]

The heavens have opened, and the voice of God the Father speaks for Edward III.

Gifts and Taxation

Thus Parliament should do Richard honour by offering gifts:

> *par manere come les paiens, c'estassavoir les trois roys de Coloigne, firent al filz Dieux, qar ils luy offrerent or, mirre et encens ...*

> in the same way as the Gentiles, that is to say the Three Kings of Cologne, did to the Son of God, for they offered him gold, myrrh, and frankincense ...

The Chancellor briefly moralizes all three gifts in the traditional fashion, then declares his intention of applying the gold and myrrh to relations between the Prince and Parliament; but *del encens je voille lesser quant apresent* ('I wish to leave the incense to one side for the present'). For the gold:

---

62   Matthew 3: 17, Haggai 2: 8. The reading from Matthew is the Gospel for the Octave of the Epiphany, and the Baptism was thought to have taken place on the thirtieth anniversary of the Epiphany: Ludolphus of Saxony *Vita Jesu Christi* edited L.M. Rigollot, 3 vols (Paris and Brussels: 1878) *1* 88. John the Baptist became Richard's patron saint: see Wilson 'Kingship and the Cult of Saints' 119–22. See also note 74 below for the use of this part of the liturgy in Royal Entries.

THE PRINCE OF PEACE AND THE MUMMERS

Et vous deivez entendre qe la loy civil dit qe luy poeple en la venue de lour prince pur signe de joie et de confort deivent espandre et jecter moneie sur le poeple, q'ils le puissent coiller, et ent par tant estre joieuse et avoir leesce en lours coers. Et si deivez vous faire, nemye soulement sur le poeple, mais doivez a luy doner et offrer or en signifiance de fait, pur luy faire riche ...

And you should understand that the Civil Law says,[63] that the people at the coming of their Prince as a token of joy and comfort should scatter and cast money on the people,[64] so that they may gather it up, and by sharing it be joyful and have delight in their hearts. And so should you do, not only upon the people, but you should give and offer *him* gold, in token of the fact, to make him rich ...

All Richard's future behaviour seems to have been modelled on this expectation: it was his subjects' duty to make him rich.

Usually *largesse* is dispensed by the ruler to his subjects, especially to his heralds as a reward (their cry of 'Largesse' at a great occasion was the cue that they now expected to receive their fees).[65] The same word (it means 'generosity') was used of the general showering of coins 'cast amongst the comone people' in celebration at great events such as a royal wedding.[66]

---

63 I have not yet discovered where the Civil Law says this, if at all. It may be an allusion to the fact that the Law of Arms (determined in the Court of Chivalry) was considered to be a branch of the Civil, not the Common Law.

64 This sounds strangely repetitive. Perhaps the practice of Royal Entries, as described below, explains it. The second group of people sound like 'the common people'; possibly the first are just 'subjects' in general.

65 The number of occasions on which the heralds were to receive largesse are listed in detail by Francis Thynne, Lancaster Herald, in 'A Discourse of the Duty and Office of an Herald of Arms' in *A Collection of Curious Discourses Written by Eminent Antiquaries* edited Thomas Hearne, 2 vols (London: Benjamin White, 1775) 139–62 at 148–51. His earliest evidence is a document from the reign of Richard II. He mentions New Year as an occasion when 'all the noblemen and knights of the court did give new years gifts to the heralds, and out of that liberality the heralds did (and to this day do) give most of the officers of the king's house new years gifts' (150–1).

66 From the *'Narrative of the Marriage of Richard, Duke of York, and Ann of Norfolk, the Matrimonial Feast, and the Grand Justing, A.D. 1478'* in W.H. Black *Illustrations of Ancient State and Chivalry* (London: William Nicol, 1840) 25–40. Many thanks to Anne F. Sutton for this reference and for pointing out that the heralds also had their

In Royal Entries, however, the process is reversed, and the King becomes the apparent recipient – except that he cannot gather it up, and so the onlookers become the beneficiaries. In Richard's subsequent coronation parade through London, four damsels 'cast fake gold coins on the young king and his charger' as he passed beneath: *florenos aureos, sed sophisticos, super eum et ejus dextrarium projecerunt.*[67] We know these coins were made of 'tinsel' because they appear in the accounts of the Goldsmiths' Company, who were responsible for this particular pageant.[68] The audience might be expected to scramble to collect the gold scattered upon the King, though in this case it was not as profitable as it seemed.[69]

Myrrh is interpreted as silver, which needs refining before it is acceptable, as the hearers will be to their Prince when they have purged all rancour from their hearts – a not too subtle way of referring to the ill-feeling between Commons and King in the events surrounding the Good Parliament. Here the Bishop is drawing on the Lesson for the Purification, from the prophet Malachi 3:1–4, familiar to us, like many Advent and pre-Lenten quotations, from Handel's *Messiah*:

> *Et quis poterit cogitare diem adventus ejus? Et quid stabit ad videndum eum? Ipse enim quasi ignis conflans, et quasi herba fullonum: Et sedebit conflans et emundans argentum; et purgabit filios Levi. Et conflabit eos quasi aurum et quasi argentum, et erunt Domino offerentes sacrificia in justitia.*

> And who shall be able to think of the day of his coming? And who shall stand to see him? For he is like a refining fire, and like the fuller's herb.

---

largesse on this occasion. At some point in its history the general largesse was of specially-struck coins or *jetons*.

67 Walsingham *Historia anglicana* 2 331–2.
68 *Wardens' Accounts and Court Minute Books of the Goldsmiths' Mistery of London 1334–1446* edited Lisa Jefferson (Woodbridge: The Boydell Press, 2003) 178–9.
69 The illustration to the Suffrages of the Three Kings in the Hastings Hours (BL Additional MS 54782 fol. 43ʳ) shows two men, not apparently heralds, casting largesse upon a mixed company of 'the people'; <www.bl.uk/manuscripts/FullDisplay.aspx?ref=Add_MS_54782>. The suffrages that follow on fols 43ᵛ–44ᵛ ask for protection and prosperity on a journey; the silencing of his enemies and his triumph over them; and that God should pour the Gifts of the Holy Spirit upon the petitioner.

THE PRINCE OF PEACE AND THE MUMMERS

And he shall sit refining and cleansing the silver, and he shall purify the sons of Levi, and refine them as gold, and as silver, and they shall offer sacrifices to the Lord in justice.[70]

The Chancellor then moves to the Gospel for the Purification and urges his listeners that as Simeon held the Christ Child in his arms, so should they embrace the Prince in their hearts, 'he whom you have desired for so long and whom you now see with your eyes, saying, "Now lettest Thou Thy servant depart in peace, for, etc."' (Luke 2:29–32, the *Nunc dimittis*). Is this valedictory tone a reflection of the increasing certainty that the old King would not last much longer? And he picks up 'peace' to refer back to the reward of the just man with his wife and many children, who shall have *pax super Israhel*, 'Peace upon Israel':

Et issint vous avez ce qe l'escripture dist, 'Pacem super Israel', 'paix sur Israel', pur quel Israel est a entendu l'eritage de Dieu, q'est Engleterre. Qar je pense vraiement qe Dieux ne voussist unqes avoir honurez ceste terre par manere come il fist Israel, par grantes victories de lour enemys, s'il ne fust q'il l'ad choise pur son heritage. La quele paix nous doine Dieux.

And thus also you will have that which the Scripture says, '*Pacem super Israel*', 'peace upon Israel', because Israel is as much as to say, the inheritance of God, which is England. For I truly think, that God would not have wished to honour this land in the way in which he did Israel, by great victories over their enemies, if it were not that He had chosen it for his inheritance. Which peace may God give us.

The statement 'because Israel is as much as to say, the inheritance of God, which is England' reminds one very strongly of the expression of the same concepts – how many years later? – in the Wilton Diptych,[71] where England

---

70 The theme of refining and purifying, though appropriate to the Feast, also suggests the mood of Advent: *Excita, Domine, corda nostra ad praeparandas Unigeniti tui vias: ut per ejus adventum purificatis tibi mentibus servire mereamur* ('Stir up, O Lord, our hearts to prepare the way of Thy Only Begotten: that by His coming we may be accounted worthy to serve Thee with purified hearts'); Collect for Second Sunday in Advent.

71 The Diptych seems deliberately to echo the standard iconography of the Three Kings: except that here the young king has taken the lead. But there are other ambiguities in the Diptych, which curiously suggest that the artist saw Richard through the

becomes the heritage of the Virgin Mary. Fascinating though these parallels are, however, they take us too far from our theme, and like the Chancellor with the frankincense, *je voille lesser quant apresent*.

From one point of view the speech is merely an ingenious way of introducing the first ever poll tax. Officially, Parliament had been summoned, as it always was summoned, in order to grant the King a military subsidy. But the tax is presented, in line with Septuagesima, as a personal offering from a cleansed and contrite Parliament to a divine child. The offertory of gold and silver may appear to be a humdrum fiscal extortion, but it is given an almost sacramentary resonance.

Mumming and the Giving of Gifts

How does this fit in with the mumming? The contrived giving of three gifts may well be a graceful reference to the Prince's Epiphany birthday. It does not take much imagination to cast the Princess Joan, despite her interesting marital history,[72] in the role of 'Mary his mother'.[73] The gold objects (I have tried and failed make them fit a coherent scheme, though one could

same bifocals as the Chancellor's speech. Is Richard offering England to the Virgin, or receiving it from her? Is John the Baptist, whose role as the precursor of Christ was celebrated concurrently with the Epiphany, and can therefore comfortably accompany the Three Kings, presenting Richard to the Virgin while saying *Ecce agnus dei*? Why has Edward the Confessor, the old king, moved into the middle of the group, ahead of the middle-aged King, Edmund of East Anglia? The Confessor's feast-day was on 5 January, the day of his death, which was also the Eve of Epiphany: he also has a liturgical right to be there. But is he also standing in for his namesake, Richard's grandfather? Did Richard have problems with the mantle of Edward III, and is this a self-affirming statement of his patronage, so stressed by the Chancellor's speech? Was the whole of the rest of his reign lived in its shadow – or attempting to live up to its image?

72 See Goodman *Joan, the Fair Maid of Kent* chapter 3 'Bigamy'.

73 Joan was a great favourite with the Londoners, and intervened as peacemaker to reconcile them with the Duke after the trouble which broke out immediately after this, when Gaunt tried to protect Wycliffe when he was summoned to answer charges of heresy in St Paul's Cathedral. Gaunt tried to intervene, and threatened the Bishop of London with physical violence. The Londoners erupted and attempted to sack the Savoy; only the intervention of the Bishop stopped a major riot. Gaunt fled to Kennington, and took refuge with the Princess of Wales: *Chronicon Angliae* 118–24, Walsingham 2 325–6; *Anonimalle Chronicle* 103–4.

argue for one that referred to the coronation)[74] may have been intended to represent the loyal largesse alluded to in the Chancellor's speech: we have no means of telling. However, gold was linked through the gifts of the Magi with the acknowledgement of a King:

Significatur enim in Christo regia potestas per aurum, quod regi solvitur in tributum: nam aurum propter sui nobilitatem munus est regale, et ideo ostendit Puerum regem esse, et se illud decere ...[75]

For the royal power in Christ is signified by gold, which is paid to the king in tribute: for gold, because of its intrinsic nobility, is a gift for a king, and thus it demonstrates that the Child is a king, and that it is fitting for him,

and in this particular context it has an important symbolic function. Though disguised as a New Year's present, it appears to anticipate the inaugural gift ceremonies of a Royal Entry.[76] Richard as heir apparent was all too clearly about to become King in reality, and the Londoners are presenting pre-emptive fealty. That they expected a quid pro quo hardly needs saying.

---

74   As gifts of the Magi, it is tempting to identify the gold ball with the orb, and the cup with myrrh, but ingenuity is defeated trying to match the gold ring with frankincense. Similarly, the ring (Edward the Confessor's) and the orb suggest the Coronation ritual, but the cup does not. They were probably just masterpieces of goldsmithry. However in the Coronation banquet the Mayor claimed the right to serve the king with his gold cup and have the cup afterwards as a reward, and the citizens to 'serve the lords in the office of butler in aid of the chief butler'. Though the official finding was that the Chief Butler had this right, the king 'in consideration of the loyalty and aid of the citizens in times past decreed' that they should assist the Butler at the main banquet, and that after dinner when the king had retired to his chamber, the Mayor should serve him as requested and have the gold cup and ewer as reward; TNA C 54/217 m. 45, 'Proceedings at the King's Coronation, 23 June 1377', translated at <www.nationalarchives.gov.uk/education/resources/richard-ii/proceedings-at-the-kings-coronation-23-june-1377/>.

75   Ludolphus de Saxonia *Vita Jesu Christi* edited Rigollot 1: 93.

76   The first fully recorded English Royal Entry is the coronation procession of Richard through London a few months later: see Gordon Kipling *Enter the King* (Oxford UP, 1998) 117–24. He shows (116–25) how one *Adventus* theme also draws on this part of the liturgy, including the Baptism of Christ with the quotation from Matthew 13: 17. Was this already a well-known theme, or did the Chancellor's speech provide the imaginative impetus for the Entry?

A Not-so-hidden Transcript

This suggests that the main political significance of the mumming probably lies elsewhere than in the obvious surface allusions. Sarah Carpenter and I suggested in our book that its message lies not in the ostensible topical detail of the procession, or even in the Magi-inflected gift-giving, but in the narrative structure of the theatrical form itself.[77] This gives a very different and distinctly provocative slant on the dynamics of the power-play.

The traditional mumming is a visit from one autonomous group (the mummers) to another (the household).[78] Mounted with this magnificence and with these characters, the Londoners' mumming almost suggests a state visit from a foreign power. In the next century, the mumming scenario was developed in civic and courtly mummings into a full-scale embassy, with herald, interpreter, and formal gift-giving. It is interesting that the antiquarian John Stow, incorporating the description (he seems to have owned a version of the manuscript)[79] in his 1598 *Survey of London*, mistakes the significance of the papal legates, and says, 'as if they had been Legates from some forrain Princes'.[80]

Consciously or not, by using this fiction, the Londoners are asserting their independence. They offer their loyalty to the Prince of their own free will: he is London's choice. There is a political subtext to this far more disturbing than the overt and safe anti-papal one of the cavalcade. At times of crisis over the succession, the Londoners had assumed the not-quite-constitutional privilege of, if not choosing, at any rate confirming the choice of a king.[81] Their acclamation was a recognizable substitute for that of the

---

77 Twycross and Carpenter *Masks and Masking* 151–3.

78 It would thus come under Tom Pettitt's classification of an Encounter custom where the power lies with the initiator: see 'Protesting Inversions: Charivary as Folk Pageantry and Folk-Law' *Medieval English Theatre 21* (1999) 21–5.

79 See *Anonimalle Chronicle* v.

80 John Stow *Survey of London* edited Charles Kingsford, 2 vols (Oxford: Clarendon Press, 1908, reprinted 1971) *1* 96. Original edition 1603.

81 May McKisack 'London and the Succession to the Crown during the Middle Ages' in *Studies in Medieval History presented to F.M. Powicke* edited R.W. Hunt (Oxford: Clarendon Press, 1948) 76–89; also Caroline Barron *London in the Later Middle Ages: Government and People 1200–1500* (Oxford UP, 2004) 26–9.

THE PRINCE OF PEACE AND THE MUMMERS

commons of the nation as a whole. The sub-text may not quite be 'Miȝt of þe comunes made hym to regne',[82] but it comes near to it.[83]

It may only be that the Londoners were trying to acquire an ingenuous ally against what they saw as Gaunt's inveterate enmity, making friends with the kitten as an insurance against the cat. But the very fact that the mumming found its way into the *Anonimalle Chronicle* in such detail suggests that making this gesture at this point in this flamboyant way was seen as significant.

If it was meant to conciliate Gaunt, however, it does not seem to have worked. The next few weeks saw his relationship with the Londoners at rock bottom. He clashed with the Bishop of London over the trial of Wycliffe, who was his (Gaunt's) protégé, threatening the Bishop with arrest by Henry Percy, the Lord Marshal of England. When the Bishop pointed out that Percy's writ did not run in the City, Gaunt menaced him with physical violence. The Londoners then attacked the Duke's palace of the Savoy, threatening to cut off his head; and he fled by barge to Kennington, where he took refuge with Richard and Richard's mother, Joan. The Londoners then reversed the Duke's arms and nailed them up at St Paul's and Westminster, implying that he was a traitor, a gesture for which they had to make public reparation.[84] Tweaking the cat's tail[85] does not seem to have been a wise move.

The diplomacy seems to have been more successful with Richard. In the following months the Londoners went out of their way to stress the special relationship between themselves and the young heir apparent and then king. They emphasize the traditional idea that London is the

---

82 *Piers Plowman* B-Text Prologue 311.

83 Later Froissart claims that Henry IV became king because the Londoners supported him and sympathized with him and his family. When Henry discovers the 1399/1400 conspiracy, Froissart has the Mayor say, 'Nous vous avons fait roi; et demeurerez roi'; *Chroniques Tome 3* edited Buchon (Paris: Wattelier, 1867) 364; Book 4 ch. 80. But see Barron *London* 27.

84 *Anonimalle Chronicle* 103–6; Walsingham *Historia Anglicana* 324–6. See on the reversing of Gaunt's arms, Marcus Meer 'Reversed, defaced, replaced: late medieval London and the heraldic communication of discontent and protest' *Journal of Medieval History 45:5* (2019) 618–45, at <https://doi.org/10.1080/03044181.2019.1669211>.

85 Thanks to Andrew Prescott for this phrase.

king's 'Chamber', a safe haven (and, it is implied, a source of revenue).[86] Walsingham says that as soon as Edward III died, a deputation of civic dignitaries went to Kennington and asked

> *ex parte civium et civitatis Londoniensis, ut habeatis recommendatam erga vestram reverentiam, civitatem vestram, Cameram scilicet vestram, qui in proximo eritis noster Rex, quem solum Regem recognoscimus ...*[87]

> on behalf of the citizens and city of London, that you should hold in your Grace's regard your city, indeed your Chamber, since you will very soon be our King, whom we acknowledge as [our] only King ...

Richard in his turn enthusiastically took upon himself the role of Prince of Peace and pushed through a reconciliation between the City and Gaunt.[88] The *Chronicon Angliae* reports that Gaunt's followers ironically said that Richard was not King of England, but *Londiniarum rex*, 'King of the Londoners', because he had been chosen more by the common people and the citizens than by the nobles.[89]

It would of course be useful to know who the mummers were and if their particular attitudes to the succession (and towards Gaunt) might have affected the message we suspect they intended to convey. *Les comunes de Londres* is tantalizingly unspecific. Did the 130 riders include the mayor and aldermen? It seems unlikely that *comunes* implies 'the ordinary citizens', given the scale of the entertainment and the expense of the gifts. The Mayor was Adam Stable, mercer,[90] and the Sheriffs John Northampton, draper, and Robert Launde, goldsmith. Among the aldermen past and present were William Walworth, fishmonger, who was later to kill Wat Tyler; Nicholas Brembre and John Hadlee, grocers; John Philipot and John Organ, mercers:

---

86   See Christian Liddy 'The rhetoric of the royal chamber in late medieval London, York and Coventry' *Urban History 29: 3* (2002) 323–49. He points out that the Entry for the Reconciliation in 1392 plays on this theme.
87   *Historia anglicana* 2 329.
88   *Chronicon Angliae* 147–9. Gaunt is said to have exchanged the kiss of peace with the citizens in the presence of the King.
89   *Chronicon Angliae* 199–200.
90   He had not yet been replaced by Nicholas Brembre.

all important names in the history of London.[91] It would take too long to map their individual stories and attitudes to the events of 1376 and 1377, but they were not by any means all on the same side. One thing many of them had in common was that they were financiers who had lent considerable sums to the Crown. The golden gifts could well have suggested that they might continue to do this; but if so, it was an anonymous offer made without obligation by masked players.

One interesting thing as far as this investigation is concerned is that Hadlee and Organ were two of London's four MPs in the first Parliament of 1377.[92] They would thus have had an opportunity of hearing and reporting on the Chancellor's opening speech. It would probably not have had any direct effect on the theme of the visit, but it might have reinforced both sides' perception of its message.

Similarly it would be useful to know what reaction they might have expected from their audience. These individuals are easier to identify. They were all, not surprisingly, of Richard's father's generation. Gaunt and his abrasive relationship with the Londoners we have spoken about; and, glancingly, of the Princess Joan and her role as peacemaker. Edmund of Langley, Earl of Cambridge, was Edward III's fourth son, later (1385) to become Duke of York. Edmund was married, precariously, to Isabella of Castille, sister of John of Gaunt's wife Constance.[93] He does not seem to have been particularly involved politically at the time.

Of the earls, Thomas Beauchamp, Earl of Warwick, William Ufford, Earl of Suffolk, and Hugh Earl of Stafford, possibly identified as the Earl of Hertford, though the title was in abeyance,[94] were also brothers-in-law as well as brothers in arms. They were a family party, but also members of

---

91 For these men and their affiliations, see *ODNB* svv *Brembre, Sir Nicholas*; *Northampton (Comberton), John*; *Philipot, Sir John*; *Walworth, Sir William*; *History of Parliament* online under *Hadley, John (d.1410)*; *Organ, John (d.1392)*.

92 *Calendar of Letter-Books: H, 1375–1399* 55; online at <www.british-history.ac.uk/london-letter-books/volh/pp49–63>. The other two were 'commoners', William Venour and William Tonge. See *History of Parliament* online under *Tong, William (d.1389)*. 'Commoners' merely means 'not currently Aldermen'; it could include ex-Aldermen.

93 See *ODNB* sv *Edmund [Edmund of Langley], first duke of York*.

94 The title was subsumed under the Earldom of Gloucester, and had died out in the male line with Gilbert de Clare, Earl of Gloucester who had died at Bannockburn in 1314. It might then have been considered to have passed down in the female line to

the court whom the Londoners had reason to think were sympathetic to their concerns.[95] The supply of gold rings to be diced for implies that it was known they would be in the audience. This seems to suggest a variety of attitudes to the situation; but we do not have enough evidence to draw up a convincing scenario, or to say whether the gold rings were propitiatory or thanks for services rendered. In any case, the main focus of attention was the heir apparent.

Starting a Trend?

This is the first recorded mumming of its kind. However, after this on more than one occasion the 1377 gesture was repeated, and recorded by the chroniclers as if it were more than just an entertainment. At Christmas 1392/3, following up the dramatic Royal Entry of Reconciliation after an even worse crisis when Richard himself *had* 'taken the city into his hand' (they had refused to lend him any more money), the Londoners appear to have mounted a similarly lavish propitiatory visit, and presented the King and Queen with a live camel and what appears to have been a pelican. The following year, 1393/4, the King held his Christmas at Westminster, and the Londoners again came *diverso apparatu* ('with different kinds of show'), some dancing, some singing, and presented him with a cargo of spices from a pageant ship. The nature of these gifts raises all kinds of questions about the possible 'meaning' of the entertainments – Were they Epiphany-themed? Did they allude to the trade symbolism of the givers? How do we deduce thematic intention when we have no surviving evidence for it? – which will have to wait for another paper.

After that there were further recorded mummings in 1395/6, and in 1400/1401, the second regnal year of Henry IV. In the fifteenth century the records add the purely civic mummings at Company feasts to the still ongoing visits of the Londoners to the royal court. The most famous crop are those in the 1420s and 1430s for which Lydgate was asked to provide narratives;[96] clearly the obligation to remain silent when the entertainment

    Stafford, whose mother was the granddaughter of Gilbert de Clare. The title was not to be renewed till 1559, for Edward Seymour.
95 See *ODNB* svv *Beauchamp, Thomas, twelfth earl of Warwick*; *Ufford, William, second earl of Suffolk*; and *Stafford, Hugh, second earl of Stafford*.
96 See John Lydgate *Mummings and Entertainments* edited by Claire Sponsler (TEAMS Medieval English Texts; Kalamazoo: Medieval Institute Publications, 2010), online at

itself had become far more complex and pageant-like was proving frustrating.

Some Conclusions

Many of these conclusions are caveats about the scope of our knowledge. We do not know if the 1377 mumming was the first of its kind, or merely the first that was reported by the chroniclers.[97] Our sense that they were politically significant may be due to our dependence on what the written records tell us, which includes the fact that they are recorded at all. There may have been others which were completely successful as celebratory gift-givings, and much enjoyed at the time, but which have disappeared without trace. The Mercers' accounts for 1395/6 mention expenses for a mumming made to the King that year. It was a costly one: *Item, pur le expenses sur un mommer fait a nostre seigneur le Roy en cel an – vi li. xiii s. iiii d.* ('Item, for the expenses of a mumming made to our Lord the King in this year, £6 13s 4d'), but it does not get into the chronicles.[98]

Again, it is hard to say whether the chroniclers chose to record these entertainments because of their intrinsic political significance, or because they happened at a politically significant time. The 1400/1401 mumming made to the King (now Henry IV) at Eltham, which is also entered into the Mercers' Account Books,[99] is chronicled, because the Emperor Manuel II of Constantinople was present on a state visit. Again frustratingly, the only report we have of it is by a late-fifteenth-century chronicler, which says, 'men of London maden a gret mommyng to hym of xij aldermen and there sones, for whiche they hadde gret thanke'.[100] This sounds strangely like one of Lydgate's later 'mummings with a commentary', in which the twelve

---

<https://d.lib.rochester.edu/teams/publication/sponsler-lydgate-mummings-and-entertainments>. As the title suggests, it is difficult to draw a line between the mumming proper and similar entertainments, especially as we do not know from the texts themselves whether the dicing component took place. See also Twycross and Dutton 'Lydgate's Mumming' 310–49.

97   The phrase *pur moummer le dit prince* could suggest that this concept was familiar.
98   *Mercers' Account Books* edited Jefferson 110–11.
99   *Mercers' Account Books* edited Jefferson 154–5 (1400–1); *Item, ils ont receu del encres del collect pur le mommer fait al Roy a Eltham, outre touz costes – xxxvs iiiid.*
100 *A Chronicle of London, from 1089 to 1483* edited (?) Nicholas Harris Nicolas (London: Longman and others 1827) 87.

aldermen and their sons are characters rather than performers, but this may simply have been what the chronicler by this time expected it to be. We are left in the dark as to what the theme, if any, might have been; it does not on the face of it sound as if it referred to the Emperor. All we know is that it did not cost as much as expected; of the proceeds of the collection taken by the Mercers for its expenses, 35s 4d was left over.

Thus we do not know if by the late 1390s the mumming to the king had become an annual event, or if it was still seen as a one-off, to be deployed in moments of crisis or where there was a need for a special declaration of loyalty. Expenses for them do not on the whole get into City Company accounts, which suggests, as does the Mercers' taking of a collection in 1400, that they were not an accepted part of an annual budget, but an initiative by an interested group when the occasion seemed to call for it.

Then, since we are not privy to the discussions of the organizing committees, we have no first-hand evidence about why they chose particular scenarios or particular gifts; certainly nothing about what they intended them to 'mean'. Any interpretation will only be a best guess. We are lucky in that the Chancellor's speech (and its close proximity in time to the mumming) gives us clues about the official line on the tense situation in 1376/7, the presented solution (clarification about the identity and role of the heir apparent, thus deflecting some of the animosity away from Gaunt, however temporarily), some of the validating imagery which could be woven around it, and the optimistic attitude that the hearers were being asked to adopt. It makes our possible interpretation of the themes of the mumming seem plausible, but we cannot go further than that.

The format of the mumming that year was relatively simple and traditional. The gifts themselves were appropriate to the occasion, but do not seem to have been as personalized, or as outré, as in future years. Gold is a gift for a king, and always acceptable. It gained an added lustre from its Epiphany setting, and an enhanced significance from its biblical parallels. But overall, it seems that the focus was more on the fact that gifts were being given, and the ingenious way in which this was contrived, than on the exact nature of those gifts.

The fact that the rules of the game dictated that all this must take place in silence and in masks is both liberating and unsettling. It is both known and not known who the mysterious visitors are. The messages being exchanged are tacit but open to interpretation. Assumptions can be made but equally they can be denied. No obligations are entered into, even if they are implied.

Even the weighted dice are ambiguous. The mummers offer a competition, but one in which the outcome is rigged to favour the opposition. The normal rules of society are temporarily suspended for the time and space of the event.

In practice, everyone knew who the visitors were, as a body if not individually.[101] The surprise visit was not a surprise. The householder and his guests were of course identifiable. But the masked anonymity and the theatrical assumption of authority give the visitors an equality they would not have had in real life, 'as if they had been Legates from some forrain Princes'.[102] In later mummings, like those of Lydgate, it was read, fictionally, as an ambassadorial status.

It was fairly clear in this case what the embassy was about. It was to be repeated *in propria persona* when the Londoners heard of the death of Edward III and sent a deputation to Kennington to assure Richard, this time in duly submissive form, of their allegiance and their desire that he should reconcile them with the Duke of Lancaster. Richard and his Council replied positively, and the Londoners returned rejoicing to pass on the message to their fellow citizens.[103] It seems reasonable to believe that the ground had been already prepared by the mumming. Even though this theatricalized version was on the surface merely a diversion offered to the Court by the City, it provided a format in which two different strata of society or indeed two different centres of power might engage in some serious if tacit negotiation, festively – no offence in the world – but on level terms.

Lancaster University

Acknowledgements

An earlier version of this paper was published in German as 'Der Prinz des Friedens und die *Mummers*' in *Theater und Fest in Europa: Perspektiven von Identität und Gemeinschaft* edited Erika Fischer-Lichte, Matthias Warstat,

---

101 It is actually much more difficult than one might think to tell who a person in a mask is, if they do not speak and are in costume. Those who were at the Medieval English Theatre meeting in York in 1998 will remember how the entire company failed to recognize Peter Happé in mummer's disguise, though they all knew him well and had spent the day in his company.
102 Stow *Survey of London* 1 96.
103 Walsingham *Historia Anglicana* 329–30.

and Anna Littmann (Tübingen and Basel: Francke, 2012). Since then, more evidence has come to light, and the experience of being involved in two recreations of mummings, one ceremonial and civic (see Twycross and Dutton 'Lydgate's Mumming'), and one domestic ('Lucy Worsley's A Merry Tudor Christmas': BBC2, 24 December 2019), has provided me with more insights and raised more questions. Very many thanks to Prof. Dr. Fischer-Lichte for her support and to Francke Verlag for confirming the contractual position. Very many thanks also to Andrew Prescott for his help and suggestions; and to Sarah Carpenter for her guidance, and suggesting tactfully that I postpone the camels to a later date.

CHIVALRIC ENTERTAINMENT AT THE COURT OF HENRY IV: The Jousting Letters of 1401

Sarah Carpenter

Phebus la principall planet du ffirmament. A tresexcellent Princesse Dame Blanche ffile au trespuissa[nt] Prince Roy Dalbion saluz & tresparfaite dileccion.[1]

Phoebus, the principal planet of the firmament, to the right excellent Princess Lady Blanche, daughter of the most mighty Prince, the King of Albion, greeting and sincere affection.

This greeting opens the first of a series of vivid imaginative letters initiating jousts for the 1401 New Year's Day celebrations at Eltham Palace. The combats proposed formed part of the spectacular Christmas entertainment offered by Henry IV to the visiting Emperor of Byzantium, Manuel II Palaeologus. The thirteen letters are miniature fictions, written in the court language of Insular French, acting in some sense as a script and storybook for the performance; they not only help us to understand what was staged, but also give insight into some of the complex ways in which chivalric performance could be deployed in late medieval courtly culture. The princess to whom the letters were addressed was the King's eight-year-old daughter Blanche, who, since Henry was at that time a widower, was acting as the lady of the jousts. In each letter, an imaginary patron – a God or Goddess, an allegorical Virtue, or mythological figure – recommends a worthy young combatant to a match in a joust with a member of Blanche's court. As theatrical texts for the entertainment, they suggest that it combined martial arts with theatrical role-play, spectacle and celebration, political compliment and ceremonial festive gift-giving.

---

[1] BL Cotton MS Nero D II fol. 260ᵛ; images online at <www.bl.uk/manuscripts/FullDisplay.aspx?ref=Cotton_MS_Nero_D_II>. Unless otherwise indicated, quotations from the letters are taken from this manuscript.

SARAH CARPENTER

The Letters

The original manuscript copies of the letters themselves do not appear to have survived in court records, but it is clear that they soon attracted heraldic attention: over the next century they were copied in at least six known manuscripts, all collections of material associated with officers of arms.[2] At least three of them are in early-fifteenth-century hands, and there are suggestions in the British Library catalogue that one of these, Additional MS 34801, may have been, as Sydney Anglo reports, 'written in the time of, and possibly for, John Mowbray, Earl Marshal 1405'.[3] Although the letters have been acknowledged by historians of heraldry and tournament for some time, they have had very little close attention.[4] Anglo, however, did point out that they 'constitute perhaps the earliest surviving fanciful challenges for an English tournament and suggest a fourteenth-century allegorical tradition of which practically all traces have disappeared'.[5] The

---

2   Until recently, five manuscripts of these letters have been known: London: College of Arms MS Arundel xxvi fols 33^r–40^v, and MS L 6 fols 145^v–150^v; London: British Library Cotton MS Nero D II fols 260^v–262^r, and Additional MS 34801 fols 36^r–42^v; Oxford: Bodleian Library MS Douce 271 fols 40^r–47^r. A sixth copy has now been located in Edinburgh: National Library of Scotland Adv. MS 32.6.9 fols 63^v–69^v.

3   Sydney Anglo 'Financial and Heraldic Records of the English Tournament' *Journal of the Society of Archivists 2* (1962) 183–95 at 189. The copy in Cotton MS Nero D II is in a group signed 'Je suis a Clarencieux Roy darmes'. College of Arms MS Arundel 26 contains signatures of John Writhe and Thomas Wriothesley, Garter Kings of Arms under Henry VII and Henry VIII, while MS L 6 was owned by William Jenyns, Lancaster Herald under Henry VIII. Bodleian MS Douce 271 contains signatures of two early sixteenth-century officers: Thomas Wriothesley, York Herald, and Christopher Barker, Norroy Herald. The NLS Adv. MS 32.6.9 is bound with a holograph copy of the 'Names and Armes of the Earles Marshalls of Englande' by Francis Thynne (antiquarian and Lancaster Herald from 1602); it also contains the signature of Thomas Ridley, a civil and ecclesiastical lawyer and contemporary of Thynne's, who appears to have connections with officers of arms.

4   The letters are discussed by Mary Anne Everett Green *Lives of the Princesses of England: From the Norman Conquest* 6 vols (London: H. Colburn, 1849–55) *3* 315; Dietrich Sandberger *Studien Über Das Rittertum in England, Vornehmlich Während Des 14 Jahrhundert* (Historische Studien; Berlin: E. Ebering, 1937) 70–4; Anglo 'Financial and Heraldic Records'; Juliet Barker *The Tournament in England, 1100–1400* (Woodbridge: The Boydell Press, 1986) 97–8. John Priestley provides a translation from the copy in Bodleian Library MS Douce 271, in *Eltham Palace* (Chichester: Phillimore, 2008) 133–8.

5   Anglo 'Financial and Heraldic Records' 188–9.

recent discovery of a set of five similar letters, written for events at the court of Edward III and dating probably from around 1357–62, has confirmed this fourteenth-century tradition.[6] The earlier letters are closely related to the 1401 collection in genre, but differ from them in various subtle ways. In their similarities and differences the two groups can throw revealing light on each other, and comparisons between them will inform the discussion of Henry IV's letters presented here.

Internal references in the 1401 letters pinpoint the date and event for which they were written. In particular, Letter 4 from Dalida, Sultan of Babylon and King of Alexandria, reports:

> *le Roy vostre pier . a cest feste de Noell tient moult solennell & loable Court & tant solennell quil a en sa Court vne Emperour & tresgrande Renommee de nobles Dames & damoiselles vaillans Chiualers & Escuiers.*
>
> fol. 261ʳ

> the King your father at this feast of Christmas is holding a most magnificent and praiseworthy Court, so magnificent that there is in his court an Emperor and a most famous company of noble ladies and maidens, valiant knights and squires.

Letter 6, from Vertu, 'mother and nurse of honour', expands:

> *nous est a entendre que deux dez plus excellent Princez de tout Crestientie sont a vostre hault & honneurable feste ce sont a ce que nous somez certiffiez le tresnoble Emperour de Constantinople & le trespuissant Prince Roy Dalbion & de Gaule.*
>
> fol. 261ᵛ

> we have been given to understand that two of the most excellent Princes of all Christendom are at your high and noble feast, who are as we have been informed the right noble Emperor of Constantinople and the most mighty Prince, King of Albion and Gaul.

Letter 7 refers to the joust being held *ycest premier Jour de lan en vostre sale* ('on this first day of the year in your hall'). Since we know from a variety

---

[6] For an edition and discussion of these earlier letters, see Philip E. Bennett, Sarah Carpenter, and Louise Gardiner 'Chivalric Games at the Court of Edward III: The Jousting Letters of EUL MS 183' *Medium Ævum* 87:2 (2018) 304–42.

of contemporary letters and observations that Manuel was entertained by Henry at Eltham over the Christmas period 1400/1401, this clearly identifies the occasion of the jousts, which is important enough to be celebrated within the letters themselves.[7]

Genre

The two groups of jousting letters between them enable us to establish a framework for their literary-heraldic genre, while also illustrating their differences of tone and purpose. All are written as if from imaginary exotic figures. In the Edward III group these are all fictional queens or ladies (e.g. 'Niolas, noble Queen of Nubia', 'Pantesilia, powerful Queen of Persia, of Femenye'). The 1401 letters are from more varied writers: a few are unidentified, but there are classical queens ('Cleopatra, Queen of Mesopotamia' or 'Penolese [Penelope], wife of the most noble Prince Ulysses') and allegorical female personifications ('Jeunesce [Youth], Queen of joy and of all pleasures', 'Naturo, nurse of life', and 'Vertu, mother and nurse of honour'). There are also both male and female planet deities ('Phoebus, principal planet of the firmament' as well as 'Venus, mother of Cupid'), and what is perhaps the key letter, addressing most directly the visit of the Emperor and the spectacles he will see, comes from another Eastern potentate: 'Dalida, Sultan of Babylon and King of Alexandria'.

Each letter congratulates the lady of the joust in reverent and affectionate courtly terms, and recommends a worthy combatant to her attention. Often, the supposed youth and inexperience of the jouster is emphasized, with the purpose of the challenge *pour apprendre le fait desbatement darmes* ('to learn the practice of the recreation of arms').[8] The court itself is

---

7   Donald M. Nicol 'A Byzantine Emperor in England: Manuel II's Visit to London in 1400–01' *University of Birmingham Historical Journal* 12 (1970) 204–25. Nicol apparently was not aware of the jousting letters, but gives details of contemporary records of the visit.

8   This seems to have been relatively standard and does not need to be taken too literally. Henry IV himself, while still Earl of Derby and a rising star of European chivalry, was recommended by his father, John of Gaunt, to the famous tournament at St-Inglevert in 1390 in similar terms. Boucicaut, one of the initiators of the joust, records that John of Gaunt: *escrivit que il luy envoyoit son fils pour apprendre de luy. Car il le sçavoit un tres-vaillant Chevalier* ('wrote that he was sending his son to learn from him [i.e. Boucicaut]. Since he knew him as a most valiant knight'); see *Mémoires ou livre des faits du bon messire Jean Le Maingre, dit Boucicaut, maréchal de France*

characterized as a place of romance splendour: in the Edward III letters it is referred to as the *Aventerouse Roiaume jadys al Roy Arthur ... la sourse et fontaigne d'amour et d'armes* ('the Adventurous Kingdom, in ancient days the kingdom of King Arthur ... the source and fountain of love and arms'), while in 1401 *la clarte du monde prennent nourriture & liesce de vostre Court Royall / comme de la vostre droit fontain donneure & de noblesce* ('the radiance of the world takes nourishment and joy from your royal Court, as from your true well-spring of honour and noblesse').[9] The combatants are sometimes given romance names which resonate with this and intensify the fictional setting of the jousts, although it is also clear that they are generally intended to be recognized and identifying details of their personal arms or history may be included, blurring together the real and the imaginary in the combat event. Following the format of more serious challenges, both sets of letters then go on to lay down the rules of the particular encounter, specifying how many runs should be made, and the type of lance and saddle to be used. The 1401 letters generally identify *bassez sellez* ('low saddles') or *haultez sellez* ('high saddles') and *coupes de lance auecques Rochez dassise sans ester liez ou attachiez* ('blows of the prescribed rebated lance, without being tied or secured [in the saddle]'); these seem to be common indications of 'jousts of peace' that aim to avoid serious injury.[10]

These defining features are shared across all the letters, but in emphasis, tone, and elaboration the two groups have some significant differences. The Edward III letters appear to be developed rather more briefly and playfully, for a relatively close-knit court community of jousters, patrons, and spectators. A stronger feminine voice plays through them, as imaginary women rulers address real adult ladies (most often Queen Philippa). These female voices are presented, in E. Jane Burns's terms, as guiding and even controlling the chivalric identities of their protégés.[11] Although framed in terms of romance fantasy, the emphasis of these earlier letters is more on

[edited Th. Godefroy] in *Collection Universelle des Mémoires Particuliers Relatif à l'Histoire de France Tome 6* (London and Paris: n.p., 1785) 69.

9   Letter 1, on fol. 260^v.

10 For discussion of this equipment, see Barker *The Tournament in England* 171-3, 178-9.

11 See E. Jane Burns 'Performing Courtliness' in *The Oxford Handbook of Women and Gender in Medieval Europe* edited J. Bennett and R. Karras (Oxford UP, 2013) 396-408 at 401.

a sometimes teasing recognition of the real identities of the combatants. And alongside their delight in affirming courtly status through magnificent display, even inextricable from it, is an intimate, jocular, and self-mocking, at times outspokenly bawdy, humour. The letters overall seem to be addressed to the elite closed community of the court; they rely on an audience who can recognize their allusions and share comfortably in their private jests.[12]

If we probe the rhetoric and the references of the 1401 letters, we find a rather different tone. Although still playfully imaginary, they are more formally developed and more elaborated. The senders' titles and greetings are expressed in more fulsome terms, drawing on more extended literary or learned decorative allusions. Naturo,[13] for example, opens her letter of recommendation:

> *Naturo Nourice de vie executeur du tout puissant Roi dez Royz / A tresexcellent Princesse Dame &c ffille au trespuissant Prince Roi Dalbion salut & tresparfite dileccion. Nous qui ordonnons a homme & best leurs viures selon le hault commaundement du creatour de tous creatures / sauons de certain que ainsi comme nostre subgiet Priapus qui est dieu de Jardins derbes & de ffleurs renouuell & refressh la face de la terre en la noble season Daurill qui estoit poure & sans vestur par limportable yver qui est le Roi de ffroidur Region & trace par entre la terre si reprent sa conjointur & subtill mantell plain de dulceur & de fflours / Droit ainsi toutz estaz du monde viuans attendans honneur sont vestuz & aournez de vertueuse science par gracious gouuernaunce & contenement de vostre excellent noble cuer Roial comme de vray mireur & exemplair de tout honneur bontie & gentillesce*
>
> Letter 5, fol. 261^r

Nature, Nurse of life, Vicegerent of the all-powerful King of Kings, to the right excellent Princess Lady [Blanche] et cetera daughter to the most mighty Prince, King of Albion, greeting and sincere affection. We who ordain to man and beast their existence, according to the high commandment of the Creator of all creatures, know for certain that, just as our subject Priapus, who is god of gardens, plants, and

---

12 For fuller discussion of these letters see Bennett, Carpenter, and Gardiner 'Chivalric Games'.

13 We would expect this writer to be the familiar personification *Natura*, but all the manuscripts consulted clearly give the name as *Naturo*.

flowers, renews and refreshes the face of the earth in the noble month of April (which had been poor and naked because of the unbearable Winter who is the King of the region of Cold) and leaves its trace over all the earth, and puts back on its robe and delicate cloak full of soft mildness and flowers, in the very same way all estates of the living world aspiring to honour are clothed and adorned with the knowledge of virtue by means of the gracious authority and guidance of your excellent and noble royal heart, as from the true mirror and model of all honour, goodness, and nobility.

The high courtesy, and extended echoes of poetic spring openings and dream visions, establish the literary status and mode of the letter, apparently addressed to a somewhat more formal audience and occasion than the earlier missives.

The recommended challengers of the 1401 letters are also more likely to be given names resonant of romance or allegory: Launcelot de Libie, Ferumbras, or *Ardent Desir*.[14] Many of these names seem to be invented (e.g. Ferrant de Ferrers, Thoret de Tollide), or to be loosely allegorical (e.g. *Joefne le Amereuz* ['Young Lover'], *Voulente Dapprendre* ['Desire to Learn']). Those given names of characters from known romances (Palamides, Ferumbras/ Fierabras) do not appear to be directly enacting the roles of these heroes: the names seem designed to evoke a romance world rather than particular tales.[15] But unlike the Edward III letters, several of the young jousters in

---

14 *Ardent Desir* is an allegorical quality regularly appearing in poems of Christine de Pisan and Alain Chartier, and a character in Philippe de Mézières' *Songe du viel pelerine*, all written around the time of the letters. (Henry IV was an admirer of Christine's work and offered her a pension and place at his court, which she refused: see J. Laidlaw, 'Christine de Pizan, the Earl of Salisbury and Henry IV' *French Studies* 36:2 (1982) 129–43.) Much later, in a Shrovetide disguising of 1522, Henry VIII's disguising troupe was 'led by one all in crimosin sattin with burnyng flames of gold, called *Ardent Desire*'; Edward Hall *The Union of the Two Noble and Illustre Families of Lancastre and Yorke* edited [by Sir Henry Ellis] as *Hall's Chronicle* (London: J. Johnson and others, 1809, reprint New York: AMS Press, 1965) 631.

15 Palamides was a Saracen knight of the Round Table, unbaptized but adhering to Christianity; see Robbins Library Digital Projects *The Camelot Project* sv Palamedes <https://d.lib.rochester.edu/camelot-project>. Fierabras (or Ferumbras), a hero of popular *chansons de geste*, was another Saracen knight who converted to support Charlemagne and his peers; see *Three Middle English Charlemagne Romances* edited Alan Lupack (TEAMS Middle English Texts; Kalamazoo: Medieval Institute

these missives are provided with quite developed allegorical or romance back-stories which offer motivation for the joust that is proposed, and sometimes allude loosely to what may have been familiar texts.

In Letter 3, for example, Jeunesce, the Queen of Joy, explains:

> *vueillez sauoir que en nostre Court a[vum] nourry vne Jeune Chiualer par son droit nomme appellee Nonsaichant qui en amours a souffert [et] soustenu plusours traualx & dangiers / Pour allegier sa peine / il est mis en la quest pour quer[ir] vne Dame de grant renom / que on appelle Grace / de la quele il na peu ne ne puet encores a[ver] aucunes nouuelles ... [Nonsaichant venoit] pour veoir & sauoir sil poura aura aucu[n] recours de la dit quest. Et aussi pour ce quil est de coustume que tous chiualers errans voulenti[ers] sacconntent de cours de Roys & haulx Princes par manier darmez ... Et oultre nostre treschier & tresame Cousin vueilliez sauoir que dit nostre norry en venant deuers vostre dit presence a encontre vne Damoisell que venoit de parde la du Royaulme de Panthaluce*[16] */ a quel il accompaigne Jusquez a vostre presence /*
>
> Letter 3, fol. 260^v

be good enough to know that in our Court we have brought up a young knight whose true name is *Nonsaichant* ('Inexperienced'), who has suffered and borne many labours and dangers in love; to relieve his suffering he has embarked upon a quest to seek out a lady of great reputation whom they call Grace, of whom he could not and still cannot obtain any news ... [*Nonsaichant comes*] to see and discover whether he might have any assistance in the said quest. And also because it is customary for all knights errant willingly to frequent the courts of kings and great princes for handling arms ... And furthermore, our right dear and well-beloved Cousin, be so good as to know that this said foster-child of ours, in coming towards your said presence, has met a maiden who was coming from overseas from beyond the kingdom of Panthaluce, whom he is accompanying as far as your presence.

Publications, 1990) Introduction to *The Sultan of Babylon* at <https://d.lib.rochester.edu/teams/publication/lupack-three-middle-english-charlemagne-romances>.

16 In some manuscripts 'Panthalice'. Perhaps a mistake or miscopying for 'Panthasile' (Penthesilea) Queen of the Amazons, who is referred to directly in Letter 4, Dalida.

The rather loose scenario outlined here does not obviously correlate with any specific known romance or allegory. The name of the jouster, literally 'Not-knowing', suggests ingenuousness or ignorance, tallying with his supposedly untried youth. It echoes, though distantly, a romance place-name, *l'Île Non Sachant*. This island appears in a popular romance widely known at the time; it was the childhood home of Ségurant, an Arthurian hero who had to leave the secluded island where he was brought up to establish his chivalric status. His key adventure was an encounter with a magical dragon (the romance is now known as *Ségurant, ou le chevalier au dragon*) and, as we shall see, the 1401 jousts appear to have featured spectacles including dragons.[17] But the letter seems not to set the scene for a dramatization of the romance, but rather alludes lightly to motifs, names, patterns, and fragments of action drawn from its audience's wide familiarity with the romance genre. The search for the Lady Grace, similarly, clearly evokes the characters and situations of love allegory, but without specific reference to the *Roman de la Rose* or any of its many analogues. Half of the 1401 letters allude to love allegory, either in brief narratives or in the naming of combatants, clearly relying on the same level of audience familiarity. There is an underlying evocation of a generalized world of love allegory and romance which provides a frame for the performance of chivalry played out in the entertainment.

Scenarios like this provide another illustration of the elaboration of the 1401 letters as literary/fictional documents in their own right. This is confirmed in a certain difference in emphasis between the two groups of letters in the relationship each establishes between fiction and actuality. The Edward III examples seem to engage rather more explicitly with the real identities of the participants. The jousters in these letters are clearly intended to be recognizable to the court audience: some combatants are identified by coats of arms, others are introduced by circumlocutions such as 'the youngest knight of the honourable company of the Garter present at your court'; or 'the best knight under fifty years'. A number of the allusions give the impression of private in-jokes and teasing references, which seem designed to make sense to the original audience, though often not to us. Who, for example, might be the honourable knight who 'knows little or

---

17 *Ségurant, ou, Le Chevalier Au Dragon* edited Emanuele Arioli (Paris: Honoré Champion, 2019).

nothing of anything except dogs and hunting'? One letter even seems to hinge on an erotic joke made about the King himself.[18]

It has often been argued that a significant element in the perceived success of Edward's long reign came from his cultivation of positive relationships and comradeship with his nobles.[19] His performance culture of chivalric tournaments and magnificent spectacle clearly aided this aim. But the jousting letters suggest another aspect of such community formation. They play with intimately oblique allusions to those involved, and the bonding force of teasing and sometimes explicit humour. These are things that arise from and can promote a sense of togetherness; they can reinforce already established affinities, and promote good-will between associates. So these performance letters might be seen as not just a symptom, but an active cause, of Edward's successful strategy of community politics.

While Henry IV's letters also occasionally invite identification of the real individuals behind the aliases, this is noticeably less frequent. In two of the thirteen letters, arms are described, and in a few more hints are given, such as the knight who 'has most often travelled into foreign lands between the ages of twenty and twenty-four'. There is one letter that could be teasingly pointed, asking to set up a joust with *le Chiualer or Escuier estant a vostre feste dessusdicte qui a plus parle damours a pluseurs Damoiselles . & qui plus souuent a changie la custume de loyaulx amans* ('the knight or squire present at your aforementioned feast who has spoken most of love to various maidens, and who has most often altered the custom of true lovers').[20] But several others are identified in similarly loosely romantic terms, such as the knight *entre lez aiges de seize & vingt ans qui a plus longuement este seruaunt damours de son aaige sans aucun guerredon* ('between the ages of sixteen and twenty years who has been the servant of love for the longest time without receiving any reward').[21] Taken together with the fictional romantic narratives created for the challengers, such descriptions may suggest not so much personal identifiers as further fictive allusion, contributing to the overall impression the letters create that these jousts inhabit and perform a world of love allegory. In the majority of letters, the descriptions of the 1401 combatants are more generic than those in the earlier group, suggesting

---

18 See Letter 2 in Bennett, Carpenter, and Gardiner 'Chivalric Games' 321–4.
19 See e.g. W. Mark Ormrod *Edward III* (New Haven: Yale UP, 2013) 363–7, 600–1.
20 Letter 5, Naturo, fol. 261[r].
21 Letter 11, fol. 262[r].

that this occasion is rather more interested in the splendid fiction of the entertainment than the real identities of the performers. Overall, Henry's letters seem more elaborate and public, less specific and personal, than Edward's, confirming the impression that they are designed for a more formal occasion in which the glorious spectacle is more important than the private games.

The Occasion

The 1401 letters and the performance they document are significantly shaped by the occasion for which they were composed. For the earlier group of letters, there is nothing to identify any specific context. Like the later group, they mention a Christmas feast, and following some of the obscure references has enabled a narrowing of the probable date to within a few years. But the jousts are not apparently designed for any particular event beyond traditional festive courtly celebration. In 1401, not only do we have a good deal of external evidence about the circumstances, but we can also see how the letters themselves acknowledge and engage with Henry IV's political situation and the Emperor's visit.

First, it is important to remember the wider political context. At this moment, New Year 1401, Henry had been king for barely one year, having been crowned on 13 October 1399 after dramatically usurping the throne from his cousin Richard II. Although his accession seems initially to have enjoyed a good deal of popular support at home, his previously positive relations with European rulers quickly fell away. During the year following, especially after the controversial death of Richard early in 1400, he began to encounter increasing political opposition at home, military setbacks and economic difficulties.[22] By Christmas 1400, his reign was not altogether certainly established, and his court was also new and uncertain as he tried to draw together his new kingdom. But Christmas festivity at court was a well-established tradition and Henry himself, like his father John of Gaunt and grandfather Edward, had been a renowned jouster, who valued chivalric

---

22 Michael Bennett 'Henry of Bolingbroke and the Revolution of 1399' in *Henry IV: the Establishment of the Regime* edited Gwilym Dodd and Douglas Biggs (York: York Medieval Press, 2003) 9–34; Chris Given-Wilson *Henry IV* (New Haven: Yale UP, 2017) 160–79.

prowess and courtly magnificence.[23] It is not surprising that he might encourage the display of those qualities in his Christmas celebration, and hope they would help to reassure his new court and assert its power and splendour. There might be good reason, however, to avoid the more intimate and jocular tones of the earlier jousting letters. Both temperamentally and politically, their playful and personal community-building was unlikely to be appropriate.

The other key feature of the occasion was the presence of the visiting Emperor of Constantinople, Manuel II Palaeologus. As a high-ranking international visitor the Emperor brought a welcome sense of authority and even validation to Henry's court at a point when his relations with France and a number of other European countries were uneasy, following his usurpation of the crown. International visits between courts were one of the important means by which courtly community and culture extended itself across Europe, and the entertainments arranged for such occasions would almost always work not only to congratulate the visitor, but also to assert the splendour and magnanimity of the host court. The jousting letters clearly support this function, although if we probe the circumstances more fully, we can also find more complex, and even ambivalent, work being done in this performance.

Manuel was a significant visitor: the Emperor of Constantinople, a high-status ruler from a far-flung land, and a bulwark of Eastern Christianity against the infidel. However, his sovereignty was somewhat less impressive than this might suggest. By the end of the fourteenth century, the Byzantine Empire had effectively been reduced to the city of Constantinople, and from 1394 the city itself had fallen under sustained attack from the Ottoman Turks. As his resources dwindled, in 1399 Manuel had left his country to go on an extended journey through Western Europe, seeking from its Christian rulers military and economic support, and a crusade against the Turks.[24] The material help he received was in the end relatively limited, but he was feted wherever he went, being honourably received by Gian Galeazzo Visconti, Duke of Milan, and Charles VI in Paris, as well as Henry

---

23 A.J. Tuck 'Henry IV and Chivalry' in Dodd and Biggs *Henry IV: the Establishment of the Regime* 55–71.

24 John W. Barker *Manuel II Palaeologus (1391–1425): a Study in late Byzantine Statesmanship* (New Brunswick NJ: Rutgers UP, 1969) 165–99; Nicol 'A Byzantine Emperor in England' 204–11.

IV in London. Manuel's visits to these European courts attracted interest and attention, and a fascination with the idea of his oriental splendour. This seems to have left a particular trace after his arrival in Paris in June 1400.[25] He was ceremoniously met and welcomed outside the city by the King with a retinue of nobles and musicians, and two thousand citizens. A contemporary French historian recorded the impression he created:

Tunc imperator, habitum imperialem ex albo serico gerens, equo albo sibi a rege in itinere oblato, et super quem tunc ascendens agiliter non dignatus fuerat pedem ad terram ponere, insidebat. Et nonnulli qui notantes ejus staturam mediocrem, thorace virile ac membris sollidioribus insignatam, subque barba prolixa, undique canis ornate, vultus eius venustatem attendebant, ipsum dignum imperio judicabant.[26]

Then the Emperor, dressed in his imperial garb of white silk, seated himself on the white horse presented to him by the King on his journey, mounting it nimbly without even deigning to set a foot upon the ground [*i.e., in transferring himself from his own horse to the white one*]. And those who – while marking his moderate stature, distinguished by a manly chest and by yet firmer limbs, though under a long beard and showing white hair everywhere – yet took heed of the grace of his countenance, adjudged him indeed worthy of imperial rule.[27]

Later, the brothers Limbourg famously drew on the Emperor as a model for one of the Magi, Melchior, in two images in the *Très Riches Heures du Duc de*

---

25 Georg Jostkleigrewe '"Rex imperator in regno suo" – An Ideology of Frenchness? Late Medieval France, Its Political Elite and Juridical Discourse' in *Imagined Communities: Constructing Collective Identities in Medieval Europe* edited Andrzej Pleszczynski, Joanna Aleksandra Sobiesiak, Michał Tomaszek, and Przemysław Tyszka (Leiden: Brill, 2018) 73–7; Charalambos Dendrinos 'Manuel II Palaeologus in Paris (1400–1402): Theology, Diplomacy, and Politics' in *Greeks, Latins, and Intellectual History 1204–1500* edited Martin Hinterberger and Chris Schabel (Leuven; Paris; Walpole, MA: Peeters, 2011) 397–422.

26 *Chronique du Religieux de Saint-Denys* edited L.-F. Bellaguet, 6 vols in 4 (Paris: Crapelet, 1839–52) 2 (1840) 756; Book 21 ch. 1.

27 Barker *Manuel II Palaeologus* 397.

Berry.[28] The first, the Meeting of the Magi, recalls his reception, being recognizably set just outside Paris; Melchior, with the flowing white beard and hair of Manuel, wears a white corslet and controls a prancing white horse.[29] In the image of The Adoration, he appears again as the leading Magus, kissing the foot of the Christ Child.

Manuel stayed in France until he visited London in December 1400. His English visit was postponed several times as Henry IV moved from military encounters in Scotland to dealing with Owen Glendower in Wales. When the time came, however, Henry seems to have been just as ready as Charles to welcome his guest and to honour his arrival in London, which was widely noted by contemporary historians (see FIG. 1). The *St Albans Chronicle* reports the Emperor's reception on 21 December 1400:

> *Cui rex occurrit ad le Blakheth cum pompa qua decuit, eumque suscepit honorificentissime; duxit Londinias in die apostoli sancti Thome, exhibuitque gloriose longo tempore, soluens pro expensis hospicii sui atque suorum, et respiciens eum dignis tanto fastigio donaciuis.*[30]

> The King met him at Blackheath with due ceremony, welcoming him with considerable splendour. He took him to London on the feast day of St Thomas the Apostle, and engaged in glorious displays over a long period, himself defraying the cost of entertaining him and his men, and honouring him with presents which were worthy of his exalted position.

The 'exalted position' of the visitor shed honour on Henry's court and was to be balanced by a reciprocal display of majesty.

---

28 Dendrinos 'Manuel II Palaeologus in Paris' 399–400; Jostkleigrewe '"Rex imperator in regno suo" 74–5; Barker *Manuel II Palaeologus* 536–7.

29 'Meeting of the three Magi' and 'The Adoration', illuminations from the *Très Riches Heures du duc de Berry*, Chantilly: MS Musée Conde 65 fols 51^v–52^r. Images available at: <https://en.wikipedia.org/wiki/Manuel_II_Palaiologos#/media/File:Folio_51v_-_The_Meeting_of_the_Magi.jpg> and <https://en.wikipedia.org/wiki/Manuel_II_Palaiologos#/media/File:Folio_52r_-_The_Adoration_of_the_Magi.jpg>.

30 *St Albans Chronicle Volume 2 1394–1422* edited Wendy R. Childs, John Taylor, and Leslie Watkiss (Oxford Medieval Texts; Oxford: Clarendon Press, 2011) 306–7. Image from London: Lambeth Palace Library MS 6 (*St Albans Chronicle*) fol. 240^r, available at: <https://en.wikipedia.org/wiki/Manuel_II_Palaiologos#/media/File:Manuel_II_Palaiologos_with_Henry_IV_of_England.png>.

The English seem to have been struck, like the French, by the exotic orientalism of the visitors, with one chronicler recording the unfamiliarity of both their dress and their religious practices:

Iste imperator semper uniformiter et sub uno colore, scilicet albo, in longis robis ad modum tabardorum formatis semper cum suis incedere solebat, multum uarietatum et disparitatem Anglicorum in uestibus deprehendendo, asserens per eas animarum inconstanciam

FIG. 1: The Meeting of Henry IV and Manuel II Palaeologus in 1400.
St Albans Chronicle, Lambeth Palace Library MS 6 fol. 240[r].
Reproduced by courtesy of Lambeth Palace Library.

et uarietatem significari. Capita neque barbas capellanorum ipsius non tetigit nouacula. In diuinis seruiciis deuotissimi errant isti Greci, ea tam per milites quam per clericos quia in eorum uulgari indifferenter cantando. Cogitaui intra me quam esset dolendum quod iste maior et ulterior Christianus uersus orientem princeps, ui per infideles compulsus, ulteriores occidentis insulas pro subsidio contra eosdem uisitare cogebatur.[31]

This Emperor and his men always went about dressed uniformly in long robes cut like tabards which were all of one colour, namely white, and disapproved greatly of the fashions and varieties of dress worn by the English, declaring that they signified inconstancy and fickleness of heart. No razor ever touched the heads or beards of his priests. These Greeks were extremely devout in their religious services, having them chanted variously by knights or by clerics, for they were sung in their native tongue. I thought to myself how sad it was that this great Christian leader from the remote East had been driven by the power of the infidels to visit distant islands in the West in order to seek help against them.

This observation not only demonstrates local fascination with Eastern customs, but perhaps also highlights the precarious position of the imperial visitor, coming not only as a fellow-ruler but also as a suppliant for aid and support.[32] For in spite of the magnificence of the encounter neither ruler was at this moment in a securely powerful position and, in spite of the promises he apparently made to Manuel, Henry's own domestic difficulties meant he was not in a position to offer real military or financial assistance. This gives the celebrations at Eltham a particular edge, as they enact magnificent welcome and splendour on both sides, while side-stepping direct commitment.

---

31 *The Chronicle of Adam Usk, 1377–1421* edited and translated Chris Given-Wilson (Oxford: Clarendon Press, 1997) 118–21.

32 It has been argued that this English report, though polite, also tended to note the relative poverty of the Byzantine Greeks and the potentially troubling otherness of their religious practices: David R. Carlson 'Greeks in England 1400' in *Interstices: Studies in Late Middle English and Anglo-Latin Texts in Honour of A.G. Rigg* edited Richard Firth Green and Linne R. Mooney (Toronto UP, 2004) 74–98.

The Entertainment Event

Although there are no eye-witness accounts, the copying of the letters into such a wide range of manuscripts suggests that the Eltham entertainment made a particular impact in its day, at least in courtly and heraldic circles. The combination of the survival of the letters with our knowledge of the specific context can help us to recover a good deal more of the performance itself and its significance than is possible for most courtly entertainments before the sixteenth century.

As the *St Albans Chronicle* makes clear, the jousts were just one part of the court's traditional twelve days of festivity at Christmas:

> *Anno gracie millesimo quadringentesimo primo, et regni regis Henrici a conquesto quarti, secundo, tenuit rex Natale gloriose apud predium suum de Eltham, ubi affuit imperator Constantinopolitanus cum Grecorum episcopis, aliisque quos necessitas hic attraxerat ea uice.*

> In the year of grace 1401, the second year in the reign of King Henry IV after the Conquest, the King spent Christmas splendidly at his manor of Eltham. The Emperor of Constantinople was also there, with Greek bishops and others whom need had drawn there on that occasion.[33]

The elements of the celebrations were themselves traditional. Entertainment was not only provided by the court, but also offered from the City of London. The *Chronicle of London*, clearly written from the point of view of the city, reports:

> In this yere was here the emperor of Constantynnoble: and the kyng helde his Cristemasse at Eltham; and men of London maden a gret mommyng to hym of xij aldermen and there sones, for whiche they hadde gret thanke.[34]

---

33   *St Albans Chronicle* 2 308–9.

34   *A Chronicle of London, from 1089 to 1483: Written in the Fifteenth Century, and for the First Time Printed from MSS. in the British Museum* edited Nicholas Harris Nicolas and E. Tyrrell (London: Longman, Rees, Orme, Brown and Green, 1827) 87. Anne Lancashire notes that the accounts of the Mercers' Guild record payments for this mumming: *London Civic Theatre* (Cambridge UP, 2002) 229 note 42. See also Twycross 'Prince of Peace' 35–6 in this volume.

SARAH CARPENTER

Christmas mummings to the king from the guilds of London seem to have become popular during the reign of Richard II.[35] It is not clear whether the 1401 mumming was particularly staged with the Emperor in mind; but it suggests the contribution of the city to his welcome, and also to the consolidation of Henry's kingship, following the disruption of his Christmas festivities the previous year by a foiled assassination attempt by a group of nobles.[36]

The twelve days of celebration were also likely to have included dancing and feasting, masks and disguisings. But the culmination of Christmas festivity appears frequently to have been a tournament or jousting. The Edward III jousting letters also refer to Christmas, and there are records of preparation for Yuletide jousts both under Richard II and in Henry's own personal accounts in the years before he assumed the throne. In the 1380s a payment is made to the *pictor regis* ('royal painter'):

Gilberto Prince, pictori London ... Pro diuersis operibus per ipsum factis pro agisamentis[37] *et ludis regis, tam apud Eltham quam apud Wyndesore, contra festa natalicia Domini, annis vij⁰ et viij⁰.*[38]

To Gilbert Prince, painter of London ... For various works done by him for the lists and the king's entertainments both at Eltham and at Windsor for the feast of Christmas, years 7 and 8.

---

35 Anne Lancashire points to records of such performances (most often from the Mercers' Company) in 1392/3, 1393/4, and 1395/6; *London Civic Theatre* 42–3. See, too, Meg Twycross's article in this volume 35–6.

36 Several histories claim that this assassination attempt was itself planned under the cover of a 'mumming': see Given-Wilson *Henry IV* 160–2; James Hamilton Wylie *The History of England under Henry IV* 4 vols (London: Longmans Green, 1884–98) *1* 93; Meg Twycross and Sarah Carpenter *Masks and Masking in Medieval and Early Tudor England* (Aldershot: Ashgate, 2002) 99. But the term seems to have been used very loosely.

37 For *agisamentum* as '(?) (erection of) lists or stands' see *ODMLBS* online at <https://logeion.uchicago.edu/agistamentum>. The entry cites, for 1397: *pro diversis operibus factis pro agisamentis et ludis regis et regine ... contra festa Natalis Domini* from Kew: TNA E361 (Wardrobe and Household Accounts 1257–1548)] 5ʳ 7ᵈ. See also *agista* [cf. *gista*], 'joist'.

38 T.F. Tout *Chapters in the Administrative History of Mediaeval England: The Wardrobe, the Chamber and the Small Seals* 6 vols (Manchester UP, 1920–33) *4* 391 note 8.

In 1391/2 Henry, then Earl of Derby, similarly paid Prince for decorating banners, saddles, shields, and helmets for Christmas jousts at Hertford.[39] It is no surprise to find that for the jousts of 1401 Gilbert Prince's successor was engaged. Wylie quotes extracts from the Wardrobe Accounts which indicate payments for a range of banners, standards, and caparisons:

> Thomas Gloucester (Pictor) of London. Pro certis agisamentis et ludis regis (*for Christmas at Eltham 1400*). Vapulat' divers' Trappur' vexillor', penon,' pencell', and standards with arms of King for hastilud' held there before Emperor of Constantinople.[40]

This entry confirms the occasion, and expenses on traditional preparations and decorative equipment for the joust. But the jousting letters themselves appear to point towards a significantly more theatrical event than usual, with an elaborated fictional frame and including spectacle beyond the individual combats.

The Performance

The letters are not just preparatory documents setting up the jousts, but will have been themselves part of the entertainment enjoyed at the court. Such extravagantly crafted rhetorical fictions are clearly not designed simply for private reading by Blanche, to whom they are addressed. Courteous epistolary exchanges between rulers and courts normally expected more public delivery. Recent work has demonstrated how such formal letters were specifically composed for reading aloud, with the *artes dictandi* even implying some training in their effective performance.[41] But the jousting letters belong to a particular kind of missive that seems especially created for performance.

---

39 Wylie *Henry IV* 4 164.
40 Wylie *Henry IV* 4 220.
41 Malcolm Richardson 'The *Ars Dictaminis*, the Formulary, and Medieval Epistolary Practice' in *Letter-Writing Manuals and Instruction from Antiquity to the Present* edited Carol Poster and Linda C. Mitchell (Columbia: University of South Carolina Press, 2007) 52–66 at 56; Martin Carmargo 'Special Delivery: Were Medieval Letter Writers Trained in Performance?' in *Rhetoric Beyond Words: Delight and Persuasion in the Arts of the Middle Ages* edited Mary Carruthers (Cambridge UP, 2010) 173–89. For comparison from academic entertainment practice, see Thomas Meacham 'Exchanging Performative Words: Epistolary Performance and University Drama in Late Medieval England' *Medieval English Theatre 32* (2010) 12–25.

Copies of challenges between noble individuals are among the most numerous kinds of documentary evidence for jousting preserved in English heraldic collections throughout the fifteenth and early sixteenth centuries.[42] While there is not much contextual evidence for the earlier examples, later in the century we find increasing records of striking performances surrounding the delivery and sharing of challenges. For large tournaments, the illustrated manuscripts of René d'Anjou's mid-fifteenth-century *Livre des Tournois* show vividly the scenes of the sending out and delivery of challenges in public court ceremonial.[43] From 1465, the letter of challenge from Anthony Woodville, Lord Rivers, to Antoine the Bastard of Burgundy includes a detailed description of the performance undertaken at the court of Edward IV to initiate the *emprise* of the 'Floure of Souvenaunce', while a full herald's account records the ceremonial delivery of the challenge to Antoine, in Philip the Good's court in Brussels.[44] Later still, under Henry VIII in 1524/5, Hall describes the delivery of a challenge for a Yuletide tournament. A group of

> Esquires of the Kynges Housholde, enterprised a chalenge of feactes of armes, against the feast of Christmas, wherefore they sent Wyndsore herault, on sainct Thomas day before Christmas, into the Quenes great chamber, the kyng being present, which herault had a coate of armes of red silke, beaten with a goodly Castle, of foure Turrettes siluer, and in euery turret a faire lady, standyng gorgiously apparelled.[45]

---

42 See Anglo 'Financial and Heraldic Records' 187–8 and Appendix B 195.

43 *Traité de la forme et devis comme on peut faire les tournois*. The original manuscript appears to be BNF MS français 2695 (1462–5), description at: <https://archivesetmanuscrits.bnf.fr/ark:/12148/cc49176v>. Images: issuing the challenge, fol. 3ᵛ <https://gallica.bnf.fr/ark:/12148/btv1b84522067/f14.item>; accepting the challenge, fol. 7ʳ <https://gallica.bnf.fr/ark:/12148/btv1b84522067/f21.item>; proclaiming the tourney, fol. 19ʳ <https://gallica.bnf.fr/ark:/12148/btv1b84522067/f45.item>.

44 See Sarah Carpenter 'Performing Chivalry: the combat between Anthony Woodville, Lord Scales, and Antoine, the Bastard of Burgundy, 1467' in *Performance, Ceremony and Display in Late Medieval England: Proceedings of the 2018 Harlaxton Symposium* (Harlaxton Medieval Studies 30; Donington: Shaun Tyas, 2020) 8–25.

45 Hall *Chronicle* 688. See also W.R. Streitberger *Court Revels 1485–1559* (Studies in Early English Drama 3; Toronto UP, 1994) 116–17.

The herald, adopting the name of *Chateau Blanche*, then outlined the romantic fiction of the tournament, in which the 'Castle of Loyalty' was to be defended by the fifteen Esquires. While there is no specific evidence of a similar performance for the 1401 letters, their nature suggests that they too would at least have been read out to the Christmas court in some kind of public ceremony, in the days preceding the jousts themselves. There are possible hints that some of the recommended jousters may have delivered the letters of challenge personally, in their fictional characters: six are referred to as *porteur de cestz* ('carrier of these [letters]'), while Jeunesce explains to Blanche that Nonsaichant will bring with him a maiden from the Kingdom of Pantaluce *a quel il accompaigne Jusquez a vostre presence* ('whom he is accompanying as far as your presence'). But whoever presented the letters, the romantic fictions and spectacular actions narrated in them are part of the performance, providing an announcement and foretaste of the entertainment to follow.

There is limited evidence of who performed in these jousts. At Edward III's court one of those challenged has been identified as Henry de Braybroke, a younger brother of the third Sir Gerard de Braybroke (c.1332–1403) and a young squire of the Black Prince.[46] The two jousters whose arms are listed in the 1401 letters seem to be similar in rank: fairly young and relatively junior members of Henry's court. The first, identified in the letter from Jeunesce as the desired opponent for Nonsaichant, *port en sez armez vn escu dont le champ est dazur a trois quintefueillez dor & vng Croissant dargent* ('bears as his arms a shield of a field azure with three cinquefoils or and a crescent argent').[47] This must belong to a member of the Bardolf family, whose arms are *Azure three cinquefoils or*.[48] The knight in question cannot have been the contemporary Thomas, fifth Baron Bardolf, who died in 1408.[49] Although Thomas Bardolf was in 1401 apparently still a

---

46 See Bennett, Carpenter, and Gardiner 'Chivalric Games' 320.

47 BL Cotton MS Nero D II fol. 260^v.

48 *Dictionary of British Arms: Medieval Ordinary Volume 4* edited Thomas Woodcock and Sarah Flower (London: Society of Antiquaries, 2014) 68.

49 An image of his arms can be seen in the Ordinary known as 'Thomas Jenyns's Book', 1410: see Yale University Library, Takamiya MS 105 fol. 66^r, top row first left: <https://collections.library.yale.edu/catalog/16161080?child_oid=16162563>.

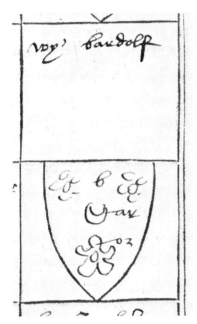

FIG. 2: Sketch of the arms of Sir William Bardolf, Norfolk and Suffolk Roll. London: College of Arms, MS Vincent 164, fol.87[r]. Reproduced by permission of the Kings, Heralds, and Pursuivants of Arms.

supporter of the newly enthroned Henry IV, he soon rebelled;[50] more decisively, the arms described are differenced by the addition of a *crescent azure*, indicating a younger son. This suggests that the jouster nominated was Sir William Bardolf, the Baron's younger brother, who remained a supporter of Henry IV throughout his reign. Jeunesce's letter also reports that the knight in question *nagares a fait armer ou Ream de Gaule si bien & vaillanment quil [a] acquis grant los & grant pris ou dit Royaume de Gaule & en pluseurs autrez contrees* ('has recently performed deeds of arms in the realm of Gaul, so well and valiantly that he has gained great praise and estimation in the said Kingdom of Gaul and several other countries'). Our records of Sir William's early career are sketchy, but we know that he served overseas under his brother Lord Bardolf in 1398, and from at least 1406 he was certainly serving in Calais with increasing distinction.[51] The Bardolf arms with the *crescent argent* difference are identified as belonging to William by a sketch in the Norfolk and Suffolk Roll (FIG. 2).[52]

The other coat of arms recorded in the letters identifies the opponent requested by Cleopatra for her knight, *Pertsapeine lieutenant de Capitain*

---

50   ODNB sv *Bardolf, Thomas, fifth Baron Bardolf (1369–1408)*, online at <https://doi.org/10.1093/ref:odnb/1360>.

51   See the entries under *William Bardolf* (years 1406–15) in *The Medieval Soldier* database: <www.medievalsoldier.org/dbsearch/>. Also Wylie *Henry IV* 4 34, 55, 57, 63.

52   College of Arms MS Vincent 164 fol. 87[r].

de nostre Citee de Troye la graunt ('Pertsapeine [*Loses-his-Labour*], lieutenant of the Captain of our city of Troy the Great').[53] He carries *vng escu dargent a vng chief Dazur a deux mellettz dore* ('a shield argent with a chief azure two mullets or'), identified as arms of the Clinton family.[54] This particular variation with two gold stars is ascribed in the Ordinary of Arms known as Thomas Jenyns' Book not to Sir William, the current Lord Clinton, but to one John Clinton.[55] Apart from the fact that Jenyns pairs him with Sir William, this John Clinton is hard to trace, but he is likely to be the man-at-arms/esquire who served under various commanders from the beginning of Henry IV's reign and into that of his son.[56] These identified participants in the 1401 jousts were not high-status nobles but appear to have been, like Braybroke under Edward III and Henry VIII's gentlemen of the household, relatively minor figures participating in combats designed more for theatrical entertainment than in defence of personal chivalric status or honour.

The jousting in which these young men took part was itself a highly theatrical sport. But the importance of its fictive framework of love allegory and romance, and the impression that the jousts were only one part of a wider spectacle, are borne out by a fascinating passage in what appears to be the central letter of the collection. The letter from Dalida, Sultan of Babylon, which most explicitly acknowledges the visiting Emperor Manuel, includes not only the story of a love quest being undertaken by the challenger, but also a vivid account of the special effects that will accompany the jousting. The recommended jouster is named as *Le Povre Perdu* ('the poor lost one'). This was the name adopted to mask his identity by Florimont, eponymous hero of the late-twelfth-century romance by Aimon de Varenne. The romance was clearly popular, surviving in many thirteenth- and fourteenth-century manuscripts and remaining in circulation into the

---

53 Letter 10, fol. 262[r]. *Pertsapeine* has associations with the *Roman de la Rose* and London was sometimes known as 'Little Troy' at this time.

54 'Arg on chf Az 2 mullets Or'; *Dictionary of British Arms: Medieval Ordinary Volume 3* edited T. Woodcock and Sarah Flower (London: Society of Antiquaries, 2009) 61.

55 Image in Thomas Jenyns's Book, Yale University Library Takamiya MS 105 fol. 48[v] (bottom row second right) <https://collections.library.yale.edu/catalog/16161080?child_oid=16162528>.

56 See entries under *John Clynton (years 1404–17)* in *The Medieval Soldier* database: <www.medievalsoldier.org/dbsearch/>.

sixteenth century.[57] Florimont was great-grandfather of Alexander the Great and wanders the Eastern world (based on a mythologized Byzantium) performing adventures, having lost the love of his fairy mistress.[58] This might fit loosely with the scenario presented in Dalida's letter:

Nostre treschier & tresamee Cousin en vostre Court a vne Dame de grant pris / que on appelle plaisance que par long temps a tenu prisoner en sez prisonez vn Chiualer du Royaume Damours nomme le pouoir perdu /. le quel Chiualer ne puet estre deliure dicelles prisonez tant quil soit dischargie de six Coupez de launcez assise en bassez sellez sans estre attachiez ne liez en selle ne en main / Pour la quel deliurance a[v]oir / Il lui semble quil lui conuendroit cheminer & errer maintes contrees chasteaulx villez & Citees montaignes valees bois & Riuiers auant quil peust trouuer vne tiel quil demaund si non quil trouuast aucun bon counseil qui luy abregast son chemin.

fol. 261^r

Our right dear and well-beloved Cousin, in your Court is a lady of great excellence who is called Pleasure, who for a long time has held prisoner in her dungeons a knight of the Kingdom of Love called The Poor Lost One, which knight cannot be released from that prison until he shall have been discharged by six blows of the lance sitting in low saddles without being attached or tied in the saddle nor by the hand. In order to obtain this release, it seems to him that he needs to travel and wander through many countries, castles, towns and cities, mountains, valleys, woods, and rivers, before he will be able to find a suitable person to challenge, unless he should find some good counsel which would shorten his journey.

More explicitly than many of the challengers, Povre Perdu's joust is thus framed as part of a romance love allegory. His entrance was apparently dramatized to support this fiction:

Icelluy pour perdu couent & mene nostre treschier & bien amee ne proneu fferebras / de Damas le Jeune generall gouuerneur de nostre

---

57 See Keith Busby *Codex and Context: Reading Old French Verse Narrative in Manuscript* (Amsterdam: Rodopi, 2002) 554–8.
58 See <https://blogs.bl.uk/digitisedmanuscripts/2016/05/florimont.html>.

Royaume Dalexandrie . A fin quil ne rompe mie sa prison & quil ne sen fuy lye & attachie dune cheyenne par my le col.

fol. 261^r

our very dear and well-beloved nephew Fierabras the Young of Damascus, Governor General of our Kingdom of Alexandria, comes with and escorts this Poor Lost One. In order that he should not break his captivity and flee, [*he is*] tied and attached by a chain round the neck.

This plays into familiar images of chivalric love. The jouster's entry to Blanche's presence, or perhaps to the joust itself, echoes the procession of combatants to the lists at Smithfield in Richard II's great tournament of 1390. This opened with '60. Ladyes of honour mounted vpon palfraies, riding on the one side, richly apparrelled, and euery Lady led a knight with a chayne of gold'.[59]

Dalida's letter not only foregrounds and elaborates the narrative frame of the joust, but also describes the fiery spectacle that apparently accompanied it. Having noted the presence of the emperor of great renown, it promises a distinguished company of

vaillans Chiualers & Escuiers qui font merueilles / comme lez vngs qui cheuauchent Dragons / les autres portent serpens sur leurs testes gettans feu & flambe / lez autres qui sont si ardans en amours / que parmy leurs targez & escuz gettent flambe de feu tout visible.

fol. 261^r

valiant knights and squires, who perform marvels; like the ones who ride dragons, others who bear serpents on their heads casting fire and flame, others who are so burning in love that through their bucklers and shields they cast visible flames of fire.

These special effects are a striking demonstration of what Philip Butterworth calls 'theatre of fire': the spectacular use of fireworks and fire-effects in theatrical display.[60] These letters provide new evidence of

---

59 John Stow *A Survey of London* edited Charles Kingsford, 2 vols (Oxford: Clarendon Press, 1908) 2 30. Also recorded by Froissart, Book 4 ch. 16: *Les chroniques de Sire Jean Froissart* edited J.A.C. Buchon, 4 vols (Paris: Desrez, 1835) 3 94–7 at 95–6.

60 Philip Butterworth *Theatre of Fire* (London: Society for Theatre Research, 1998).

such pyrotechnics in England, evidence which also significantly pre-dates what is often referred to as the earliest such English fire-spectacle, at the coronation of Henry VII's wife Elizabeth of York in 1487.[61]

The display envisaged enhances both the romance and love-allegory elements of the jousting. On the one hand the emphasis is on dragons: both those that were ridden and those 'serpents' spouting fire, mounted on the riders' helms. Battling dragons is a common trope of romance; and where the letters give names of romance heroes to the 1401 jousters, they are of protagonists with dragon associations. The romance of Florimont (a.k.a. Povre Perdu) tells how his conception was accompanied by a dragon dream, and the monster from which he saves his father's kingdom is described as having the body of a flying serpent.[62] As the mythical grandfather of Alexander the Great, he is also associated with Alexander's dragon battles.[63] Nonsaichant, as we have seen, recalls the romance of Ségurant, *le chevalier au dragon*. On the other hand, the knights whose shields throw out fire because they are *si ardans en amours* ('so on fire with love') seem to be enacting love allegory. Both dragons and love are, of course, widely associated with fire, giving grounds for the spectacle. While dragons breathe out flames,[64] fire as an allegorical image of passionate love is common both visually and in literature throughout the period. The Castle of Jalosie in the *Roman de la Rose* is won when Venus shoots and fires it with her flaming torch, while the mid-fifteenth-century collection of Italian love-sonnets in the British Library is profusely illustrated with burning hearts.[65]

---

61   Butterworth *Theatre of Fire* 9.

62   Joanne Marie Young 'A Study of Aimon de Varennes' *Florimont*' (PhD thesis, University of Sheffield, 2010) online at <https://etheses.whiterose.ac.uk/14977/1/527245.pdf p.129>; Aimon de Varennes *Florimont* edited A. Hilka (Gesellschaft für romanische Literatur 48; Halle: Niemeyer, 1932) line 1975.

63   See <https://blogs.bl.uk/digitisedmanuscripts/2016/05/florimont.html>.

64   See e.g. <http://ica.themorgan.org/manuscript/page/18/76973>.

65   For Venus see: National Library of Wales MS 5016D (Roman de la Rose) fol 129ᵛ. Image available at: <https://en.wikipedia.org/wiki/File:Roman_de_la_Rose_f._129v_(Venus_aims_at_the_castle).jpg>. This image is interestingly resonant of that of the eleventh-century military portable flame thrower in Codex Vaticanus Graecus 1605 fol. 36ʳ. Image available at <https://commons.wikimedia.org/wiki/File:Hand-siphon_for_Greek_fire,_medieval_illumination.jpg>. For burning hearts see BL MS King's 322, fol. 1, at <www.bl.uk/catalogues/illuminatedmanuscripts/ILLUMIN.ASP?Size=mid&IllID=2314>.

We have no further evidence of whether the spectacle described in this letter was in fact realized, or if so how it was created. But the letter is specific enough in the performance it promises to make its possibilities worth investigating further. Although we have no further documentary evidence of firework displays in England from this early date, it seems clear that the technologies needed to create what the letters describe would have been available. A variety of ingredients for explosive effects were commonly supplied for military purposes to gunners, whose expertise was generally involved in early firework displays, and the British Library holds a manuscript of a fourteenth-century collection that contains 'Recipes for fireworks, rockets, the burningglass, &c'.[66] The well-known stage direction in *The Castle of Perseverance*, thought to date from the first quarter of the fifteenth century, suggests that firework effects were already in use in theatrical performances:

> ... he þat schal pley belyal loke þat he haue gunnepowdyr brennynge
> In pypys in hys handys and in hys erys and in hys ars whanne he gothe to batayl.[67]

> ... he that shall play Belyal, look that he have gunpowder burning in pipes in his hands and in his ears and in his arse when he goes into battle.

The prime fire-effect the 1401 event called for is to 'throw' flames, either from the *serpens* mounted on the performers' heads, or from the shields they carried. By the end of the century there are certainly accounts of such fire-spewing dragons. The aforementioned account of the coronation of Elizabeth of York reports that the river pageantry included:

---

66 BL catalogue entry for Royal MS 12 B XXV, #26 fols 245–7. For ingredients see Butterworth *Theatre of Fire* ch. 1, especially 13–20. Wylie cites extracts from the Wardrobe Accounts listing stores of gunpowder including e.g. in 1404: '1300 lbs. of gunpowder made in Tower from 1360 lbs. of saltpetre and 400 lbs of sulphur' (*Henry IV* 4 234).

67 *The Macro Plays* edited Mark Eccles EETS OS 262 (1969) 1.

FIG. 3: Two crests representing fire-breathing dragons.
Wapenboek Gelre, Brussels, KBR MS 15652–56, pages 112 and 122, details.
Reproduced by permission of the Koninklijke Bibliotheek van België.

a Barge called *The Bachelers Barge*, garnysshed and apparellede, passing al other, wherin was ordeynede a great red Dragon spowting Flamys of Fyer into Temmys.[68]

A few years later this effect was repeated indoors, in the Westminster Hall, when a pageant of St George led in 'a Terryble and huge Rede dragun, The which In sundry placys of the halle as he passyd spytt ffyre at hys mowthe'.[69] Philip Butterworth gives us evidence of the technology employed for this particular kind of display, including a Berlin manuscript recipe dating from 1425–50.[70]

Dalida's letter does not suggest that a similar dragon would appear at the jousting; the fire-breathing serpents mounted on the performers' heads probably provided a smaller-scale and more mobile display. The likeliest staging for this would have involved making use of the decorative crests normally mounted on jousting helms, which often took the shape of heraldic beasts (FIG. 3). A striking Aragonese dragon crest has survived from the thirteenth century, the *Cimera de Jaime I*, which suggests the impressive effect.[71] It is clear that these crests were detachable from the helm itself, as seen in the image from René d'Anjou's *Livre des Tournois* that shows the stages of assembling the tournament helmet.[72] Such a crest could support the fire-apparatus associated with larger artificial dragons, or else those used for flaming devils.[73] A later, fuller, stage direction from John Heywood's *A Play of Love* (1534) gives an idea of how the display might have been achieved, as well as the theatrical spectacle it could provide:

---

68   John Leland *Johannis Lelandi Antiquarii de Rebus Britannicis Collectanea* edited Thomas Hearne, 6 vols (London: Benjamin White, second edition 1774) 4 218.

69   *The Great Chronicle of London*, edited A.H. Thomas and I.D. Thornley, Guildhall Library (London: Jones, 1938) 251.

70   Butterworth *Theatre of Fire* 79–98, especially 80.

71   See <www.factumfoundation.org/pag/1374/the-cimera-de-jaime-i>. There are paintings in armorials of the crest of the King of Aragon in Bibliothèque de l'Arsenal MS 4790 res. fol. 108[r]; *Equestrian Armorial of the Golden Fleece* (1433–5); <https://en.wikipedia.org/wiki/Crown_of_Aragon#/media/File:Roy_d'Arag%C3%B3n.jpg>, and in the *Gelre Armorial*, Brussels: KBR MS 15652–5 fol. 62[r]: <https://commons.wikimedia.org/wiki/Category:Gelre_Armorial#/media/File:Gelre_Folio_62r.jpg>.

72   René d'Anjou *Livre des Tournois*; BNF MS français 2692 fol. 20[r], at <https://gallica.bnf.fr/ark:/12148/btv1b10532593m/f46.item>.

73   Butterworth *Theatre of Fire* 21–7.

Here the vyse cometh in ronnyng sodenly aboute the place among the audyens with a hye copyn tank [*tall hat*] on his hed full of squybs fyred, cryeng 'Water, water, fyre, fyre, fyre, water, water, fyre' tyll the fyre in the squybs be spent.[74]

Fire does not seem to have been envisaged for the performers *qui cheuauchent dragons* ('who ride on dragons'), and although the construction of rideable pageant creatures would no doubt have been possible, the chivalric nature of the display seems to make it more likely that these dragons were costumed horses.[75] There is evidence of a long history of horses used in chivalric spectacles being disguised in a variety of ways. In 1298 the Guild of Fishmongers passed through London with a series of pageants followed by forty-six knights 'riding on horses, made like Luces of the sea' [i.e. hake].[76] Images in Sir Thomas Holme's *Book of Arms* (from before 1448) show jousters riding horses with chaffrons (face armour) made in the form of fantastic beasts.[77] One such chaffron from the late fifteenth century, later re-decorated for the future Henry II of France, actually survives in the Metropolitan Museum of New York.[78] But perhaps the most intriguing possible analogue is the mid-fifteenth-century drawing by Jacopo Bellini, now in the Louvre, of a 'rider on a palfrey with a fantastic harness' (FIG. 4): this looks as if it could easily be a flamboyant costume for a theatrical spectacle of the kind that Dalida's letter envisages.[79]

The third element of the spectacle promised in the letter is those knights *qui sont si ardans en amours / que parmy leurs targez & escuz gettent flambe de feu tout visible* ('who are so on fire with love that through the middle of their targes and shields visible flames of fire shoot out'). Fifteenth- and

---

74 *The Plays of John Heywood* edited Richard Axton and Peter Happé (Cambridge: D.S. Brewer, 1991) 174 *sd* at line 129. A *copyn tank* was 'A high-crowned hat of the form of a sugar-loaf' (*OED* sv *copintank*).

75 For the possibilities for representing dragons see Stephen Wright 'Wrangling Livestock, Dragons and Children: Practical Stagecraft and Its Thematic Consequences in the Augsburg St George Play (ca. 1486)' *Research Opportunities in Medieval and Renaissance Drama 48* (2008) 51–70 at 55–60.

76 Lancashire *London Civic Theatre* 48.

77 <www.bl.uk/manuscripts/Viewer.aspx?ref=harley_ms_4205_fs001ar> fols 9ʳ–40ᵛ.

78 For image see <www.metmuseum.org/art/collection/search/25403>.

79 Paris: Louvre, Cabinet des Dessins, at <http://arts-graphiques.louvre.fr/detail/oeuvres/60/113201-Cavalier-sur-un-palefroi-au-harnachement-fantastique-max>.

FIG. 4: Jacopo Bellini: Rider on a palfrey with a fantastic harness (RF 1515, 57). Paris: Louvre, Cabinet des Dessins, Réserve des grands albums. Album Bellini Jacopo fol. 47ʳ. © RMN-Grand Palais – Photo G. Blot <http://arts-graphiques.louvre.fr/detail/oeuvres/60/113201-Cavalier-sur-un-palefroi-au-harnachement-fantastique-max>.

early-sixteenth-century accounts of tournaments suggest that the flames of love remained a popular and often central motif in chivalric games. Records more often refer to visual decoration than to real fire: jousts at the Field of Cloth of Gold in 1520, for example, featured a company apparelled in 'blew Veluet enbrodred with a mans hartburnyng in a ladies hand holding a garden pot stillyng with water on the hart', and another 'apparelled and barded in crimosyn Sattin full of flames of golde, the borders ribbed with crimosyn Veluet'.[80] At Shrovetide in 1525, the King's caparison was 'richely embraudered, with a mannes harte in a presse, with flames about it', while the Marquess of Exeter jousted against him 'in Grene Veluet, & crimosyn sattyn embroidered with hartes burnyng, and ouer euery harte a Ladies

---

80   Hall *Chronicle* 613–4.

hand commyng out of a cloude, holdyng a garden water pot, which dropped siluer droppes on the harte'.[81]

Jousting shields were frequently decorated, either with the bearers' arms or with other devices reflecting the themes of the tournament. Before he became king there are regular payments for Henry's own shields to be adorned before jousts in this way.[82] The adaptation of shields to cast real flame is one step further along this established path. Intriguingly, one mid-fifteenth-century heraldic device directly links the flames of chivalric love with Greek fire, the name given to an intense incendiary mixture first developed in the Byzantine Empire. This was used to create both military and artificial fire, hugely impressing European knights who encountered it during the crusades.[83] Jean, Sire de Joinville, records in his memoirs the experience of Greek fire during the Seventh Crusade (1248–54): 'the tail of fire that trailed behind it was as big as a great spear; and it made such a noise as it came, that it sounded like the thunder of heaven. It looked like a dragon flying through the air'.[84] The device appears on a 1447 seal of Charles de Bourbon, in which his arms are surrounded by *pots d'or cassés, dont yssoit grans flammes de feu grégeoys* ('broken golden pots from which flow great flames of Greek fire').[85] René d'Anjou included the shield in the armoury of the *hôpital d'Amour* in his *Livre de Cœur d'Amour épris*, with verses that explain the significance of the fire-pots: *Charles de Bourbon fuys, qui grant renom avoye ... par l'ardeur d'amours je prins, comme scavez, | Por mon mot, feu grégeoys* ('I was Charles de Bourbon, of great renown ... through the ardour of love, as you know, I took for my device Greek fire').[86] This heraldic

---

81 Hall *Chronicle* 707. Compare with images of burning hearts in BL MS King's 322, fol. 1ʳ (see note 65).

82 See e.g. 1392 payment for 'covering of 6 shields palez white, red and black with white and red bands written with white and red letters (2/6 each)' (Wylie *Henry IV 4* 161).

83 See J.R. Partington *A History of Greek Fire and Gunpowder* (Baltimore and London: Johns Hopkins UP, 1999; first edition 1960) 21–8. BL Royal MS 12 B XXV (see note 66) includes a recipe for *Puluis ad ignem Grecum iactandum*.

84 Jean, Sire de Joinville, *The Memoirs of the Lord of Joinville: a New English Version* translated Ethel Wedgwood (London: John Murray, 1906) 98.

85 See <https://devise.saprat.fr/embleme/feu-gregeois>. A pursuivant of the Duke in the 1430s was given the name *Feu grégeois*.

86 Paris: BNF MS français 24399 fol. 86ʳ illustrates the episode; <https://gallica.bnf.fr/ark:/12148/btv1b60005361/f245.item>. Quotation on fol. 86ʳ⁻ᵛ.

adoption of the artificial fire of pyrotechnics as the image for ardent love is a resonant parallel to the fire-throwing shields of the 1401 jousters.

Political Implications

So far I have concentrated primarily on the 1401 jousting performance simply as a courtly chivalric entertainment. But we can also learn from the letters something about how the event was shaped to its occasion, and the diplomatic work it was designed to do beyond normal Christmas festivity. It is possible that the jousts had already been planned for the court, before being repurposed towards the Emperor Manuel's visit. Certainly, few of the letters acknowledge his presence directly. Five of the thirteen letters, noticeably briefer than the others, are relatively rudimentary: they do not name a sender, or an occasion, and while most of them give the challengers imaginative names and claim they are from distant lands, beyond that they focus solely on the terms of the requested joust. The remaining nine are all in more elaborately developed style, with exotically imagined senders and expanded literary or narrative elements. But only two of these letters address the visit of the Emperor directly. Both of them also give more specific details of the event: the letter from Dalida includes the details of the fire-spectacle, and that from Vertu sets up the ceremonial gift-giving to the imperial guest.

There is no way of telling whether these various differences between the letters are incidental, or whether they suggest changes developed during the planning of the show. Manuel had been planning to solicit a visit to Henry's court since June 1400, but had been advised to delay for some months while the King was on military expeditions to Wales and to Scotland. A letter from Henry dated 18 October reports that the Emperor's ambassadors have finally arrived and that a decision about the requested visit would be made by his Council in due course.[87] Manuel finally arrived in England with his retinue around 12 December. While there might well have been enough time to prepare for the show in full knowledge of the impending imperial visit, it might equally be that the event was moved to a more spectacular level after initial preparations had begun, or even that the letters from Dalida and Vertu were specific late additions to the programme.

---

87 *Anglo-Norman Letters and Petitions From All Souls MS. 182* edited M. Dominica Legge (Anglo-Norman Texts 3: Oxford: Blackwell, 1941) 465–6 #410.

SARAH CARPENTER

The overall themes of love and romance that dominate the entertainment are entirely traditional within European courtly culture, with no particular reference to the Emperor's situation or presence. But the official rhetoric of the letters, and the content of those from Vertu and Dalida, reveal more about the diplomatic issues at stake. Manuel is honoured with the expected formal titles of courtesy. He is paired in status with Henry, his host, Vertu having heard that:

> *deux dez plus excellent Princez de tout Crestientie sont a vostre hault & honneurable feste ce sont a ce que nous somez certiffiez le tresnoble Emperour de Constantinople & le trespuissant Prince Roy Dalbion & de Gaule*
>
> fol. 261ᵛ

two of the most excellent Princes of all Christendom are at your high and noble feast, who are as we have been informed the right noble Emperor of Constantinople and the most mighty Prince, King of Albion and Gaul.

According to Dalida, Manuel is ranked as the chief guest of the *moult solennell & loable Court & tant solennell quil a en sa Court vne Emperoure* ('most magnificent and praiseworthy Court, so magnificent that there is in his court an Emperor').

Manuel's imperial position is thus acknowledged in gracious terms, although these are no different from the normal courtesies used between rulers. It is also clear that the event presents the glory as shared between host and guest, each enhancing the other's position. This is particularly clear in Vertu's account of the gift-giving. The exchange of often lavish and costly New Year gifts in English royal courts was already well established by 1401, and there are many records of high expenditure on jewellery and goldsmith's work for this purpose in Henry's accounts both as Earl of Derby and as king.[88] The festive jousting spectacle on New Year's Day is thus an ideal occasion to perform the generosity of the King to the Byzantine Emperor. But interestingly, Vertu's letter suggests this was staged as a double gift-giving, not from Henry to Manuel, but from herself, 'the mother

---

88 See Jenny Stratford *Richard II and the English Royal Treasure* (Woodbridge: The Boydell Press, 2012) 66–7, 119–21, and throughout. For Henry, see Wylie *Henry IV 4*, Index under *New Year's Day*.

and nurse of honour', to the two of them together. Hearing of the presence of 'the noble Emperor of Constantinople and the most powerful Prince King of Albion', Vertu explains: *Nous enuoyons deuers eulx nonmie pour don mais pour remembraunce de cest primier Jour de lan deuz petitz entreseignes* ('We are sending to them, not so much as a gift but more as a memento, on this first day of the year, two small tokens').[89] There is no indication of what these gifts might be, but it is certain that they would have been more than 'small tokens'.[90] Manuel and Henry are presented as equal recipients of Vertu's favour, within the fiction.

The letters also do work for Henry's own status. While paying due reverence to the Emperor's presence, their fictions pay significantly more attention to the king's own position at this uncertain early stage of his reign. He is generally referred to as the 'King of Great Britain' or 'King of Albion', the poetic name for England that suits the romance world of the jousts. But he is also given a range of other titles which expand his regal and mythic heritage. He is *seigneur de pays dez merueilles / & vray successour Du puissant Emperour Arthur* ('Lord of the Country of Marvels, and true successor of the mighty Emperor Arthur'), *herieter & successeur de tresnoble Emperour Charlemaine* ('heir and successor of the right noble Emperor Charlemagne'), *Roi de lisle dez Geans* ('King of the Isle of Giants'), *tresnoble Roi vray successeur du Roy saint Louys & du vaillant villam le Conquereur* ('the right noble King, true successor to the King St Louis and of the valiant William the Conqueror'). Similar quasi-romance titles appear in the Edward III letters; but those here are more varied, and have an extra resonance. With whatever popular and noble support at the time, Henry had nonetheless taken the throne barely a year earlier, by usurpation rather than by inheritance, and at this stage of his reign there remained a degree of challenge to his kingship both at home and, significantly, abroad, especially in France. The titles accorded to him in these letters seem designed to assert the mythic security of his title, to England and the land of Arthur, to the imperial European heritage of Charlemagne, and to the realm of France through St Louis. The spectacle of the jousts offers a romance validation of Henry's royal legitimacy.

89 Letter 6, Vertu, fol. 261^v.

90 According to the *St Albans Chronicle*, Manuel left England *magnificis donaciuis ... remuneratum* ('rewarded with magnificent gifts'): *St Albans Chronicle 2* edited Taylor, Childs, and Watkiss 10–11.

Yet apart from the power of compliment, how far does the jousting event actually acknowledge or address the purpose of Manuel II Palaeologus' visit to Henry's court? It was not a visit of courtesy or congratulation, but one urgently soliciting military and economic help against the Turks who were blockading Constantinople. In 1398 envoys had already been sent to Europe, and to Richard II, Henry's predecessor. A year later, an appeal to Pope Boniface had resulted in a papal call for a Crusade to relieve the city and a Europe-wide collection of funds, which Richard reinforced with his own collection scheme. By the beginning of 1401, however, England had not yet sent either military or financial aid.[91] Not unlike Richard, Henry was sympathetic to the Emperor's position; he was also eager to appear generous and powerful, and was personally committed to chivalry and crusade. But, again like Richard, he was short of both funds and troops to offer to the cause. It is possible to read the jousting letters as treading a diplomatic tightrope through this problematic situation.

It is the letter from Dalida where this is clearest. Its opening salutations present a vivid combination of allegiances:

Dalida par la grace de Mahomet dieu de tous vrayz Infidelz & Sarrazins Soudan de Babilon & Roy Dalexandrie / A hault & puissant Princesse & nostre treschier & tresamee Cousin &c par la grace de celluy a qui lez troys Roys offrirent ore ensence & mirre / Ainsne fille de tresnoble Roi Dalbion herieter & successeur de tresnoble Emperour Charlemaine / Soudanal & Alexandrinal dileccion.

fol. 261[r]

Dalida, by the grace of Mahomet God of all true infidels and Saracens, Sultan of Babylon and King of Alexandria, to the high and mighty Princess and our right dear and well-beloved Cousin &c, by the grace of Him to whom the Three Kings offered gold, frankincense, and myrrh, eldest daughter of the right noble King of Albion, heir and successor of the right noble Emperor Charlemagne: Sultanal and Alexandrinal affection.

This is the only letter sent as from an Eastern potentate, loosely echoing – at least for its local audience – the origin of the Emperor of Constantinople.

---

91   For an account of this complex situation, see Nicol 'A Byzantine Emperor in England' 205–10.

It may now seem surprising that the letter-writer is framed as Muslim, honouring the 'god of all true Infidels and Saracens' since, although he is the ruler of Babylon, this might appear to link him to the Ottoman Turks, the enemies against whom Manuel was seeking support from European Christendom. However, romances frequently include 'Saracen' and other infidel rulers; romance seems to constitute a safe fictional space in which both hostile and amicable interactions between Christian and non-Christian characters can be explored.[92] The Edward III letters similarly include several fictional women writers identified with Islamic countries. Dalida elegantly balances himself, ruler by the grace of Mohammed, with Blanche, whom he courteously acknowledges as princess 'by the grace of Him to whom the Three [*Eastern*] Kings offered gold, frankincense, and myrrh'. This is followed by the association of King Henry with Charlemagne, the heroic emperor whose romances present various crusading tales of Saracen heroes ultimately converted to Christianity.[93] One of these, Fierebras (or Ferumbras), is invoked later in the letter as warden of the recommended challenger Povre Perdu – who himself has mythologized Byzantine connections. Altogether, while avoiding any direct reference to Manuel's homeland or military situation, Dalida's letter establishes a mingled fictive world which enables chivalric encounters between Eastern and Western protagonists and rulers without regard to political actualities.

It is in the conclusion of the letter that we get an intriguing closer brush with the contemporary situation. Setting up the joust for Povre Perdu, the letter requests that his opponent should be:

le Chiualer de vostre Court qui plus grande desir a de fair le Conquest du Royaume de Jerusalem soit Roy Prince Duc ou Conte Chiualer ou Escuier.

fol. 261^r

the knight of your court who has the greatest desire to accomplish the conquest of the Kingdom of Jerusalem, whether he be King, Prince, Duke or Count, knight or squire.

---

92 See e.g. Siobhain Bly Calkin 'Saracens' in *Heroes and Anti-Heroes in Medieval Romance* edited by Neil Cartlidge (Cambridge: D.S. Brewer, 2012) 185–200.

93 See Leila K. Norako 'Charlemagne Romances' in *The Crusades Project: Medieval Insular Literature* (University of Rochester; Robbins Library Digital Projects: no date) at <https://d.lib.rochester.edu/crusades/text/crusades-medieval>.

It is hard not to read this as a possible allusion to Henry himself. He had travelled to Jerusalem in 1392; he appears to have held a lasting desire to join a crusade to free the city, and various stories and allusions suggest that his interest was well known.[94] The phrasing, unique to this letter, also seems to suggest the possibility that the King himself might take up this challenge. Henry had always been an enthusiastic and admired participant in tournaments and jousts, and there are regular records of his taking part in hastiludes as well as overseas campaigns during the 1390s, including a crusade in Prussia.[95] There is no evidence that he did in fact take part in these jousts, but even raising the possibility seems a theatrical gesture to his readiness to support embattled Christendom.

However, the desire attributed to this jouster is not the relief of Constantinople, but the conquest of Jerusalem. While it asserts a general crusading intention, it sidesteps any commitment to Manuel's prime objective. The letters outline a performance that was a spectacular show of generosity, shared values, and military engagement, but the material help that Henry provided to the Emperor was in the end modest. Manuel certainly expressed gratitude for his welcome and hospitality. In a letter written from London during his visit he talks of 'the ruler with whom we are now staying, the king of Britain the Great, of a second civilized world, you might say, who abounds in so many good qualities ... he honours us to the greatest extent and loves us no less ... he has gone to extremes in all he has done for us'.[96] His account of Henry almost seems to mirror the formal courtly congratulation of the jousting letters themselves. Yet, however hospitable, Henry could make no commitment to send or lead troops to support Constantinople. Although he did apparently make a significant parting gift of £2000, even that seems to have been collected and transferred by a kind of smoke and mirrors set of transactions, drawing on the undelivered proceeds of the funding collections set up in 1399.[97]

Henry's generosity seems to have been genuine at a local and personal level, but did little to address the real purpose of the Emperor's visit. This is

---

94 Wylie *Henry IV* 4 105–10; Given-Wilson *Henry IV* 150–1, 398–9, 515–6.
95 Tuck *Henry IV and Chivalry* 58–62.
96 George T. Dennis *The letters of Manuel II Palaeologus: Text, Translation, and Notes* (Corpus fontium historiae Byzantinae 8, Dumbarton Oaks Texts 4; Washington: Dumbarton Oaks Center for Byzantine Studies, 1977) 102.
97 Nicol 'A Byzantine Emperor in England' 216–19.

explicitly recognized in the *St Albans Chronicle*, which reports on Manuel's departure:

> *rex uero ipsum magnificis donaciuis et grandi summa pecunie remuneratum, cum gloria summa deduxit extra Londonias ... Causa peregrinacionis sue in hanc terram fuerat ut militare subsidium optineret a rege ... Sed tunc insurgencibus Scocis ex parte una, et Wallicis uel Hibernicis ex parte altera, excusauit se rex non posse carere propria manu bellica, qui tot aduersantibus urgeretur: et ideo ipsum habundancioribus donariis onerauit.*[98]

> The King lavished magnificent gifts upon him and gave him a large sum of money, and then conducted him out of the city of London with a show of great honour ... The reason for the Emperor's journey to this land had been to obtain military aid from the King ... But then the Scots had begun hostilities in one part of the kingdom, and the Welsh and Irish in another part, so the King explained that he could not allow himself to be deficient in his own armed forces, when he was being threatened by so many enemy troops: and that was the reason why he heaped so many presents upon the Emperor.

We can read the jousting letters as a conscious response to this context. The letter from Dalida seems crafted to create a fiction of a chivalric spectacle which draws together the Byzantine and British courts. The letter is full of mythologized Byzantine and Eastern references. It implies that the magnificent origins, heritage, and aims of the two courts are shared, and enacted together. We might almost see the performance of the jousts, and the New Year gift-giving, as replacing the real military support that Henry could not in the end supply.

It is also worth bearing in mind that the nuance of the letters must have been directed at Henry's own court rather than the imperial visitors. There was a significant language barrier, and Manuel and his retinue were unlikely to have understood the courtly French in which these letters were composed.[99] For them the entertainment probably gave no more than a

---

98   *St Albans Chronicle 2* edited Taylor, Childs, and Watkiss, 10–13.

99   Manuel himself commented on 'the change of language, which did not allow the contacts we wished' on his arrival in France in 1400: Barker *Manuel II Palaeologus* 174.

general impression of magnificence. The performance insists on and enacts a community between the two courts. But it may well be that in the end its meanings were designed as much or more for the home audience as for the Byzantine visitors.

The survival of these two sets of letters from the courts of Edward III and Henry IV point to a developed genre of courtly chivalric entertainment. They are, as early commentators remarked, 'fanciful' and 'imaginary', linking literary romance and allegory with theatrical displays of 'the recreation of arms'. They emphasize the delights of playful spectacle and festivity, overtly engaging only lightly with the serious concerns of their day. But they can give us some real insights into those concerns, and how they were perceived. Even more revealingly, they show us the different and nuanced ways in which such chivalric performances could be used to shape relationships, both within and between the courts of late medieval Europe and their rulers.

University of Edinburgh

Acknowledgements

This article arose from work with Philip Bennett and Louise Gardiner on 'Chivalric Games at the Court of Edward III: The Jousting Letters of EUL MS 183' *Medium Ævum 87:2* (2018) 304–42. My thanks to them both for their insight and collaboration. I am also grateful to Philip Bennett for much expert guidance on Old French language and literature, and to him and Meg Twycross for the transcription and translation which follows.

Fig. 5. London: British Library Additional MS 74236 (The Sherborne Missal, c.1399–1407) page 216, bas-de-page. © British Library Board. Artist: John Siferwas.
<http://access.bl.uk/item/viewer/ark:/81055/vdc_100104060212.0x000001>

Contemporary image of two jousters in high saddles with rebated spears. The coronals are shown as three spikes. The saddles have leg-protectors which go right down to the foot, and the jousters do not appear to be wearing leg armour; however, the only visible armour is their helmets, and this may be partly a fantasy joust, or they may be tilting at the quintain above their heads.

APPENDIX:
BL Cotton MS D II fols 260ᵛ–262ʳ

Meg Twycross and Philip Bennett

This transcription and translation was roughed out by Meg Twycross, and then received thorough and very much appreciated scrutiny from Philip Bennett. It would be difficult now to unpick their contributions from each other, so we have left them unattributed.

The following does not purport to be a scholarly edition of the text of the challenges, merely a transcription and tentative translation of the version in BL Cotton MS Nero D II. (For the manuscript, see <www.bl.uk/manuscripts/Viewer.aspx?ref=cotton_ms_nero_d_ii_f252r>). It preserves the rhetorical punctuation, which gives a sense of how the challenges might have been delivered.

Since this version, like the others, is a later copy, it has inaccuracies and miscopyings. Some of the more obvious are marked in the transcription, though otherwise there is minimal editorial intervention. Occasionally the version in National Library of Scotland Advocates' MS 32-6-9 fols 63ʳ–69ᵛ provides a suggestion, but that version too has its problems.

The translation also attempts the slightly archaic vocabulary and syntax of a royal proclamation, though it is of course a moot point quite how archaic it would have sounded to the original audience – especially since it was delivered in Insular French, much of which has become the accepted vocabulary of honorifics. The syntax is rhetorical and declamatory and proceeds by accumulation. It often defers the important point to the end of the sentence, as is the custom: 'EDWARD VI, by the grace of God King of England, France, and Ireland, defender of the faith and of the Church of England and also of Ireland in earth the supreme head, to all our most loving, faithful, and obedient subjects, and to each of them, greeting'.

Some vocabulary is almost impossible to translate because it encapsulates a system of courtly values the modern descendants of which to us sound stilted: *noblesse* ('nobility'), *gentilesse* ('gentility'), *bontie* ('bounty'). The ethos of jousting is another problem. The young knights ask to be instructed in *le fait desbatement darmes*, 'the fact/performance of the entertainment of arms'. We have translated this as 'the practice of the recreation of arms'.

The names of the challengers are another problem. Many of them come from the vocabulary of love-literature and again we do not have a direct equivalent. As concepts they are perfectly transparent: *Povre Perdu*, 'Poor Lost One'; *Non Saichant*, 'Not-Knowing'; but the modern equivalents sound patronizing or dismissive. Then there are nuances: for example, does *le Joefne Amereuz* imply 'Young-and-in-Love' or 'Young-and-Susceptible'?

The challengers frequently ask to encounter their opponents *sans estre attachiez ne liez en selle ne en main* ('without being attached or tied in the saddle nor by the hand').[1] Occasional regulations against being tied into the saddle specify that this is a form of cheating, to prevent the jouster from being unhorsed:

> the said jousters shall not use any contrivance for cheating either in the saddles or in the weapons, such as hidden girths or other devices which would prevent their being thrown from the saddle, on pain of losing his horse: and of being expelled from the joust in disgrace.[2]

The Beauchamp Pageant recounts and illustrates an episode in which the Earl is accused of cheating in this way, and proves the contrary by leaping out of his saddle.[3] Being tied by the hand is less easy to decipher. In other types of combat it makes it less possible for the jouster to lose his weapon (see the notes to the translation below), but in a joust with lances this would defeat the object. Marina Viallon suggests that this might be a stock phrase repeated because it was expected in a challenge.[4]

Each of the challenges has been given a title with its number in the sequence and the name of the challenger. These are not in the original, but are supplied for ease of reference.

On the first page of this section of the manuscript, fol. 260ᵛ, some words at the ends of lines have disappeared into the binding. It is usually fairly clear what they should be; suggestions are shown in square brackets.

Universities of Lancaster and Edinburgh

---

1 Challenge 4: Dalida.
2 J. Rühl 'Regulations for the Joust in Fifteenth-Century Europe: Francesco Sforza Visconti (1465) and John Tiptoft (1466)' *The International Journal of the History of Sport* 18:2 (2001) 193–208; <https://doi.org/10.1080/714001557>.
3 BL Cotton MS Julius E IV art. 6 fol. 16ʳ; *The Beauchamp Pageant* edited Alexandra Sinclair (Donington: Richard III and Yorkist History Trust / Paul Watkins, 2003) 112–13.
4 Private communication 12 October 2021.

MEG TWYCROSS AND PHILIP BENNETT

BL Cotton MS Nero D II: Transcription

fol. 260ᵛ
¶ Au tresexcellent & tresnoble Princesse Dame Blanche
ffile a trespuissant Prince le Roy Dalbyon /

[*1 Phebus.*]

Phebus la principall planet du ffirmament. A tresexcellent Princesse Dame Blanche ffile au trespuissa[nt] Prince Roy Dalbion saluz & tresparfaite dileccion. Comme nous qui par nostre continuell course enuironnant le hault cercle du ffirmament. Voians par nostre clere inspeccion la gouuernance de tous choses terriennes sachant de certain que tout ainsi comme nostre suer[1] la lune prent sa course & lumier de noz droit aussi tost la clarte du monde prennent nourriture & liesce de vostre Court Royall / comme de la vostre droit fontain donneure & de noblesce Nous desirans lencrese de nostre tresame enfaunt de nostre Chambre fferombras de la ffontain luy enuoyons deuers vostre haultesse pour veoir le contenement de vostre Court Roial & pour apprendre le fait desbatement dar[mes] vous enpriant que vous plaise commander aucun de lez honurablez chiualers estans en vostre feste a deliurer n[ostre] dit enfans de six coups de lance auecques Rochez dassise en haultez sellez sans estre liez ou attachiez a fin que nostre dit enfant puisse retourner deuers nous le mieulx aprins / de lesbatement dessusdicte. come nous affions trese[n]tierment en vous / Et si chose soit deuers nous que fair pouons / a vostre aise ou consolacion. nous lu vueillez certiff[ier] par nostre dit enfaunt / & nous laccomplirons de treslie & Joyeulx cueur. Vostre excellent & honurable estat en[..?] honneur Joye & farfait[2] prosperitie garde & gouuerne le createur de toutez creaturs

---

1 The flourish on the r might be an abbreviation for *-e*, but it also occurs on *pour* and *veoir* six lines down.
2 *Farfait* for *parfait*?

82

APPENDIX: BL COTTON MS D II

BL Cotton MS Nero D II: Translation

fol. 260ᵛ

¶ To the most excellent and right noble Princess, the Lady Blanche, daughter of the most mighty Prince, the King of Albion

[*1 Phebus.*]

Phoebus, the principal planet of the firmament, to the right excellent Princess Lady Blanche, daughter of the most mighty Prince, the King of Albion, greeting and sincere affection. Since we, who by our continuous circuit encompassing the high circle of the firmament, seeing by our clear gaze the government of all earthly things, surely know[ing] that just as our sister the Moon takes her course and light from us, so equally the radiance of the world takes nourishment and joy from your Royal Court, as from your true well-spring of honour and noblesse, we, wishing for the advancement of our much-loved young knight of our Chamber,[1] Ferombras of the Fountain, send him to Your Highness to see how your Royal Court is conducted, and to learn the practice of the recreation of arms, praying you that it would please you to command any one of the honourable knights present at your feast to deliver to our aforesaid new knight six blows of the rebated lance[2] in high saddles,[3] without being tied or secured [in the saddle], to the end that our said new knight may return to us the better instructed in the aforementioned recreation. As we rely most entirely on you. And if there is anything in our power that we may do for your ease or pleasure, be so good as to inform us by our aforementioned new knight, and we will fulfil it with a most cheerful and joyful heart. May the Creator of all creatures

---

1 Implies that Ferombras is directly attached to the household of Phebus.

2 Fitted with a coronal or *roche* (possibly the same word as chess *rook* or castle?); see Juliet Barker *The Tournament in England 1100–1400* (Woodbridge: The Boydell Press, 1986) 178, and for an image <www.worldhistory.org/image/8979/jousting-lance-head/>.

3 A 'high saddle' had a very high saddle bow and was continued downwards so as to protect the legs; Marina Viallon 'A German High Tournament Saddle in the Royal Armouries, Leeds' *Arms and Armour* 12:2 (2015) 103–23. See <https://collections.royalarmouries.org/object/rac-object-17499.html>, also BL Additional MS 74236 (Sherborne Missal, c.1399–1407) page 216: <http://access.bl.uk/item/viewer/ark:/81055/vdc_100104060212.0x000001>, bas-de-page, left.

/ Donne en nostre merveilleu[se] mansion du firmament plain destoilles /

[2 *Vng Jeune & non saichant Escuier*]

Atresexcellent & tresnoble Princesse Dame Blanche ffille au trespuissant Prince Roi de la grant Breta[igne] Moustre treshumblement vng Jeune & non saichant Escuier porteur de cestes qui est venu de longt[ain] parties pour veoir le contenement de vostre Court Roial / & en especial pour apprendre le fait desbatem[ent] darmes / Suppliant a vostre haultesse que vous plaise commaunder le plus vailant Bachiller ou Escuie[r] dessoubz laaige de trent deux ans esteans en vostre feste a deliurer le dit suppliant en bassez sellez de do[..] Coupes de lance auecques Rochez dassise sans estre liez ou attachiez a fin de lui apprendre le fait e[t] esbatement[3] dessusdicte / Et ce par voye de vostre tresnoble bonte & gentilesce /

[3 *Jeunesce.*]

Ieunesce par la grace de dieu Damours Roigne de Joye & de tout liesce / A hault & puissant Princ[esse] & nostre treschier & tresamee Cousin Blanche ainsne ffille du treshault & puissant Prince Roi de Bretaign le grand & de Gaule / seigneur de pays dez merueilles / & vray successour Du puissant Emperour Arthur ou quel honneur &

---

3   NLS Advocates' MS 32 6 9 has *apprendre le dit fait & esbatement Darmes.*

preserve and guide your excellent and honourable estate in honour, joy, and all prosperity. Given in our marvellous mansion in the star-filled firmament.

[2 Vng Jeune & non saichant Escuier]

To the right excellent and noble Princess Lady Blanche, daughter to the most mighty Prince, King of Greater Britain,[4] there humbly presents [himself][5] a young and unschooled squire, the bearer of this, who has come from distant parts to see how your royal court is conducted, and especially to learn the practice of the recreation of arms, begging Your Highness that it would please you to command the most valiant knight-bachelor or squire present at your feast below the age of thirty-two to deliver to the said suppliant, in low[6] saddles, twelve[?] blows of the prescribed rebated lance, without being tied or secured, to the end of instructing him in the practice of the abovementioned recreation. And this through your most noble favour and generosity.

[3 Jeunesce.]

Youth, by the grace of the God of Love, Queen of Joy and of all pleasure, to the high and mighty Princess[7] and our right dear and well-beloved cousin Blanche, eldest daughter of the most high and mighty Prince, King of Greater Britain and of Gaul,[8] Lord of the Country of Marvels, and true successor of the mighty Emperor Arthur, in whose person honour

---

4   Not 'Great Britain' in our sense, but in the Arthurian sense of Britain as contrasted with Little Britain, Brittany.

5   The formula in appeals to the Chancellor in the courts begins 'Showeth ...' What is shown is the plaintiff's or defendant's case. Here the challenger seems to be showing both himself, and his request to be allocated an answerer.

6   For a low saddle (though a ceremonial instead of a jousting one), see <https://collections.royalarmouries.org/object/rac-object-524.html>. It was easier to knock a jouster out of a low saddle than out of a high one. Thanks to Marina Viallon for the reference.

7   This is a customary style in royal proclamations in the sixteenth and seventeenth centuries; e.g. 'our Soveraigne Ladie, the High and Mightie Prince, Elizabeth late Queene of England, France, and Ireland ...'; Larkin and Hughes *Royal Stuart Proclamations* (Oxford UP, 1973) 1 1.

8   France: as appears later in the sentence there is a conscious equation of Henry IV's kingdom with the lands of Arthurian romance.

prouesce de hault ch<u>iua</u>lrie est plus grant habond[ament] en sa p<u>e</u>rsonne que en Prince qui soit au Jo<u>ur</u>duy viuant . Car moult approuuee est la prouues[ce] de sa hault ch<u>iua</u>lrie . en pluso<u>ur</u>s estraunge Regions / Dont la reno<u>m</u>mie en Court par tout le mond[e] salut & plaisant dileccion / Nostre treschier & t<u>re</u>same Cousin vueillez sauoir que en n<u>os</u>tre Court a[vum] nourry vne Jeune Ch<u>iua</u>le<u>r</u> par son droit no<u>m</u>me appellee Nonsaichant qui en amours a souffert [et] soustenu plusours traualx & dangiers / Pour allegier sa peine / il est mis en la quest pour quer[ir] vne Dame de grant renom / que on appelle Grace / de la quele il na peu ne ne puet encores[4] a[ver] aucunes nouuelles / Et de p<u>re</u>sent a entendu que vne moult noble & belle assemblee de pluseurs no[bles] Dames & Damoiselle<u>s</u> & de vaillans ch<u>iua</u>ler<u>s</u> & Escuiers doit estre deuers v<u>os</u>tre Prince / a cest p<u>re</u>sen[te] feste de Nouuell. Si cest trait & to<u>ur</u>ne vers celle part pour veoir & sauoir sil poura aura[5] aucu[n] recours de la dit quest. Et aussi pour ce quil est de coustume que tous ch<u>iua</u>ler<u>s</u> errans voulenti[ers] sacconntent[6] de cours de Roys & haulx Princes par manier darmez / Nous qui auons entend[u] que ycelle solempnell feste & noble assemblee entre les autres vaillans Ch<u>iua</u>lers & Escuiers. I[l] ya vng Ch<u>iua</u>le<u>r</u> qui nagares a fait armer[7] ou Ream de Gaule si bien & vaillanment quil [a] acquis grant los & grant pris ou dit Royaume de Gaule & en pluseurs autrez contrees dont il puet mieulx estre prisie & loe. Desirant que le dit nonsaichant n<u>os</u>tre nourry soit aprins es faiz dez esbatemens darmes / par lez mains de celluy noble ch<u>iua</u>ler . Vous prions tresaffectuesement que Icelluy mesmes n<u>os</u>tre nourry faciez deliurer de six coups de lance ass<u>is</u> en sellez Rasses[8] par le dessusd<u>icte</u> noble ch<u>iua</u>ler qui port en sez armez vn escu dont le champ est dazur a trois quintefueillez dor & vng Croissant dargent/. Et que ce soit sans estre attachiez ne liez en main[9]

4   These three words are joined together wrongly, as *peuten cores*.
5   Probably copied wrongly echoing the ending of the previous verb. One would expect *aver*.
6   Probably a minim too many, for *s'accointent*, 'get to know, frequent'.
7   Probably a mistake for *armes* – the noun fits the syntax and general sense better than the verb.
8   *Selles rasses* (modern French *selles rases*, literally 'flat saddles') was the term used in French-speaking Flanders for low saddles. Thanks to Marina Viallon for this information.
9   There is a distinct abbreviation mark or flourish in the margin. It might be an abbreviation for *er*, or a flourish on a final *n*. The latter seems more likely; compare

and prowess of high chivalry more greatly abounds than in any Prince this day living; for the prowess of his high chivalry has been experienced in many distant regions, of which the fame runs throughout the whole world: greeting and warm friendship. Our most dear and well-beloved Cousin, be good enough to know that in our Court we have brought up a young knight whose true name is Inexperienced, who has suffered and borne many labours and dangers in love; to relieve his suffering he has embarked upon a quest to seek out a lady of great reputation whom they call Grace, of whom he could not and still cannot obtain any news. And now he has understood that a very noble and handsome assembly of many noble ladies and maidens and of valiant knights and squires is to come to your Prince for this present Feast of Christmas, he is drawn and diverted towards this region to see and discover whether he might have any assistance in the said quest. And also because it is customary for all knights errant willingly to frequent the courts of kings and great princes for handling arms, We, who have understood that in this solemn festival and noble gathering, among the other valiant knights and esquires, there is a knight who has recently performed deeds of arms in the realm of Gaul, so well and valiantly that he has gained great praise and estimation in the said Kingdom of Gaul and several other countries, through which he can be the more esteemed and praised. Desiring that the said Inexperienced, our foster-child, should be instructed in the practice of the recreation of arms by the hands of this noble knight, we pray most warmly that you should cause this same foster-child of ours to receive six blows of the lance, seated in [low?] saddles, by the aforementioned noble knight, who bears as his arms a shield of a field azure with three cinquefoils or and a crescent argent. And that this should be without being attached or tied in hand[9]

---

9   There seems to be no reason why he should be attached 'by the hand'. The phrase is apparently common in fifteenth-century French-language challenges, but refers to handheld weapons: there are images in the *Livre des Tournois* of René d'Anjou which show the sword attached to the gauntlet by a chain, and the mace hanging from the belt; BNF MS français 2962 fols 32^V–33^r; see <https://gallica.bnf.fr/ark:/12148/btv1b10532593m/f71.item>.

ne en selle / Et en ce fais[10] vous nous ferez tresingulier plaisir / Saichant que se voulez chose que soit en no̲s̲tre Royaulme . nous le ferons liement. Enpriant celluy qui sur tous a puissans quil vous mainteine tousiours en bone pros̲p̲eritie / donneur & de liesce. Escript en no̲s̲tre Chastel de plaisance le Jour le mois pre̲sent. Et oultre no̲s̲tre treschier & tre̲same Cousin vueilliez sauoir que dit no̲s̲tre norry en venant deue̲r̲s vo̲s̲tre dit pre̲sence a encontre vne Damoisell que venoit de parde la[11] du Royaulme de Panthaluce / a quel il accompaigne Jusquez a vo̲s̲tre pre̲sence /

fol. 261ʳ

[*4 Dalida.*]

D alida par la grace de Mahomet dieu de tous vrayz Infidelz & Sarrazins Soudan de Babilon & Roy Dalexandrie / A hault & puissant Princesse & no̲s̲tre treschier & tre̲samee Cousin &c par la grace de celluy a qui lez troys Roys offrirent ore ensence & mirre / Ainsne fille de tre̲snoble Roi Dalbion herieter & successeur de tre̲snoble Empe̲rour Charlemaine / Soudanal & Alexandrinal dileccion /

   with *assise en bassez sellez sans estre attachiez ne liez en selle ne en main* in the following challenge.
10 This appears to have an (unlikely) abbreviation mark through the double s.
11 For *de par dela*, 'from beyond'.

or in saddle. And in doing this you will give us the most especial pleasure. Knowing that if you wish for anything which might be in our kingdom, we will do it with delight. Praying to Him who has power over all that He should keep you forever in good prosperity of honour and pleasure. Written in our castle of Delight the [X] day of the present month. And furthermore, our right dear and well-beloved Cousin, be so good as to know that this said foster-child of ours, in coming towards your said presence, has met a maiden/young lord[10] who was coming from overseas from beyond the kingdom of Panthaluce,[11] whom he is accompanying as far as your presence.

fol. 261ʳ

[*4 Dalida.*]

Dalida,[12] by the grace of Mahomet God of all true infidels and Saracens, Sultan of Babylon and King of Alexandria, to the high and mighty Princess and our right dear and well-beloved Cousin &c,[13] by the grace of Him to whom the Three Kings offered gold, frankincense, and myrrh, eldest daughter of the right noble King of Albion, heir and successor of the right noble Emperor Charlemagne: Sultanal and Alexandrinal affection.

---

10 Despite the copyist's *vne*, a *damoisel* could be a 'young lord' instead of 'a young lady'. It is of course possible that Penthesilea had sent an Amazon to the jousts, or (in practice) a knight costumed as an Amazon; but the young person comes from *beyond* (*de par dela*) Penthesilea's kingdom, which suggests a young lord coming from an unimaginable distance.

11 Probably Penthesilea, Queen of the Amazons. She was one of the B-list of the Nine Female Worthies, one which concentrated on military prowess rather than matching the tripartite division of the Nine male Worthies. Many of them were Amazons. Her name is spelt as Panthasilee. She appears in Christine de Pisan's *Epitre d'Othea* ch. 15: *Panthasellee fu vne pucelle royne damazonie et moult fu belle et de merueilleuse proece en armes*; BL Harley MS 4431 fol. 103ᵛ: <www.bl.uk/catalogues/illuminatedmanuscripts/ILLUMIN.ASP?Size=mid&IllID=35754>.

12 Though Dalida uses masculine titles, like 'Sultan' and 'King', the name is recognisably that of Delilah the mistress of Samson. When s/he says that Blanche will give her *tresfeminal plaisir*, 'most womanly pleasure', is she referring to the Princess or to her[?]self? Delilah was not one of the Nine Female Worthies. She does, however, appear in later fantasy catalogues as one of the armigerous Nine Unworthy Women, in the company of Semiramis and Jezebel. In Munich: Bayerische Staatsbibliothek Hs cgm 1952 fol. 16ʳ, her arms are a pair of shears; <www.digitale-sammlungen.de/en/view/bsb00016900?page=35>.

13 Fill in 'Blanche'.

Nostre treschier & tresamee Cousin en vostre Court a vne Dame de grant pris / que on appelle plaisance que par long temps a tenu prisoner en sez prisonez vn Chiualer du Royaume Damours nomme le pouoir perdu /. le quel Chiualer ne puet estre deliure dicelles prisonez tant quil soit dischargie de six Coupez de launcez assise en bassez sellez sans estre attachiez ne liez en selle ne en main / Pour la quel deliurance a[v]oir[12] / Il lui semble quil lui conuendroit cheminer & errer maintes contrees chasteaulx villez & Citees montaignes valees bois & Riuiers auant quil peust trouuer vne tiel quil demaund si non quil trouuast aucun bon counseil qui luy abregast son chemin / Et pour ce que nous auons entendu que nostre treschier & bien amee Cousin le Roy vostre pier . a cest feste de Noell tient moult solennell & loable Court & tant solennell quil a en sa Court vne Emperour & tresgrande Renommee de nobles Dames & damoiselles vaillans Chiualers & Escuiers qui font merueilles / comme lez vngs qui cheuauchent Dragons / les autres portent serpens sur leurs testes gettans feu & flambe / lez autres qui sont si ardans en amours / que parmy leurs targez & escuz gettent flambe de feu tout visible & plousours autres Chiualers auentureux & errans qui vennent deuers vous tant depar lempereys Pantasile come depar la Roigne de Cartaige. Nous luy auons conseillie / quil se tire & adresce deuers vous[13] dominal[14] & Jouuensall[15] presence et Icelluy pour perdu couent & mene nostre treschier & bien amee ne proneu[16] fferebras / de Damas le Jeune generall gouuerneur de nostre Royaume Dalexandrie . A fin quil ne rompe mie sa prison & quil ne sen fuy lye & attachie dune cheyenne par my le col / Si vous prions tresaffectueusement que au dit Chiualer poure perdu vous vueilliez deliurer le Chiualer de vostre Court qui plus grande desir a de fair le Conquest du Royaume de Jerusalem soit Roy Prince Duc ou Conte Chiualer ou Escuier pour le deliuerer & dischargier de six coups de lance dessusdit.

12   In MS, *aioir*.

13   *Vous* is an acceptable form of the plural possessive adjective in Anglo-Norman, corresponding to Continental French *vos/voz*. The presence of two adjectives seems to have led the scribe, or even the original writer, to use the plural possessive; though it might also be the equivalent of *nous*, 'we', used by a royal person.

14   *Dominal* is not recorded elsewhere, but is a reasonable coinage, though it might be a miscopying of *dominical*, 'lordly, appertaining to a lord' (Godefroy). Should *vous* be *vostre*?

15   AND sv *jovencel* etc. = 'youthful'.

16   Probably a mistake for *nepneu*, 'nephew'. Possibly the original had something like *bien amé et prou neveu*, 'well-beloved and excellent nephew'.

APPENDIX: BL COTTON MS D II

Our right dear and well-beloved Cousin, in your Court is a lady of great excellence who is called Pleasure, who for a long time has held prisoner in her dungeons a knight of the Kingdom of Love called 'The Poor Lost One' which knight cannot be released from that prison until he shall have been discharged by six blows of the lance sitting in low saddles without being attached or tied in the saddle nor by the hand. In order to obtain this release, it seems to him that he needs to travel and wander through many countries, castles, towns and cities, mountains, valleys, woods, and rivers, before he will be able to find a suitable person to challenge, unless he should find some good counsel which would shorten his journey. And since we have understood that our right dear and well-beloved Cousin the King your father at this feast of Christmas is holding a most magnificent and praiseworthy Court, so magnificent that there is in his court an Emperor and a most famous company of noble ladies and maidens, valiant knights and squires, who perform marvels; like the ones who ride dragons, others who bear serpents on their heads casting fire and flame, others who are so burning in love that through their bucklers and shields they cast visible flames of fire, and many other adventurous and wandering knights who are coming towards you, as much on the behalf of the Empress Penthesilea[14] as on behalf of the Queen of Carthage.[15] We have advised him that he should draw and direct himself towards your sovereign and youthful presence; and our very dear and well-beloved nephew Fierabras the Young of Damascus, Governor General of our Kingdom of Alexandria, comes with and escorts this Poor Lost One. In order that he should not break his captivity and flee, [he is] tied and attached by a chain round the neck. So we beg you most affectionately that to the said knight Poor Lost One you would be willing to present as challenger the knight of your court who has the greatest desire to accomplish the conquest of the Kingdom of Jerusalem, whether he be King, Prince, Duke or Count, knight or squire, to deliver and discharge upon him[16] six blows of the lance aforesaid. And you will do us right womanly pleasure.

14   Seems to suggest that *Panthaluce* in Letter 3 is indeed Penthesilea.
15   Dido does not appear as a letter-writer in the surviving challenges, but seems a good candidate for one.
16   Impossible to reproduce in English: he is to be delivered and discharged *by* and *of* six blows of the lance. The blows are delivered, but he will also be delivered from his quest.

Et vous nous ferez tresfeminal plaisir / Enpriant a Alpha & Oo quil vous doint reignier perdurablement. Donne en nostre Citee de Jherico le Jour de la translacion Appolin. /

[*5 Naturo.*]

Naturo Nourice de vie executeur du tout puissant Roi dez Royz / A tresexcellent Princesse Dame &c ffille au trespuissant Prince Roi Dalbion salut & tresparfite dileccion. Nous qui ordonnons a homme & best leurs viures selon le hault commaundement du creatour de tous creatures / sauons de certain que ainsi comme nostre subgiet Priapus qui est dieu de Jardins derbes & de ffleurs renouuell & refressh la face de la terre en la noble season Daurill qui estoit poure & sans vestur par limportable yver qui est le Roi de ffroidur Region & trace par entre la terre si reprent sa conjointur & subtill mantell plain de dulceur & de fflours / Droit ainsi toutz estaz du monde viuans attendans honneur sont vestuz & aournez de vertueuse science par gracious gouuernaunce & contenement de vostre excellent noble cuer Roial comme de vray mireur & exemplar de tout honneur bontie & gentillesce / a cest vostre noble feste / pour veoir la gouuernaunce de vostre excellent estat & pour apprendre le fait desbatement darmes / Nous desirans lencres de nostre bien amee

APPENDIX: BL COTTON MS D II

Praying to Alpha and Omega that he will grant you to reign for ever and ever. Given in our City of Jericho the day of the translation of Appolin.[17]

[5 *Naturo.*]

Nature, Nurse of life, Vicegerent of the all-powerful King of Kings, to the right excellent Princess Lady [Blanche] etcetera daughter to the most mighty Prince, King of Albion, greeting and sincere affection. We who ordain to man and beast their existence, according to the high commandment of the Creator of all creatures, know for certain that, just as our subject Priapus, who is god of gardens, plants, and flowers, renews and refreshes the face of the earth in the noble month of April (which had been poor and naked because of the unbearable Winter who is the King of the region of Cold),[18] and leaves its trace over all the earth,[19] and puts back on its robe[20] and delicate cloak full of soft mildness and flowers, in the very same way all estates of the living world aspiring to honour are clothed and adorned with the knowledge of virtue by means of the gracious authority and guidance of your excellent and noble royal heart,[21] as from the true mirror[22] and model of all honour, goodness, and nobility. At this noble festival of yours, in order that he may see the conduct of your excellent estate, and to learn the practice of the recreation of arms, we, desiring the advancement of our well-beloved

17   Appolin (Apollo) is another of the many gods attributed to Saracen ('pagan') religion in *chansons de geste*; the expression *translacioun Appolin* is obviously borrowed from the idea of the translation of relics from one holy site to another.

18   He is possibly thinking of the Frigid Zone. Medieval writers were familiar (through Macrobius's *Commentary on the Dream of Scipio* if nowhere else) with the concept of two frozen areas around the Poles, where winter is permanent.

19   It is not clear from the syntax whether it is Priapus or April which is the subject.

20   This is difficult. *Conjointure* in the MS should mean 'joining together', 'conjunction'. One suggestion is that it refers to the conjunction of the stars which heralds spring; but *conjunction* usually refers to the coming together of the planets, which does not occur in a regular annual pattern. Spring is heralded by the rising of the constellations of the fixed stars. The Advocates' manuscript has *couuerture*, which at least has the merit of being a doublet of *subtill mantell*, but may well be a *lectio facilior*. See Charles of Orléans: *Le temps a laissié son manteau | De vent, de froidure et de pluye, | Et s'est vestu de brouderie, | De soleil luyant, cler et beau.*

21   Possibly a mistake for *cour*, 'court', but *cuer* is also apposite.

22   As in *Mirror for Princes*; see *OED* sv mirror n. I. 'A model or example'.

93

nourry fferrant de fferers porteur de cestz / luy enuoyons deuers vous / priant que par laduis de nobles de vostre feste / vouz plaise commaunder le Chiualer or Escuier estant a vostre feste dessusdicte qui a plus parle damours a pluseurs Damoiselles . & qui plus souuent a changie la custume de loyaulx amans / Deliurer nostre dit Escuier de six coupes de lance en hautez ou en bassez selles auec Rochez dassise / sans estre liez ne attachiez / A fin que nostre dicte nourry puisse en sa Jeunesce aprendre a eschiuer destre double ou faulx en amours que dieu deffend comme nous affions tresespecialment a vostre bonte & noblesce / Tresexcellent Princesse nous prions a dieu Damours de vous octroir[17] honneur parfite saincte & Joyeux vie & longue aduree / Donne en nostre palaice de plaisance plain de delicez. /

[6 Vertu.]

Uertu mere & Nourrice Donneur Dame de parfait plaisance / A tresexcellent Princesse nostre trescheir & tresamee Cousine & Dame de cest hault feste Dame &c ffille au trespuissant Prince le Roi de lisle dez Geans salut & dileccion / Nous de plain entent auons ordonne & deppute vostre noble persone pour generall executeresce de toutz chosez qui

fol. 261ᵛ

appartiennent a lexcellence de nostre office a nous garanties par le Roy dez Royz./ Comme a tresnoble Dame predestinate[18] de dieu de laccomplir loyalment & honneurablement . enuoyons deuers vostre noblesce vng Chiualer de nostre Chambre appelle Jeune lapprenant qui a grant voulentie & especiall desir pour veoir le noble deuis & execucion de nostre commission a vous dicte par nostre prouidice prudence & pour apprendre le fait du honneurable esbatement

17   The precise form *octroir* is not registered in *AND*, but the forms *ottohir* (inf.) and *ottruyz* (p.p.) would justify it.
18   This appears to be a latinate Middle English form first recorded in the late fourteenth century; see *MED* sv *predestinaten* p.p. *predestinate*. It is not recorded in *AND*.

fosterling Ferrant de Ferrers, bearer of these letters, send him to you, praying that by the advice of the noblemen of your feast, it should please you to command the knight or squire present at your aforementioned feast who has spoken most of love to various maidens, and who has most often altered the custom of true lovers, to deliver to our said squire six blows of the lance in high or low saddles with the prescribed rebated points, without being tied or attached [in the saddle], so that our said fosterling may in his youth learn to renounce double-dealing and faithlessness in love – which God forfend! – as we place our faith most especially in your generosity and nobility. Right excellent Princess, we pray to the God of Love to grant you honour, the best of health, and a long and joyful life. Given in our palace of Pleasure full of delights.

[6 *Vertu.*]

Virtue, mother and nurse of Honour, Lady of perfect Pleasure, to the right excellent Princess our right dear and well-beloved Cousin and Lady of this exalted feast, Lady etc., daughter to the most mighty Prince, the King of the Isle of Giants, greeting and affection. We, being fully resolved, have ordained and appointed your noble self as executrix with full powers over all things which

fol. 261ᵛ

belong to the excellence of our office, as warranted to us by the King of Kings, as to a most noble Lady predestinate by God to fulfil them loyally and honourably: we send to Your Nobility a knight of our Chamber called 'The Enterprising Youth'[23] who has a great resolve and special desire to see the noble planning and execution of our commission to you directed by Our foreseeing[24] prudence, and to learn the practice of the honourable recreation

---

23 One variant of the verb *emprendre*, 'to undertake (enterprises)' is *apprendre* (see *AND*), present participle thus *apprenant* 'active, enterprising'.

24 *Providice* is probably a nonceword from *providere* 'to foresee'. *Prudentia* is a contracted form of *providentia*, 'fore-seeing'. The iconography of the cardinal virtue of Prudence is connected with faculty of sight: she is often shown gazing into a mirror ('know thyself'), or with two or three heads – like Janus, she uses the experience of the past to act in the present so as to secure the future. As Lydgate puts it, 'Dame Prudence, | The which with hir mirrour bright, | By the pourveyaunce of hir foresight | And hir myrrour, called provydence, | Is strong to make resistance | In hir

darmes, vous especialment / priant qui vous plaise commaunder le plus honneurable & noble Chiualer destate ou de compte qui a plus viel temps este armes sur le mescreant[es] a present estant a vostre hault & Roial feste / a apprendre nostre dit Chiualer de nostre Chambre le fait de desbatement darmes dessusdicte Et tresexcellent Princesse pour ce que donne nous est a entendre que deux dez plus excellent Princez de tout Crestientie sont a vostre hault & honneurable feste ce sont a ce que nous somez certiffiez le tresnoble Emperour de Constantinople & le trespuissant Prince Roy Dalbion & de Gaule / Nous enuoyons deuers eulx nonmie pour don mais pour remembraunce de cest primier Jour de lan deuz petitz entreseignes pour nostre dit Chiualer. En vous priant que nostre present lettre nous puisse Recommaunder aux haux & honneurables estaz dez excellentz Princez dessusdiz comme nous en vostre parfite & honneurable bontie / Tresexcellent & tresnoble Princesse lespecial cause de nostre creacion vous garde & gouuern en honneur & parfite saincte & vous octroye Joyeuse vie & longue aduree / Donne en nostre noble Donjon de parfite diligence voide de vices /

[7 *Ardant Desireux.*]

A tresexcellente & tresnoble Princesse Dame &c ffille au trespuissant Roi de la grande Britaign Moustre treshumblement vng Jeune chiualer nomme Ardant desireux qui est venu de longtaines parties de la terre de Inde a cest vostre noble feste pour veoir le contenement de vostre excellence & pour apprendre la fait desbatement darmez / vous suppliant humblement quil vous please commaunder le Chiualer de cest feste qui a plus cheuauchie en estraunge pais entre lez aaigez de vingt & xxiiij ans crut ait[19] & deliurer le dit suppliant de six coupes de lance de mesure sans vilain Rochet & sans estre liez ne attachiez ycest premier Jour de lan en vostre sale au soir en basses selles & celluy qui aura Jouste le mieuleurs courses par vostre tresnoble Jugement aura de son compaignon a chacun

---

19 This is clearly an error (misheard in dictation?). The Advocates' manuscript misses it out altogether. It seems to be intended for a doublet to *deliurer*, an infinitive depending on *commaunder*. The only other doublet is *baillier & deliurer* in (10) Cleopatra.

of arms; praying you most specially that it should please you to command the most noble and honourable Knight of rank or standing who has from the longest way back taken up arms against the infidels, and who is at present at your high and royal feast, to teach our said Knight of our Chamber the practice of the recreation of arms abovesaid. And, right excellent Princess, because we have been given to understand that two of the most excellent Princes of all Christendom are at your high and noble feast, who are as we have been informed the right noble Emperor of Constantinople and the most mighty Prince, King of Albion and Gaul, we are sending to them, not so much as a gift but more as a memento, on this first day of the year, two small tokens by the hand of our said knight. Praying you that our present letter may recommend us to the high and honourable estate of the excellent princes aforesaid, as it may us to your perfect and honourable bounty. Right excellent and right noble Princess, may the Primary Cause of our creation protect and guide you in honour and the best of health, and grant you a joyous and long life. Given in our most noble keep of perfect Diligence free from vices.

[7 Ardant Desireux.]

To the right excellent and right noble Princess Lady &c daughter to the most mighty King of Britain the Great, I most humbly present a young knight named Ardent Desire[25] who has come from distant regions of the land of India to this your noble feast to view the conduct of Your Excellence and to learn the practice of the recreation of arms, praying you humbly that it would please you to command the knight in this feast who has ridden the most into foreign parts between the ages of twenty and 24 years to receive and deliver to the said suppliant six blows of the lance of standard length[26] without disallowed spear-points and without being tied or attached, on this first day of the year in your hall in the evening, in low saddles; and he who shall according to Your right noble judgement have jousted the best

forsight, as it is right, | Ageyns Fortune and al hir might': *Disguising at London* 140-6. He gives her three eyes, for past, present, and future.

25 Literally 'Burning Desirous'.
26 Juliet Barker says that 'Jousting challenges for all hastiludes and chivalric combats commonly specified that the lances should be *de mesure*, that is, of equal length as measured against a standard provided by the organizer. This prevented any knight having an unfair advantage of length'; *Tournament in England* 178.

course vne vierge dor par voye de bone Escuier / Cest pour supplicacio[n] vous plaise grantier & accomplir & le nomme du Chiualer qui me deliurera me fera assauoir par voye de bontie & gentillesce /

[*8 Penolese.*]

Atresexcellent Princesse Dame &c fille au trespuissant Roi Dalbion Penolese femme a tresnoble Prince Ulixes salutz & tresparfait dileccion / Pour ce que la commune fame Damours nous a infourmez que vous tenez a present vne feste Roial comme vouz esteez tousdiz accoustumee. A la quelle maints bons chiualers & Escuiers sont pour Jouster dancier & Joyeuse vie mener / Si enuoyons a vostre haultesce vne nostre bien amee enfaunt Palamides le loyal porteur de cestz qui a grant desir destre aprins[20] en fait desbatement darmez Suppliant a vostre bontie & haultesce de commaunder vne noble Chiualer estant a vostre feste qui porte a sa deuise trois diuerse fueillez en guise de vne treffoile a deliure[r] nostre dit enfaunt de six coupes de launce sans vilain Rochet en bassez selles a fin que nostre dit enfau[nt] puisse retourner deuers nous le mieulx aprins de fait de lesbatement dessusdicte. Nous certifians par luy vostre plaisir soit a vostre excellence droit nouuelle de vostre hault & honneurable estate pour especiall consolacion de nostre cuer comme nous affions tresentierment de vous / Tresexcellent Princesse le vray dieu Damours vous octroy honneur Joye & parfite saintie & bon vie & long a durer /

20 MS *a prins.*

courses[27] will have from his partner in each course a rod of gold by the hand of[28] a good Squire. May it please you to grant and fulfil this poor request and he will inform me by Generosity and Nobility the name of the knight who is to deliver[29] me.[30]

[8 Penolese.]

To the right excellent Princess Lady &c daughter to the most mighty King of Albion, Penolese[31] wife to the right noble Prince Ulysses: greeting and sincere affection. Because the common report of Love has informed us that at this very moment you are holding a royal feast, as is your established custom, at which many good knights and squires are [present] in order to joust, dance, and lead a joyful life, thus we send to Your Highness a well-beloved young knight of ours, Palamides,[32] the loyal bearer of these [letters], who has a great desire to be instructed in the practice of the recreation of arms. Beseeching Your Beneficence and Highness to command a noble knight present at your festival who bears in his coat of arms three distinct leaves in the form of a trefoil to deliver to our said child six blows of the lance without disallowed spear-points, in low saddles, to the end that our said child may return to us the better instructed in the practice of the above-mentioned recreation. Informing us by him, should it please your Excellence, correct news of your high and honourable estate, for the special solace of our heart, as we trust most entirely in you. Right excellent Princess, the true God of Love grant you honour, joy, and the best of health, and a good and long-lasting life.

27 The technical term: see *MED* sv *cours* n. 2a. 'A charge in battle or tourney; a passage at arms', with examples. Also *OED* sv *course* n. 5.
28 Literally 'by means of'.
29 The opponent delivers the blow, but also releases (delivers) the challenger from the onus of his challenge.
30 There seems to be confusion in this sentence between the (unnamed) sender of the letter and the knight Ardent Desire. There is also a strong suggestion that *bontie & gentillesce* through whom the name of the knight is to be made known are allegorical characters.
31 Penelope.
32 Palamides, though ostensibly Greek, is in French romance a Good Saracen. In the *Prose Tristan*, he is the unsuccessful rival of Tristan, adoring Iseut from afar like a true *fin amant*.

[9 Venus.]

Uenus mere de Cupido dieu Damours / A tresexcellent Princesse Dame de cest hault fest fille au trespuissant Prince Roi de la grant Britaign salut & tresparfit dileccion / Pour ce que nous auons plain entendement par la Relacion de nostre feal messagier appelle loial Rapport que en vostre noble Court sont grant partie des mieuleurs Chiualers du monde a cest vostre Royal feste pour Jouster Dancier & Joyeuse vie mener / Nous qui tresvoulentiers desirons lencresse de nostre petit enfant appelle le Joefne le Ameruez[21] porteur de cestez le enuoyons pardeuers vostre haultesce pour apprendre nourretur & le fait desbatement darmes / En vous priant de commaunder a aucun chiualer de vostre feste a deliurer nostre dit enfaunt de six coups de launce sauns vilain Rochet en haultz sellez. Par oultre nostre

fol. 262ʳ

dit enfaunt puisse retourner deuers nous auec nouuelles / [de] vostre honneurable estate & parfite saincte le mieulx aprins de lesbatement dessusdit Tresexcellent Princesse le hault & puissant Roi dez Roys vous garder & gouuerner[22] en tresparfite saincte & vous octroye honneur & Joyeuse vie long adurer/ Donne en nostre merueilleuse mansion de Monsicheron[23] Lan depuis nostre creacion cinque milles cinque cens & seize /

[10 Cleopatra.]

Cleopatra par la grace de Saturnus et de toutz lez autrez planetz Roigne de Mesolopolitanie & de Gobosse[24] / Ainsne fille de treshault Empereur Dynde la maieur appelle prester Johane Capitain des bassez Courtz de paradix terrestre / A hault & puissant Princesse & nostre treschier & bien

---

21 On the model of Letter 6, *Jeune lapprenant*, it looks as if the first article should be omitted; the repetition of the article is not impossible, but may well be a dittography following the last syllable of *appelle*.

22 These infinitives are syntactically impossible here: it needs the two 3 sing. pres. subj. *garde & gouuerne*.

23 'Mount Cithaeron', home of Venus in the mythographers. See Chaucer's *Knight's Tale* (*CT A* 2222): 'Thow gladere of the mount of Citheron'.

24 This might refer to Gabaza, where according to Quintus Curtius, Alexander's men nearly perished of extreme cold; *Historiae Alexandri Magni* Book 8, ch. 4 #14–15.

APPENDIX: BL COTTON MS D II

[9 Venus.]

Venus, mother of Cupid, God of Love, to the right excellent Princess, Lady of this high feast, daughter to the most mighty King of Britain the Great, greeting and sincere affection. Because we have full understanding by the report of our faithful messenger named Loyal Report that in your noble court there are most of the best knights in the world at this your royal feast to joust, dance, and lead a joyful life, We, who most willingly desire the advancement of our page called Young Lover, bearer of these [letters], send him to Your Highness to be instructed in good breeding and the practice of the game of arms. Beseeching you to command any knight at your feast to deliver to our said page six blows of the lance without disallowed spear-points in high saddles. Furthermore, may our

fol. 262ʳ

said page return to us with news of your honourable estate and excellent health the better instructed in the abovesaid recreation. Right excellent Princess, the high and mighty King of Kings keep and govern you in the best of health and grant you honour and a joyful life, long to last. Given in our marvellous mansion of Mount Cithaeron, the year after our Creation 5516.

[10 Cleopatra.]

Cleopatra by the grace of Saturn and all the other planets Queen of Mesopotamia and of Gobosse, eldest daughter of the exalted Emperor of Greater India who is called Prester John, Captain of the Lower Courts of the Earthly Paradise.[33] To the high and puissant Princess and our right dear and

---

33 'According to the fictitious letter of Prester John to the Emperor Emanuel Comnenus, Paradise was situated close to – within three days' journey of – his own territories'; <https://blackcentraleurope.com/sources/1000-1500/a-letter-from-prester-john-ca-1165-1170/>. Mandeville speaks of Prester John (*Travels* chs 30 and 32). He tells of a king under Prester John who built a castle which he named 'Paradise'; the story is that of the Old Man of the Mountains and the Assassins. Chapter 32 explains 'wherefore the Emperor of Ind is clept Prester John'. Prester John's empire abuts the Terrestrial Paradise.

amee Cousin Blanche par la grace dicellui par qui[25] lez oyseaulx volent en lair ainsnee fille de tresnoble Roi vray successeur du Roy saint Louys & du vaillant villam le Conquereur / pardon salut & feminal dileccion. Nostre treschier & bien amee Cousin nous auons entendu que maints Chiualers & Escuiers de pluseurs estraunge Royaumes se adrescent vers vostre presence pour apprendre & veoir le deduit[26] dez armes que lez vailllans Chiualers & Escuiers de vostre Court font a cest noel / Pourquoy nous enuoyons deuers vous nostre tresbien amee Chiualer appelle Pertsapeine lieutenant de Capitan de nostre Citee de Troye la graunt qui [a] graundement desir destre aprins de la science dudit fait darmes auecques lez autres Chiualers & Escuiers dessuisditz / Pourquoy tresaffectueusement vous prions que a nostre dit Chiualer vous vueilliez baillier & deliurer vng Chiualer de vostre Court qui port en sez armez vng escu dargent a vng chief Dazur a deux mellettz dore / pour le dischargier de six Coupes de lancez assis en basses sellez sans estre attachiez ne liez / et ne le nous tenez pas longuement considere le grant Chemyn quil luy conicient[27] retourner / Donne en nostre Citee de Troye dedeins le temple Jubiter ce Jour de sa defendacion[28] / Celluy qui fait croistre le pain & vine. vous doint reigner sans fin /

[*11 Thoret de Tollide.*]

A Tresexcellent & tresnoble Princesse Dame de cest hault feste Dame &c fille &c Moustre treshumblement vng petit & Jeune homme nomme Thoret de Tollide porteur de cestes qui est venuz destraungez partiez pour veoir le contenement de vostre Court Roial a fin dapprendre nourritur & le fait desbatement darmes / humblement suppliaunt a vostre haultesce que vous plaise commaunder le plus Jolis chiualer de vostre feste entre lez aiges de seize & vingt ans qui a plus longuement este seruaunt damours de son aaige sans aucun guerredon receuoir a deliurer le dit suppliaunt de six coupes de launce de mesur sans vilain Rochet en vostre excellent presence

25 MS *parqui*.
26 The scribe seems to have written *deduct* but it is certainly a mistake for *deduit*, synonym of *esbatement* used in all the previous letters.
27 Almost certainly an error for *convient*.
28 This word is not recorded anywhere else. It may well have been a cross between *defension* ('prohibition') and *defendement* ('protection, defence' or 'prohibition'). It sounds like a parody of a festival like a Translation or a Martyrdom.

APPENDIX: BL COTTON MS D II

well-beloved Cousin Blanche by the grace of him by whom the birds fly in the air, eldest daughter of the right noble King, true successor to the King St Louis and of the valiant William the Conqueror, [whom God] pardon,[34] greeting, and sisterly affection. Our right dear and well-beloved Cousin, we have heard that many knights and squires from many foreign realms are making their way to your presence in order to learn and witness the sport of arms which the valiant knights and squires of your court are practising this Christmas. For this reason we are sending to you our well-beloved knight named Loses-his-Labour, lieutenant of the Captain of our city of Troy the Great, who has greatly longed to be instructed in the science of the said exploit of arms with the other knights and squires abovesaid. Therefore most affectionately we beg you that you should present and deliver to our said knight a knight of your court who bears in his arms a shield Argent with a chief Azure two mullets Or to discharge on him six blows of the lance seated in low saddles without being attached or tied, and not to keep him from us for long, considering the great journey which he will have to make to return. Given in our City of Troy in the temple of Jupiter the day of his Prohibition.[35] He who causes bread and wine to grow grant you to reign without end.

[*11 Thoret de Tollide.*]

To the right excellent and noble Princess, Lady of this high feast, Lady &c daughter &c I present most humbly an insignificant and young man called Thoret de Tollide bearer of these [letters], who has come from foreign parts to observe the conduct of your Royal Court in order to acquire nurture and the practice of the recreation of arms, humbly beseeching Your Highness that it should please you to command the merriest knight of your feast between the ages of sixteen and twenty years who has been the servant of love for the longest time without receiving any reward to deliver to the said suppliant six blows of the standard lance without disallowed spear-points in your excellent presence in your hall when it shall please

---

34 Possibly due to eye-skip: Advocates' MS fol. 68^v has *du vaillant guillaume le Conquereur cui dieu pardone* ('the valiant Willliam the Conqueror, whom God pardon').

35 *Defendacion* (see textual note) could mean 'prohibition' or 'protection'. Exactly what it implies is unclear.

103

en vostre sale quant il plaira a Vostre Haultesce a fin que le dit pour & petit suppliant puisse retourner a le straunge pais dont il est venu le mieulx aprins de lesbatement dessusdit . et ce par voye de vostre excellent bontie & noblesce /

[*12 Lancelot de Libie.*]

A Tresexcellent & noble Princesse Dame &c fille &c Moustre treshumblement vng Jeune homme nomme lancelot de libie qui est venu de longtaines parties dorient pour cercher la droit eschole de nourritur & damours / Aiant plain enfourmacion que vostre Court Roial est vray vniuersitie de toutz excellentz vertues / Si vient a vostre hault pouoir apprendre nourretur & le fait desbatement darmez / Suppliant a vostre excellent noblesce que vous plaise commaunder le Chiualer demourant en vostre Court qui porte en sa deuise vne manier de best appelle ffoliart[29] a deliurer vostre[30] dit enfaunt de six coupes de lance en bassez sellez auecquez Rochez dassise sans estre liez ne attachiez pour apprendre le Jeune suppliant du dit fait desbatement . Et ce par voy de vostre benigne courtoisie /

[*13 Voulente dapprendre.*]

A Tresexcellent Princesse Dame de ceste hault feste &c fille &c Moustre treshumblement vng Jeune petit enfant appelle voulente dapprendre porteur de cestz venu de loingtaines parties pour veoir le noble contenement de vostre Court Roial & pour apprendre le fait desbatement darmes / A vostre excellent haultesce humblement suppliaunt / que vous

---

29   *Fulmart*, 'polecat'? Another source suggests *fol liard* 'silly grey horse': *Lyard/lyart* OED a. 'Of a horse: Spotted with white or silver grey. In northern English dialects "a white lyared horse means a grey one, or one dappled with white and black; and a red lyared one is dappled with bay or red and white" (Eng. Dial. Dict.)'. A *liard* is also a cross between a lion and a leopard. Leopards were also thought to be crosses.

30   *Sic*: but a mistake for *nostre*.

Your Highness, to the end that the said poor and insignificant suppliant may return to the foreign country from which he has come the better instructed in the abovesaid game; and this by means of your excellent generosity and noblesse.

[*12 Lancelot de Libie.*]

To the right excellent and noble Princess Lady &c daughter &c I present most humbly a young man named Lancelot of Libya who has come from distant parts of the East to seek the true school of nurture and of love. Having clear information that your Royal Court is the true university of all excellent virtues, he therefore comes to Your Sovereignty to learn manners and the practice of the recreation of arms, beseeching Your High Nobility that it should please you to command the knight staying in your Court who bears in his arms a kind of beast called a polecat to deliver to our[36] said young knight six blows of the lance in low saddles with statutory rebated points without being tied or attached, in order to instruct the young suppliant in the said practice of the recreation. And this by means of your gracious courtesy.

[*13 Voulente dapprendre.*]

To the right excellent Princess lady of this high feast &c daughter &c, I present most humbly a young child[37] called Willingness to Learn, bearer of these [letters], who has come from distant lands to observe the noble conduct of your Royal Court and to learn the practice of the recreation of arms, humbly beseeching Your Excellent Highness that it should please

---

36 Copying mistake: *vostre* for *nostre*.
37 The expression *jeune petit enfaunt* almost certainly identifies this person as what we would call a 'child' – distinguished from the young knights (*enfants*) of other letters.

plaise co<u>mm</u>aunder le plus Jolis & mieulx Joustant Ch<u>iua</u>ler de v<u>ost</u>re feste qui est droit Cousin au tresdoubte Prince le Roy de lisle des Gians a deliurer aux premier Joust[i]ure /

THE REST IS MISSING.

APPENDIX: BL COTTON MS D II

you to command the merriest and best jousting knight of your feast who is close Cousin to the redoubted Prince, Lord of the Isle of Giants,[38] to deliver at the first encounter ...

THE REST IS MISSING.

[38] According to Geoffrey of Monmouth, the only inhabitants of the Islands of Britain before the arrival of the Trojans under Brutus were 'a few giants': *Erant tunc nomen insulae Albion, quae a nemine, exceptis paucis gigantibus, inhabitabantur.* Brutus's companion Corineus enjoyed wrestling with them, and cleared the land by throwing the last one, Gogmagog, over a Cornish cliff; *Historia Regum Britanniae* Book 1 Ch. 16. *Des Granz Geanz* appeared either separately or as a preface to the chronicles known as *Brut*. Gogmagog and his companion Gog became favourite giants in city pageants, e.g. London and Norwich.

'MASKERYE CLAYTHIS' FOR JAMES VI AND ANNA OF DENMARK

Michael Pearce

In 1603 James VI of Scotland inherited the throne of Elizabeth I and moved to London with his wife, Anna of Denmark, to become James I of England. Their English court is renowned for its masquing activity, with Anna and her ladies, in particular, enthusiastic participants in the spectacular masques designed and composed by Inigo Jones and Ben Jonson. Until now little has been known of the couple's involvement in such performances during their reign in Scotland; scarcity of evidence of masquing at the Scottish court has contributed to a loose impression that James was indifferent and that Anna's interest flowered only in England. But surviving evidence in clothing accounts, at least during the early years of their marriage, shows the King and Queen both engaging in *maskerie* on a number of occasions. This essay explores what this as yet little-known evidence can show us about the materials, activities, and occasions of royal *maskerie* in Scotland.

We are dependent on the records of expenditure on royal clothing for this evidence. In the early years of James's reign, these are recorded in the Scottish Treasurer's Accounts.[1] But in 1590, perhaps following James's marriage, it seems to have been decided that the King's and Queen's wardrobe should be funded directly out of the yearly subsidy granted to James by Elizabeth I throughout most of his reign.[2] From that time onwards, most wardrobe payments disappear from the Treasurer's Accounts. However, there survives a detailed account of materials supplied for clothing for James VI and Anna of Denmark at the Scottish court through the 1590s, made by the merchant and financier Robert Jousie, and funded

---

1. For almost full publication of these accounts between 1473 and 1579 see *Accounts of the Lord High Treasurer of Scotland* 13 vols (Edinburgh: H.M. General Register House, 1877–1978). For entries related to performance between 1579 and 1592, see 'The Royal Court of Scotland' edited Sarah Carpenter in *REED Pre-Publication Collections* <https://reedprepub.org/royal-court-of-scotland/>.
2. Julian Goodare 'James VI's English Subsidy' in *The Reign of James VI* edited Julian Goodare and Michael Lynch (East Linton: Tuckwell Press, 2000) 110–25; Miles Kerr-Peterson and Michael Pearce 'James VI's English Subsidy and Danish Dowry Accounts, 1588–1596' *Miscellany of the Scottish History Society XVI* (Woodbridge: The Boydell Press, 2020) 1–94.

largely from the subsidy paid by Queen Elizabeth.[3] On at least four occasions in 1591 and 1592, fabrics for clothes were bought for *maskerie*. These entries will be discussed below. The records give a vivid picture of colours and fabrics but describe ensembles only as 'maskerie clothes' rather than giving any particular garment names. These costumes and the masques at the Scottish court in early 1590s are not well known. No *maskerie* costumes appear to have been bought after 1592, perhaps because of a lack of occasion, or the pregnancies of the Queen.

This kind of *maskerie* seems to have been especially associated with marriages. Some, perhaps all, of these costumes were made for entertainments at weddings, at least one being worn at an *infare* celebration. An *infare* is defined in the *Dictionary of the Older Scottish Tongue* as 'The feast in the bridegroom's house after the wedding', with one of its examples from 1595 describing it more generally as 'the infair, the banket after the bridall'.[4] The seventeenth-century history of the Somerville family describes two *infare* celebrations at bridegrooms' homes in the reigns of James IV and James V; they claim the personal attendance of the two Kings, though this is now doubted.[5] Several of the *maskerie* occasions in the 1590s, discussed below, were celebrations hosted by the brides' or grooms' families in the days after the wedding.

Maskerie, like the English traditions of courtly disguising, centrally involved highly costumed dance.[6] James VI and Anna of Denmark dressed in special clothes, and presumably danced and performed in person, though not necessarily with each other. Records of earlier masques in Scotland give some clues to the possible nature of the entertainments in the 1590s. At a wedding at Castle Campbell in January 1563, attended by Mary, Queen of Scots, courtiers and musicians apparently dressed as shepherds entered

3 Edinburgh: National Records of Scotland (NRS) E35/13 and E35/14; see Jemma Field 'Dressing a Queen: The Wardrobe of Anna of Denmark at the Scottish Court of King James VI, 1590–1603' *The Court Historian* 24:2 (2019) 152–67 at 154.

4 *DOST* sv *infare* (2); <www.dsl.ac.uk/entry/dost/infare>.

5 Walter Scott *Memorie of the Somervilles* 2 vols (Edinburgh, 1815) *1* 297–9; James Cameron *James V* (East Linton: Tuckwell, 1998) 224.

6 For the various forms of courtly masking see Meg Twycross and Sarah Carpenter *Masks and Masking in Medieval and Tudor England* (Aldershot: Ashgate, 2002) 'Courtly Masking' 128–90.

the castle and joined the guests in celebrations in the great hall. The royal wardrobe accounts record:

> *Plus vne aulne et demie de damas blanc pour faire six gibesieres de bergers pour des masques au nopces de Monsieur Sainct Cosme.*
>
> *Plus jay deliure a Jacques le tailleur deux manteaux de masque faictz de taffetas blanc pour faire daultre sorte dhabillementz a ceux qui jouoient du lut pour la dicts masques.*[7]

Also one ell and a half of white damask to make six shepherds' satchels for the masques at the wedding of M. Sainct Colme.

Also I delivered to Jacques the tailor two masque gowns made of white taffeta to make another kind of costume for those who played the lute for the said masques.

The English diplomat in Scotland, Thomas Randolph, seems to have associated this event with John Knox's disapproval of dancing, since on sending news of the wedding to Cecil he observed that Knox 'is so harde unto us, that we have layde a syde myche of our dansynge'.[8] Mary herself took active part in *maskerie* activities.[9] On 11 February 1565, the Queen and her husband made 'maskrie and mumschance' for the benefit of a French ambassador. While *maskerie* most often seems to involve disguised and costumed dancing, *mumschance* generally also includes an exchange of gifts through some kind of game of chance.[10] On this occasion, Mary and her ladies were all reported to be clad in men's apparel, and presented gifts of daggers to the French ambassador and his gentlemen.[11] Randolph had also

---

7   Joseph Robertson *Inventaires de la Royne Descosse* (Edinburgh: Bannatyne Club, 1863) 136. The second of these entries is crossed out, but annotated *Efface pour ce quil est escript en vng aultre endroict* to indicate it is entered elsewhere in the accounts.

8   *Calendar of the State Papers Relating to Scotland and Mary, Queen of Scots, 1547–1603* (*CSPS*) edited Joseph Bain, 13 vols (Edinburgh: H.M. General Register House, 1898–1969) *1* 674 #1157.

9   See Sarah Carpenter 'Performing Diplomacies: the 1560s Court Entertainments of Mary, Queen of Scots' *The Scottish Historical Review 82:2* (2003) 194–225.

10 See Twycross and Carpenter *Masks and Masking* 151–68.

11 Thomas Thomson *A Diurnal of Remarkable Occurrents* (Edinburgh: Bannatyne Club, 1833) 87.

reported that Mary attended a wedding on a Sunday in October 1564 and returned and 'that nyght she danced longe and in a maske playing at dyce loste unto my Lord of Lenox a prettie jewel'.[12] Randolph again mentioned wedding-day dancing customs when describing the marriage of Mary to Lord Darnley, 'after the marriage followethe commenlye cheare and dancinge' and 'after dynner theie dance awhyle', and after supper, 'some dancinge ther was, and so theie go to bedde'.[13]

Some of the entertainment at Scottish court weddings may have followed a disguising tradition in which masquers and musicians who entered in costume to dance subsequently invited selected members of the audience or wedding guests to dance with them.[14] Such an event at the French court of Henry III in 1580 was described by the English diplomat Henry Cobham. In a Shrove-tide masque held after supper, a group of dancers, including the King, dressed as German knights and women. After the team had danced 'some newly devised measures' together, the King 'came up and took his Queen, and his other maskers danced around with the ladies of state'. The King subsequently spent the rest of the night taking his team of fellow-maskers to dance in various other houses.[15] Elements of this sequence are present in references to dancing at Mary's court, and in an unruly incident in which the Earl of Bothwell visited Alison Craik, the daughter of an Edinburgh burgess 'in a mask', which may have been in some respects a similar 'amorous' masquerade.[16]

Biographers of James VI and I have supposed that the King was averse to dancing, following the observations of the French ambassador Fontenay, who reported from a visit in 1584 that the teenage King hated dance and music in general.[17] Descriptions of masques and dancing at court during the

12 *CSPS 2* 88 no. 110; Kew: TNA SP 52/9 fol. 44[r].

13 Henry Ellis *Original Letters, Illustrative of English History* (Series 1; London: Harding, Triphook, and Lepard, 1824) 2 204; British Library MS Cotton Caligula B IX (1) fol. 228[r–v].

14 Twycross and Carpenter *Masks and Masking* 169–83.

15 *Calendar of State Papers, Foreign, Elizabeth 1579–1580* edited Arthur Butler (London: HMSO, 1904) 162–4 no. 172.

16 Sarah Carpenter 'Masking and politics: the Alison Craik incident, Edinburgh 1561' *Renaissance Studies 21:5* (November 2007) 625–36.

17 See e.g. Alan Stewart *The Cradle King: a Life of James VI and I* (London: Pimlico, 2004) 183; *HMC Manuscripts of the Marquis of Salisbury at Hatfield* (London: HMSO, 1889) 3 60.

MICHAEL PEARCE

reign of James VI are rare, possibly due to the absence of an observer like Thomas Randolph. But he was taught to dance in the early 1580s by William Hudson, one of the well-established family group of English musicians at the Scottish court, who is sometimes referred to as the King's *balladin* or dance master.[18] The first record of James's participation in *maskerie* appears to be for the wedding of the Earl of Murray in January 1581. This was a two-centred celebration involving a wedding and a celebration in Fife, when the fourteen-year-old King took part in the tournament game of 'running at the ring', and a second event eight days after, with more running at the ring and a pageant on the Water of Leith in Edinburgh.[19] The Treasurer's Accounts list materials for a set of white satin 'masking claithis' for James, as well as one of his master stablers and one of his pages, who clearly accompanied him:[20]

Item aucht eln of quhyit sating to be ane slip to his ma*ies*ties masking claithis the tyme of the erle of m*ur*rayes mariage price of the eln [viij] sex pund. Inde	xlviij li
Item four eln of laun theirto price of ye eln iiij li Inde	xvj li
Item f*our* elnis of ca*m*marage to the said vse at iiij li x s the eln Inde	xviij li
Item sex elnis of quhyit taffatie of the coird to be ane of his hienes maister staiblairis ane garmonth at xl s the eln Inde	xij li
Item fyve eln of quhyite taffatie of the coird to be ane of his ma*ies*ties peadges ane garmo*n*th p*r*ice of the eln xl s Inde	x li
Item xxvij elnis lyni*ng* fustiane to the saidis claithis at x s the eln Inde	xiij li x s

18 Carpenter 'The Royal Court of Scotland' *1579–80* 8, *1581–82* 10, *1582–85* 8. For the Hudson family see Helena M. Shire *Song, Dance and Poetry of the Court of Scotland under King James VI* (Cambridge UP, 1969) 71–5.
19 *CSPS* 5 611.
20 Edinburgh: NRS E22/4 fol. 75ʳ, E21/62 fols 111–2; transcribed in Carpenter 'The Royal Court of Scotland' *1581–82* 1–2.

Item thre elnis of stiff buckrum to lyne the heidis of the saidis play claithis at viij s the elne Inde	xxiiij s
Item ane bolt of silkin rybbenis to his hienes masking claithis contening lxviij elnis	viij li x s
Item four vnce of quhyit silk to the saidis claithis at xviij s the vnce Inde	iij li xij s

While this reveals little about the nature of the garments, or the *maskerie* itself, it is revealing of the materials used for *maskerie* clothes. Lightweight fabrics like taffeta and relatively inexpensive gold and silver 'tocks' or gauzes are the defining feature of these and other masque costumes. *DOST* defines *tock* as 'A type of cloth, chiefly, tok of silver, gold'; Randle Cotgrave glossed *tocque* as 'plated cloth of gold, or siluer; a kind of tinsell, or stuffe that is striped with gold, or siluer'.[21] Mary, Queen of Scots, and her companions performed in a masque at Blois on Holy Innocents Day, 28 December 1550, before Henry II, Catherine de Medici, and Mary of Guise, dressed in costumes involving *tocque d'argent faulx*.[22] The *tocque* was 'false', an imitation of cloth of gold or cloth of silver, but apparently made with real metal thread.

In Scotland in 1553, *tok de argent* was bought to line silk hoods worn by Anne Hamilton, the youngest daughter of Regent Arran, at 18 shillings the ell.[23] Mary, Queen of Scots, bought a large quantity of silver tock at 20s the ell in December 1565; William Fowler, the merchant father of the poet, supplied *tuk* in February 1566 at 18s an ell; and his stock, inventoried after his death, includes a 'tok craip rayit with silk & gold' at 14s 4d the ell.[24] *Touke* of gold and silver costing 20s the ell was used in the King's costume at the Opening

---

21 *DOST* sv *tok* <https://dsl.ac.uk/entry/dost/tok>; Randle Cotgrave *A Dictionarie of the French and English Tongues* (London: Adam Islip, 1611) sv *Toque d'or*; <www.pbm.com/~lindahl/cotgrave>.

22 Paris: BNF MS français 11207 fols 264ᵛ–265ʳ, 271ʳ, 278ᵛ, 338ʳ. Excerpts from this manuscript were printed by Alphonse de Ruble *La première jeunesse de Marie Stuart* (Paris: E. Paul, L. Huard, et Guillemin, 1891) 290, but he misread the word as *tregne*. Incarnate taffeta and red satin for a *juppe* were also purchased for the masque.

23 Melanie Schuessler Bond *Dressing the Scottish Court: 1543–1553* (Woodbridge: The Boydell Press, 2019) 473.

24 *Treasurer's Accounts* 11 439, 466; Will of William Fowler, Edinburgh: NRS CC8/8/3 721.

of Parliament in July 1578.[25] The King's viol players were dressed in 'touke of silver', which cost 20s the ell, for a masque at Christmas time in 1579.[26] This *tock*, a kind of crepe or gauze, was obscure to the editor of Mary's accounts, who mistakenly compared it with coloured *tewkes* or *tuke* canvases found in earlier English records.[27] *Tocque* seems to be an Italian word in origin, *tocca*, perhaps a material link to Italian court custom.[28] Florio's 1611 edition of *Queen Anna's New World of Words* has 'Tócca d'óro, *Gold-tinzell or Tissue*'.[29]

These fabrics were much cheaper than true cloth of gold or cloth of silver, which are rarely mentioned in the inventories of Edinburgh merchants, and infrequently in the royal wardrobe accounts of the 1590s. Anna of Denmark used both types of metallic cloth in her gowns. In October 1590 she ordered 'foure ellis of gold: and foure ellis of sillver tok of the doubill sort to cut out upone _ £16.' Another order in the same week involved 'twentye foure ellis of fin clayth of sillver of doubill threid figuret with incarnadine to be hir majestie ane goun and ane wylicoit att xxv li the elle _ £600'.[30] This fine cloth was £25 Scots an ell, compared with tock at £1.

James VI chose the most expensive metallic fabrics for six suits worn at the baptism of Prince Henry in 1594. The 'clayth of silver argentyne', 'clayth of gold', and 'fyn clayth of sillver' used to cut out these garments cost £30 the ell.[31] William Fowler noted that female masquers, probably Anna's maids of honour, who appeared in the tableaux at the baptism wore costumes enriched with *togue* and *tinsal* of pure metal:

> About the table, were placed six Gallant dames, who represented a silent Comedie, three of them clothed in Argentyne Saten, and

25 *Treasurer's Accounts* 13 210.
26 Roderick J. Lyall *Alexander Montgomerie: Poetry, Politics, and Cultural Change in Jacobean Scotland* (Tempe AZ: Arizona Center for Medieval and Renaissance Studies, 2005) 66; Maria Hayward *Stuart Style: Monarchy, Dress and the Scottish Male Elite* (New Haven and London: Yale University Press, 2020) 59; *Treasurer's Accounts* 13 301.
27 *Treasurer's Accounts* 11 lxvii.
28 Francisque Michel *Recherches sur le commerce, la fabrication et l'usage des étoffes de soie, d'or et d'argent en Occident, principalement en France pendant le moyen age* 2 vols (Paris: Crapelet, 1854) 2 243.
29 John Florio *Queen Anna's New World of Words, or Dictionarie of the Italian and English Tongues* (London: Edward Blount and William Barret, 1611) sv *Tócca d'óro*.
30 Edinburgh: NRS E35/13 Section 2 page 7.
31 Edinburgh: NRS E35/13 Section 3 pages 9–16.

three in Crimson Saten: All these six garments, were enriched with Togue and Tinsal, of pure gold and siluer, euery one of them hauing a Crowne or Garland on their heades, very richly decked with fethers, pearles, and Iewels vpon their loose haire, in *Antica forma*.[32]

The fabrics embellishing the satin costumes worn by maidens of the household of Anna of Denmark were described by Fowler as *toque* and *tinsel*, but using pure gold and silver, suggestive of luxury. *Toque* was apparently a lightweight material suited to theatrical display and movement. Cloth of gold may have been employed differently, like the appliqué flames recycled from cushion covers used in a masque of Mary, Queen of Scots.[33]

Maskerie in the 1590s

On 20 February 1591, fabric was bought for a lightweight black silk taffeta suit for James VI made with black buttons, long black silk stockings, and ten ells (940 cm) of black ribbon to be 'strings' to the costume. A marginal note, 'wes to be maskerye claythis to his majestie', identifies the suit as a masque costume, though it seems to suggest that the clothes were not made. The use of black Spanish taffeta certainly suggests a lightweight and ephemeral costume suitable for a masque.

> [*margin*: wes to be maskerye claythis to his majestie]
>
> Item the 20 of Februar thre ellis and ane half of doubill blak Spanis taffetie for his majestie att vj li x d the ell   xxiiij li x d.
>
> Item half ane unce and half ane quarter ane unce black silk to sew this taffetie   xj s iij d

---

32 William Fowler *A true reportarie of the most triumphant, and royal accomplishment of the baptisme of the most excellent, right high, and mightie prince, Frederik Henry; by the grace of God, Prince of Scotland* (Edinburgh: Robert Waldegrave, 1594) fol. 3^{r-v}.

33 Robertson *Inventaires de la Royne Descosse* lxxxvi, 162; Thomas Thomson *A Collection of Inventories and Other Records of the Royal Wardrobe and Jewelhouse* (Edinburgh: Bannatyne Club, 1815) 148. The *toylle dor plainne* for the flames, recorded in the Robertson (French) inventory, was cross-referenced by the clerks to the Thomson (Scots) inventory which records the supply of 'thrattene little cusscheonis of plane claith of gold', providing a useful contemporary translation.

MICHAEL PEARCE

Item ane pair lang blak silk hois to serve with thir taffetye clayths	xxvj li.
Item fyve quarteris of blak boukessye[34] to band thir taffetye clayths	xv s.
Item thre dossane of blak silk bouttons to thir taffetye clayths	xv s.
Item tene ellis of blak Florence rubanes to be stryngis to thir taffetye clayths	xxxv s.[35]

The record of this costume was made a few days after a wedding attended by James at Thirlestane Castle on 15 February, when the chancellor's niece married the Laird of Lugton.[36] The black taffeta *maskerie* clothes may have been intended for this occasion, or alternatively for another wedding projected around this time between the children of the Earl of Morton and Lord Maxwell, which seems never to have taken place.[37] Whatever its original purpose, the marginal note seems to suggest that the fabric was not used, perhaps to indicate that it was still available for other purposes.

The next record of *maskerie* clothes was for the wedding of Lilias Murray to John Grant of Freuchie at Tullibardine, north-west of Edinburgh, on 21 June 1591.[38] The clothing account details 'ane stand of maskerie clayths to his majestie att the mariage of the laird of Tullebarne dochter', that is, Lilias Murray.[39] The laird of Tullibardine, John Murray, had long been a member of the King's household, and held various roles including Master of the Household.[40] He lived at the Gask and the nearby Tullibardine Castle

---

34 A kind of buckram: see *DOST* sv *Buckasie* <www.dsl.ac.uk/entry/dost/buckasie>.
35 Edinburgh: NRS E35/13 Section 1 page 21 / fol. 13ʳ; Carpenter 'The Royal Court of Scotland' *1590–92* at September 1591.
36 *HMC Salisbury Papers at Hatfield* 13 428.
37 *CSPS 10* 449, 467.
38 Hayward *Stuart Style* 59.
39 Edinburgh: NRS E35/13 Section 1 page 33 / fol. 19ʳ; *CSPS 10* 533–5.
40 *CSPS 6* 560; TNA SP52/32 fol. 112; Amy Juhala '"For the King Favours Them Very Strangely": the rise of James VI's chamber 1580–1603' in *James VI and Noble Power* edited Miles Kerr-Peterson and Steven J. Reid (Abingdon: Routledge, 2017) 155–75 at 173; William Fraser *Chiefs of Grant: Charters* 3 vols (Edinburgh: privately printed, 1883) 3 402.

'MASKERYE CLAYTHIS' FOR JAMES VI AND ANNA OF DENMARK

at Auchterarder, where the King was a frequent visitor in the 1590s.[41] Both houses are now long demolished but the Murrays' Tullibardine Chapel remains.

Joussie's clothing account includes the following entries:

Item the 18 of June deliverit to Allexander Miller[42] aucht ellis of incarnedin Spainze taffetye to be ane stand of maskerie clayths to his majestie att the mariage of the laird of Tillebarne dochter att vij li the elle	lvj li.
Item fyve quarteris of reid cramosye Spainze taffetye to be ane pair sleiffis to this garment att vij li the elle	viij li xv s.
Item aucht ellis of incarnet taffetie to be ane stand of maskerye clayths to hym that wes his majesties vallet att thatt tyme	xxiiij li.
Item sex ellis of tock of gold to serve bayth thir garments	xij li.
Item seventene ellis of yallow canves to lyn bayth thir garments of maskerye clayths cost xiiij s the elle	xj li xv s.
Item sex quarters of hard boukrame to be thair heid peces	xviij s.
Item twellfe elles of incarnet Florence rubanes: and twellfe elles of blew Florence rubanes to thir tue garments	iiij li xvj s
Item fyve unces of reid silk to work thir tue garments	vj li xiij s.
Item tua wenyss maskis the ane to his majestie the udir to his vallet	vj li.

---

41 *CSPS 11* 659; TNA SP 52/56 fol. 64, 29 July 1595.
42 Alexander Miller, the tailor who made the King's masque clothes, followed the court to London in 1603 (Hayward *Stuart Style* 54); he died in 1616 and was buried in Greyfriars' Kirkyard, Edinburgh; William Maitland *History of Edinburgh from Its Foundation to the Present Time* (Edinburgh: Hamilton, Balfour, and Neil, 1753) 192–3.

Item deliverit to Robert Abircromy thatt saming tyme auchtt ells of incarnet taffetye to be ane capparessone for his majesties horss	xxiiij li
Item tene ellis of canues to lyn this hors capparessone	viij li
Item tene unces of Reid silk to work this capparesone	liij s iiij d.[43]

James performed with his gentleman of the bedchamber, probably John Wemyss of Logie. Logie left the King's service before August 1592, joining the rebel Francis Stewart, Earl of Bothwell, and is remembered for escaping from Dalkeith Palace with the help of his Danish fiancée, Margaret Vinster.[44] At Tullibardine, both King and valet wore Venetian carnival masks ('tua wenyss maskis') with headpieces made from stiff buckram fabric. James wore rose-red Spanish taffeta and the valet wore a costume of cheaper taffeta possibly of a different shade; the colour terms are *incarnadine* and *incarnate*.[45] The clothes were lined with yellow and embellished with gold tock fabric and pink and blue ribbons.

The saddler Robert Abercromby also made a taffeta horse-caparison or sumpter cloth of the same *incarnet* taffeta for the King, which seems to have been an ephemeral costume piece for use at the masque. Taffeta was regularly used in the 1630s to make or line items of saddlery for Henrietta Maria and her ladies, but not for caparisons or horsecloths, which were generally made of more substantial velvet and lined with buckram.[46]

It is unclear if Anna of Denmark attended this wedding or stayed at Linlithgow, but at the end of month she made her formal Entry to Perth, not far from Tullibardine. On 19 June 1591 the English diplomat Robert Bowes wrote:

---

43 Edinburgh: NRS E35/13 Section 1 pages 33-4 / fol. 19^{r-v} at June 1591; Carpenter 'The Royal Court of Scotland' *1590–92* at June 1591.

44 *The Historie and Life of King James the Sext* edited Thomas Thomson (Edinburgh: Bannatyne Club, 1825) 253–4.

45 *DOST* sv *incarnate*: 'Fleshcoloured, pale pink or crimson, carnation-coloured'; Cotgrave *A Dictionarie of the French and English Tongues* sv Incarnadin: 'A carnation; or more properly a deep, rich, or bright carnation; (This word hath often th'addition of, d'Espagne.)'.

46 Arthur MacGregor 'Horsegear, Vehicles and Stable Equipment' *Archaeological Journal 153* (1997) 176, 195.

The K[ing] being lately greeved with a troublesome rewme in his cheeke, supposed to drawe to a Quynancye, is well recovered and ready to ride this day to the mariage of the Lairde of Tyllybarnes daughter with the laird of Grant, and afterwards to repayre with the Queene to St. Johnston, that the Queene may make her entry there on the 24th hereof.[47]

James returned to Edinburgh on 24 June, to deal with a crisis involving the rebel Francis Stewart, Earl of Bothwell. The next day he left to join Anna of Denmark at Perth, for her Entry, now planned for 29 or 30 June. Anna may have been at the wedding at Tullibardine, and although evidence for this is lacking, older historians asserted she was present.[48] Little is known of the Entry at Perth apart from a disagreement about precedence, the Earl of Errol claiming precedence as Constable of Scotland over the Earl of Atholl, who was Provost of Perth.[49]

Lilias Murray's first child, born in 1594, was called Annas after the Queen.[50] There is no evidence that she had been a maiden in the Queen's household. In October 1594 Anna of Denmark bought clothes for Lilias's sister Anne Murray, who had been reputed to be the King's mistress,[51] including a new bodice and sleeves of blue satin, and silver cordons to upgrade her 'freis' gown.[52] This suggests that Anne Murray was then a member of the Queen's household. Anne Murray then married the Master of Glamis in June 1595 and James gave her a three-tailed gown of cloth of silver, a purple velvet gown, and a black velvet gown with three *vasquines* or skirts. The cloth-of-silver gown was for her wedding day.[53] The marriage was planned to be an important event at Stirling Castle intended to reconcile

---

47   *CSPS 10* 531; TNA SP/52/47 fol. 67[r].
48   William Fraser *Chiefs of Grant: Memoirs 1* 192.
49   James Maidment *The Chronicle of Perth* (Edinburgh: Maitland Club, 1831) 60; *CSPS 10* 536, 540; TNA SP/52/47 fols 71, 75; Anna J. Mill *Mediaeval Plays in Scotland* (Edinburgh: Blackwood, 1927) 90.
50   William Fraser *Chiefs of Grant: Memoirs 1* 195, *3* 221.
51   *Calendar of letters and papers relating to the borders of England and Scotland* edited Joseph Bain, 2 vols (Edinburgh: HM General Register House, 1894) 2 30–1, 34.
52   Edinburgh: NRS E35/14 fol. 34[r].
53   Edinburgh: NRS E35/14 fol. 33[r]; E35/13 Section 6 page 3.

factional differences, but was scaled back because of the Queen's illness.[54] George Nicholson, a servant of the English agent, reported on 19 May that 'Some say that the marriage of Lord Glamis is to be at Gask, Tullibardine's house, to-morrow, and that the King rides thither to-morrow'; a week later he wrote that 'the banquet of Lord Glamis's marriage is to be on Sunday next with great triumph (after the fashion of the country) at Stirling'.[55] This may be a reference to the *infare* celebrations.

Anna of Denmark had a set of masque clothes made in September 1591, possibly for a group of dancers. These were in red, silver grey, green, blue, and yellow taffeta. The clothes were enhanced with gold and silver cloth. The occasion is unknown, and there is no record of clothes for James at the same time. As James danced with his valet, Anna may have danced with her 'maidens' and her Danish male servants, as well as other courtiers.

Item the 3 day of September deliverit to Petter Rannald auchttene ellis reid: auchttene ellis quhit graye: foure ellis grene: foure ellis blew: and foure ellis yallow. Making in the haill ffourtye auchtt ellis of taffetyis to be maskerye clayths to hir majestie at Liij s iiij d the ell	j^c xxvi li
Item auchttene ellis of tok of gold and auchttene ellis of tok of sillver to thir maskerye clayths att xl s the ell extending	iij^{xx} x li
Item thre unces of reid silk and ane unce quhit silk to work thir clayths	vli vjs viij d.
Item fourtye auchtt ellis of [New][56] small boukerame to lyn thir maskerye clayths	xliij li iiij s.
Item sex grit plumages reid and quhit to thir garmentis	xviij li.[57]

54 *CSPS* 11 588, 597.
55 *CSPS* 11 597, 600; TNA SP/52/55 fol. 115.
56 The reading and meaning of this word is unclear.
57 Edinburgh: NRS E35/13 Section 2 pages 28–9 at 3 September 1591; Carpenter 'The Royal Court of Scotland' *1590–92* at September 1591.

The next record of masque costume, from December 1592, may have been for the wedding of Marie Stewart, daughter of James's early favourite Esmé Stewart, Duke of Lennox, to John Erskine, Earl of Mar, celebrated around the time of Anna's birthday on 12 December. Marie's sister Henrietta had married George, Earl of Huntly, in 1588, and James VI wrote a masque for this which seems to include a part for himself. However, the masque appears to have remained unfinished and may not have been performed.[58]

Anna bought clothes for Marie Stewart, who was one of the younger maidens in her household, described in 1591 as 'ane tender bairn' who ought to have an allowance for her breakfast.[59] Marie Stewart's banns were read at Stirling on 17 September 1592, but the marriage was delayed because of the Earl of Mar's illness. Probably with her marriage in mind, Anna bought clothes for Marie Stewart in September 1591 including an elaborate purple crimson gown with inner sleeves and bodice of cloth of gold, at £25 the ell.[60] In December 1592 James bought her gowns for her marriage of Lucca rose velvet, another of black velvet, and a chamber gown of red figured velvet.[61] On 10 November, Anna had given her cloth of silver (at £25 the ell) to be sleeves and bodice to an existing cloth-of-gold gown, and 40 ells of gold passments 'at the tyme of hir marriage'.[62] This was the gown for the wedding day, and perhaps to wear to join in masque with the Queen dressed in the taffeta and tock of gold recorded on the previous day:

Item the Nynt of December 1592 twentie fyve ellis quarter and half quarter taffetie of the cord to be your majestie maskerie claithis at Liij s iiij d the ell	lxvij li xiij s iiij d.
Item twentie ane ellis of gold tock to thir maskrie claithis	xlij li.

58 *The Poems of James VI of Scotland* edited James Craigie, 2 vols (Edinburgh: Scottish Text Society, 1955) 2 134–45.

59 Edinburgh: National Library of Scotland Adv. MS 34.2.17 (Papers concerning the Exchequer and King's rents).

60 Edinburgh: NRS: E35/13 Section 2 page 30.

61 Edinburgh: NRS: E35/13 Section 2 pages 61–2, October 1592.

62 Edinburgh: NRS E35/13 Section 2 pages 61–3; E35/14 fol. 16^v at 10 November 1592.

Item twentie twa ellis of small traillie to thir maskerie claithis	xix li xvj s.
Item sex ellis of lyning cloth to thir claithis	iij li.
Item sex ellis of quhyt Florence rubanes to thir clothes	xxiiij s.[63]

The *infare* celebration of the wedding took place at Alloa Castle, and it is likely that the masque took place there rather than at Holyroodhouse. James was at Alloa by 17 December according to Robert Bowes.[64] One of the Queen's gentlemen, John Elphinstone of Selmes, wrote on 22 December that 'My Lord of Mar was married fifteen days since, and the King and Queen's majesties are ridden to Allowmay (Alloa) to the "In forz"', and that they planned to go to Tullibardine afterwards.[65] Instead, because of news of the 'Spanish blanks' conspiracy, they returned to Edinburgh on 3 January.[66] Although the dates of payment in the clothing account are likely to be approximate, the date of 9 December may suggest that these *maskerie* clothes were made for use at the wedding celebration in Alloa.

Although there are no further mentions of *maskerie* clothes in the accounts, James VI and Anna continued to attend *infare* wedding celebrations, including Anne Murray's discussed above. Both King and Queen also continued to dance: the household of Anna of Denmark was censured by the kirk in 1596 for *balling* (dancing),[67] and the Dutch ambassadors at the baptism of Prince Henry in August 1594 mentioned that James VI led a dance or danced for them, after some persuasion, at Stirling Castle.[68] The record of costume purchases in the 1590s has recently attracted scholarly

---

63 Edinburgh: NRS E35/14 fol. 1ʳ⁻ᵛ at 9 December 1592; Carpenter 'The Royal Court of Scotland' *1590–92* at December 1592.
64 *CSPS 10* 824.
65 *HMC Salisbury Papers at Hatfield 4* 252.
66 Thomson *Historie and Life of King James the Sext* 260; David Calderwood *History of the Kirk of Scotland* 8 vols (Edinburgh: Wodrow Society, 1844) *5* 214.
67 David Calderwood *History of the Kirk of Scotland 5* 409.
68 James Ferguson *Papers Illustrating the History of the Scots Brigade* 3 vols (Edinburgh: Scottish History Society, 1899) *1* 161–3.

attention.[69] It also demonstrates that festival costume and dance, and James VI and Anna of Denmark's active participation in masking activity, were more frequent features at the Scottish court of the 1590s than previously supposed.

Edinburgh

Acknowledgements

This article was suggested by Jemma Field's researches into the household of Anna of Denmark and I am grateful to Sarah Carpenter for discussions and several references.

---

69 Jemma Field 'Dressing a Queen'; Michael Pearce 'Anna of Denmark: Fashioning a Danish Court in Scotland' *The Court Historian* 24:2 (2019) 138–51.

PEERS AND PERFORMERS IN THE REIGN OF HENRY VI

James H. Forse

The ongoing volumes of the University of Toronto's *Records of Early English Drama* (*REED*) and the online *REED Patrons and Performances* provide information concerning performance activities from about half of medieval and early modern England: 17 counties, 9 municipalities. It also includes Wales.[1] When augmented by information found in other sources, like Ian Lancashire's *Dramatic Texts and Records of Britain*, the Malone Society's *Plays and Players in Norfolk and Suffolk*, and others, the data reveal thousands of performances in large and small communities throughout the kingdom.[2] A survey and analysis of these records during the reign of Henry VI has revealed an unusual increase in payments to travelling and visiting performers, unmatched in the surviving record evidence from before or after his reign. This paper presents an exploration of this striking pattern.

For purposes of analysis I use a master spreadsheet created from data in the *REED* volumes and various other sources. The spreadsheet lists travelling performers from one of the earliest records, King Edward I's *ystrioni* at Christ Church Priory (1277),[3] until the end of the reign

---

1 For *REED* volumes published to date, see <https://reed.utoronto.ca/print-collections-2/print-collections/>.

2 *Records of Plays and Players in Norfolk and Suffolk* edited David Galloway and John Wasson (Malone Society Collections 11; Oxford UP, 1980/1981) provides the only collection of dramatic records published to date for Norfolk and Suffolk in that period. Ian Lancashire's *Dramatic Texts and Records of Britain to 1558* (Toronto UP, 1984), and other sources offer some dramatic records from the following counties for which there are as yet no *REED* volumes: Bedford, Buckingham, Derby, Durham, Essex, Hertford, Leicester, Northampton, Northumberland, Nottingham, Surrey, Warwick, and Wiltshire. For online *Patrons and Performances* see <http://link.library.utoronto.ca/reed>. Other printed sources giving information about touring performers include: E.K. Chambers *The Elizabethan Stage* 4 vols (Oxford: Clarendon Press, 1965); John T. Murray *English Dramatic Companies* 2 vols (London: Constable, 1910); Glynne Wickham *Early English Stages* 3 vols (London: Routledge and Kegan Paul, 1958, 1963, 1972, and 1981); *The Register of Thetford Priory Part 1: 1482–1517* edited David Dymond (Oxford UP for the British Academy, 1995); *Extracts from the Account Rolls of the Abbey of Durham* edited J.T. Fowler Surtees Society 99, 100, 103 (1898–1901).

3 *REED: Kent* 28.

of James I (1625). At present it contains over 9,000 entries from most areas of medieval and early modern England. The spreadsheet includes: performers identified by patron or place of origin, types of performers, dates and places of performances, and payments to performers if such were recorded. The terms *performers* or *entertainers* are used to cover a variety of activities. The terminology in the records is often very loose. Until records began to be written in English rather than Latin (c.1525), dramatic records refer to *histriones*, *mimi*, *luditores*, and *lusitores*. *Histriones* and *mimi* could designate 'actors' of some sort, and *luditores* and *lusitores* are generic terms for 'players' (which could mean game players and/or actors). Performers designated as *minstrels*, which dominate the records examined here, were most often musicians but could be actors, dancers, or all of these. Entertainers such as bearwards, keepers of animals in the royal menageries, jugglers, and jesters are usually specified, and musicians are sometimes identified as trumpeters, pipers, harpists, drummers, or waits. Therefore for the following discussion and tables, in the absence of more specific designation, the Latin terms *histriones*, *mimi*, and *luditores* are all translated as 'entertainers' or 'performers'.[4] Furthermore, the focus here is not on the types of entertainers, nor their numbers, should an individual entry note that fact.[5] Rather the emphasis is on how the number of patrons and appearances by touring entertainers under their patronage expanded during the reign of Henry VI, and how these appearances may have directly or indirectly enhanced the prestige and status of their patrons as well as reflecting the political situations of the times.

Sorting the master spreadsheet by years seems to indicate that entertainers patronized by royalty and aristocrats toured more frequently during the troubled reign of Henry VI than before and after that reign. Starting with Henry's succession as a baby-king in 1422 and ending in 1462, when he was deposed by Edward IV, the spreadsheet yields a total of 631 records of provincial performances by royal and aristocratic entertainers –

---

4   See <https://reed.utoronto.ca/wordbook/>. Terms such as *histrio* (plural *histriones*) and *mimus* (plural *mimi*) sometimes were used to denote actors in farces or ritual dramas. The words *luditor* (plural *luditores*) and *lusitor* (plural *lusitores*) sometimes meant 'game-player' but also were used to mean 'actor' and/or 'performer'.

5   Future research may explore the significance of type and number of performers. See article by Alexandra Johnston 'Travelling Entertainers and their Patrons: York, 1446-9' in *Medieval Travel* edited Martha Carlin and Caroline Barron (Harlaxton Medieval Studies 32; Donington: Shaun Tyas, forthcoming).

including players, minstrels, musicians, bearwards, jugglers, jesters, and the like. Entertainers were provided with liveries, and paid by their respective patrons, but when not performing for their patrons may have toured to augment their incomes.[6]

Provincial records before Henry VI's reign (1277 to 1421) number only 258 performances. In other words, during Henry's forty years on the throne there are records of almost 2.5 times more provincial performances by royal and aristocratic entertainers than in the 144 years that preceded his reign. The records also reveal a sharp increase in the number of aristocrats whose performers appear in the provinces. For those 144 years before Henry VI, 84 peers and knights are named as patrons. During Henry's reign the number jumps to 109. One might attribute some of that increase to a greater survival of records from the 1400s, but it seems unlikely that locales began to better preserve their accounts only after 1422. Alexandra Johnston's forthcoming article discusses the survival of documents in York for certain years giving fuller itemization of expenditures than the official Rolls. Perhaps documents from other localities may be discovered which shed more light on performance activities.[7] Yet to date there is no indication in pre-1400 sources that suggests touring by aristocratic entertainers was already a common practice. These numbers not only far exceed anything seen before in provincial records, but also exceed the number of provincial performances during the reigns of Henry's three successors: Edward IV, Richard III, and Henry VII.

The Minority of Henry VI

To move to the main focus, touring under Henry VI, it must be recalled that even at the beginning of his reign Henry's situation was unusual. He succeeded to the throne as a nine-month-old infant. According to Henry V's will, the King's brother John, Duke of Bedford, was to be Regent for his son in France, and his other brother, Humphrey, Duke of Gloucester, was named 'principal guardian and protector' of his heir – in effect Regent in England. However, the Minority Council side-stepped Henry's will. Humphrey's role was described as 'protector and defender and principal councillor', but

---

6   See Richard Rastall Secular *Musicians in Late Medieval England* (PhD Thesis: University of Manchester, 1968), especially chapters 1, 4, and 7. The thesis is online at <www.townwaits.org.uk/richardrastall.shtml>.

7   Johnston 'Travelling Entertainers' forthcoming.

the Council deemed the person and office of king 'inseparable'. This subtle phrasing meant Gloucester could not exercise authority as Regent.[8]

Did Henry's Minority Council arrange extensive touring by royal entertainers, perhaps to advertise the legitimacy of the boy-king (and implicitly thereby its own)? In the next century, Kings Henry VII and Henry VIII certainly did so for their under-age children. For instance, performers attached to Henry VIII's son Prince Edward were touring the provinces within months of his birth.[9] However, touring by the boy-king's entertainers does not seem to present a similar story (TABLE 1).

TABLE 1: Tours by Henry's Performers during His Minority

Patron	Year	Place	County	Type	Source
King Henry	1425	Exeter	Devon	minstrels	REED Dev 88
King Henry	1425	Robertsbridge	Sussex	minstrels	REED Sus 187
King Henry	1426	Exeter	Devon	minstrels	REED Dev 88
King Henry	1428	Exeter	Devon	minstrels	REED Dev 90
King Henry	1429	Coventry	Warks	minstrels	REED Cov 10
King Henry	1429	Coventry	Warks	trumpeter	REED Cov 10
King Henry	1429	Westminster	Middlesex	minstrels	REED Ken 324
King Henry	1432	Canterbury	Kent	minstrels	REED Ken 83
King Henry	1432	Canterbury	Kent	minstrels	REED Ken 156
King Henry	1433	Cambridge	Cambs	minstrels	REED Cam 27
King Henry	1433	Canterbury	Kent	minstrels	REED Ken 244
King Henry	1434	Cambridge	Cambs	minstrels	REED Cam 27
King Henry	1435	Cambridge	Cambs	minstrels	REED Cam 27
King Henry	1436	Cambridge	Cambs	minstrels	REED Cam 28
King Henry	1436	Canterbury	Kent	minstrels	REED Ken 299

Of 98 total appearances by Henry's performers between 1425 and 1462, only 15 appearances in four counties occurred during his minority, the first when he was four years old. Of those 15 appearances, 6 occurred in the

8   Bertram Wolffe *Henry VI* (New Haven: Yale UP, 2001) 29–34.
9   James H. Forse 'Advertising Status and Legitimacy: or, Why Did Henry VIII's Queens and Children Patronize Travelling Performers?' *Early Theatre* 16 (2013) 69–76.

years between 1429 and 1432, when the boy-king was involved in travel and ceremonies connected with his anointing and coronation as King of England at Westminster (1429) and King of France at Paris (1431). And 2 of those 6 performances coincide with Henry's progress with members of his Council to Canterbury after his coronation in France, when his entertainers were probably part of the entourage.

Did the appearance in the provinces of aristocratic entertainers sponsored by the lords of the Minority Council reflect rivalries within the Council? When tours by performers of Humphrey, Duke of Gloucester, are excluded (see TABLE 3), the data, as seen in TABLE 2, suggests on the whole this was not so. Of the seventeen members of Henry's Minority Council, ten lords' entertainers appear in provincial records during his minority. Entertainers of seven of those ten lords average less than once a year on tour. Among the lords of the Council, the entertainers of Sir Walter Hungerford, Earl of Huntingdon, and John Holland,[10] Duke of Exeter, appear most often in Exeter's records, as do those of Thomas Beaufort, Earl of Dorset, and later Duke of Exeter. That probably does not indicate any rivalry among the three. Both Hungerford and Holland held substantial properties in Devon – hence, probably, the performances of their entertainers in Exeter. Similarly, the presence of Beaufort's entertainers in Exeter is perhaps due to his numerous titles in England's South-West, as well as his holding office as JP in Devon and Dorset.[11]

TABLE 2: Tours by Performers of Lords of the Minority Council (excluding Humphrey, Duke of Gloucester)

Patron	Year	Place	County	Type	Source
Cardinal Henry Beaufort, Bishop of Winchester	1429	Exeter	Devon	jester	REED Dev 91
Henry Beaufort	1429	Dover	Kent	minstrels	REED Ken 324
Henry Beaufort	1429	Dover	Kent	minstrels	REED Ken 326
Henry Beaufort	1431	Dover	Kent	minstrels	REED Ken 326

10   The family name 'Holland' is also rendered 'Holand'.
11   For Hungerford see <https://reed.library.utoronto.ca/node/316108>; for Holland see <https://reed.library.utoronto.ca/node/316110>; for Beaufort see <https://reed.library.utoronto.ca/node/315926>.

Patron	Year	Place	County	Type	Source
Henry Beaufort	1432	Exeter	Devon	minstrels	REED Dev 94
Henry Beaufort	1432	Dover	Kent	minstrels	REED Ken 326
Henry Beaufort	1434	Exeter	Devon	jester & tabor	REED Dev 95
Humphrey Stafford, Duke of Buckingham	1425	Dover	Kent	minstrels	REED Ken 320
Humphrey Stafford	1426	Exeter	Devon	minstrels	REED Dev 89
Humphrey Stafford	1431	Canterbury	Kent	minstrels	REED Ken 61
Humphrey Stafford	1436	Shrewsbury	Salop	minstrels	REED Shr 131
John Scrope, Baron Scrope of Masham	1431	Exeter	Devon	minstrels	REED Dev 93
John of Lancaster, Duke of Bedford	1422	Cambridge	Cambs	entertainers	REED Cam 22
John, Duke of Bedford	1422	Dover	Kent	entertainers	REED Ken 321
John, Duke of Bedford	1426	Dover	Kent	minstrels	REED Ken 324
John, Duke of Bedford	1426	Dover	Kent	minstrels	REED Ken 324
John, Duke of Bedford	1431	Dover	Kent	minstrels	REED Ken 326
John, Duke of Bedford	1432	Dover	Kent	minstrels	REED Ken 326
John, Duke of Bedford	1433	Exeter	Devon	entertainers	REED Dev 94
John, Duke of Bedford	1434	Exeter	Devon	minstrels	REED Dev 95
John, Duke of Bedford	1433	Dover	Kent	taborer	REED Dev 95
John, Duke of Bedford	1434	Dover	Kent	minstrels	REED Ken 329
John, Duke of Bedford	1434	Exeter	Devon	minstrels	REED Dev 95

Patron	Year	Place	County	Type	Source
John, Duke of Bedford	1434	Dover	Kent	minstrels	REED Ken 329
John Holland, Earl of Huntington	1425	Exeter	Devon	minstrels	REED Dev 85
John Holland	1427	Cambridge	Cambs	minstrels	REED Cam 25
John Holland	1427	Exeter	Devon	minstrels	REED Dev 90
John Holland	1428	Exeter	Devon	minstrels	REED Dev 90
John Holland	1429	Exeter	Devon	minstrels	REED Dev 91
John Holland	1431	Exeter	Devon	minstrels	REED Dev 92
John Holland	1432	Exeter	Devon	minstrels	REED Dev 93
John Holland	1433	Canterbury	Kent	minstrels	REED Ken 333
John Holland	1434	Exeter	Devon	minstrels	REED Dev 95
John Holland	1435	Barnstaple	Devon	minstrels	REED Dev 30
John Mowbray, Duke of Norfolk	1416	King's Lynn	Norfolk	entertainers	Malone Nor 43
John Mowbray	1423	Cambridge	Cambs	entertainers	REED Cam 23
John Mowbray Junior	1434	Lydd	Kent	entertainers	REED Ken 649
Richard Beauchamp, Earl of Warwick	1425	Exeter	Devon	minstrels	REED Dev 88
Richard Beauchamp	1427	Exeter	Devon	minstrels	REED Dev 89
Richard Beauchamp	1427	Dover	Kent	minstrels	REED Ken 323
Richard Beauchamp	1428	Exeter	Devon	minstrels	REED Dev 89
Richard Beauchamp	1428	Dover	Kent	minstrels	REED Ken 322
Richard Beauchamp	1431	Exeter	Devon	minstrels	REED Dev 92
Richard Beauchamp	1433	Exeter	Devon	minstrels	REED Dev 94

Patron	Year	Place	County	Type	Source
Richard Beauchamp	1433	Canterbury	Kent	minstrels	REED Ken 322
Richard Beauchamp	1434	Dover	Kent	minstrels	REED Ken 328
Richard Beauchamp	1435	Dover	Kent	minstrels	REED Ken 329
Richard Beauchamp	1436	Dover	Kent	minstrels	REED Ken 330
Thomas Beaufort, Duke of Exeter	1423	Exeter	Devon	minstrels	REED Dev 87
Thomas Beaufort	1424	Cambridge	Cambs	entertainers	REED Cam 24
Thomas Beaufort	1424	Exeter	Devon	minstrels	REED Dev 88
Thomas Beaufort	1425	Exeter	Devon	minstrels	REED Dev 88
Thomas Beaufort	1425	Exeter	Devon	minstrels	REED Dev 88
Thomas Beaufort	1425	Dover	Kent	minstrels	REED Ken 320
Thomas Beaufort	1426	Exeter	Devon	minstrels	REED Dev 88
Thomas Beaufort	1426	Dover	Kent	minstrels	REED Ken 321
Sir Walter Hungerford	1427	Exeter	Devon	minstrels	REED Dev 90
Sir Walter Hungerford	1428	Exeter	Devon	minstrels	REED Dev 90
Sir Walter Hungerford	1428	Dover	Kent	minstrel	REED Ken 324
Sir Walter Hungerford	1429	Exeter	Devon	minstrel	REED Dev 91
Sir Walter Hungerford	1429	Dover	Kent	minstrel	REED Dev 92
Sir Walter Hungerford	1420	Exeter	Devon	minstrel	REED Dev 92
Sir Walter Hungerford	1431	Exeter	Devon	minstrel	REED Dev 92
Sir Walter Hungerford	1433	Exeter	Devon	minstrel	REED Dev 93

The one exception among the lords of the Minority Council is Humphrey, Duke of Gloucester. Though blocked by the Minority Council from asserting his authority as Regent, Gloucester strove to gain that status. In 1422 he petitioned Henry VI's first Parliament to recognize his status as Regent, citing Henry V's will. In March of 1428 he ceased participation in the Council for a time, again hoping to force the lords to acknowledge him as Regent.[12] Whatever Gloucester's reasons were, his entertainers appeared in the provinces during Henry's minority more often than the boy-king's – 30 times in five counties – and equals one-half of the combined total of the other lords of the Minority Council.

TABLE 3: Tours by Performers of Humphrey, Duke of Gloucester, during Henry's Minority

Patron	Year	Place	County	Type	Source
Humphrey, of Gloucester	1420	Exeter	Devon	entertainers	REED Dev 91
Humphrey of Gloucester	1422	Cambridge	Cambs	entertainers	REED Cam 23
Humphrey of Gloucester	1423	New Romney	Kent	entertainers	REED Ken 733
Humphrey of Gloucester	1425	Cambridge	Cambs	minstrels	REED Cam 24
Humphrey of Gloucester	1426	Cambridge	Cambs	entertainers	REED Cam 24
Humphrey of Gloucester	1426	Dover	Kent	entertainers	REED Ken 320
Humphrey of Gloucester	1426	Dover	Kent	minstrels	REED Ken 321
Humphrey of Gloucester	1426	Shrewsbury	Salop	minstrels	REED Shr 130
Humphrey of Gloucester	1427	Cambridge	Cambs	entertainers	REED Cam 25
Humphrey of Gloucester	1427	Shrewsbury	Salop	minstrels	REED Shr 130

12 S.B. Chrimes 'The Pretensions of the Duke of Gloucester in 1422' *English Historical Review 45* (1930) 101–3.

Patron	Year	Place	County	Type	Source
Humphrey of Gloucester	1429	Dover	Kent	minstrels	REED Ken 323
Humphrey of Gloucester	1429	New Romney	Kent	entertainers	REED Ken 736
Humphrey of Gloucester	1430	Dover	Kent	entertainers	REED Ken 324
Humphrey of Gloucester	1430	Exeter	Devon	entertainers	REED Dev 92
Humphrey of Gloucester	1430	Lydd	Kent	entertainers	REED Ken 647
Humphrey of Gloucester	1430	New Romney	Kent	entertainers	REED Ken 734
Humphrey of Gloucester	1431	Canterbury	Kent	entertainers	REED Ken 63
Humphrey of Gloucester	1431	Dover	Kent	entertainers	REED Ken 325
Humphrey of Gloucester	1431	Lydd	Kent	entertainers	REED Ken 647
Humphrey of Gloucester	1432	Exeter	Devon	entertainers	REED Dev 93
Humphrey of Gloucester	1432	Lydd	Kent	entertainers	REED Ken 648
Humphrey of Gloucester	1433	Oxford	Oxford	entertainers	REED Oxf 15
Humphrey of Gloucester	1433	Canterbury	Kent	entertainers	REED Ken 333
Humphrey of Gloucester	1433	Exeter	Devon	entertainers	REED Dev 94
Humphrey of Gloucester	1433	Lydd	Kent	entertainers	REED Ken 648
Humphrey of Gloucester	1433	Lydd	Kent	entertainers	REED Ken 649
Humphrey of Gloucester	1435	Dover	Kent	entertainers	REED Ken 328

Patron	Year	Place	County	Type	Source
Humphrey of Gloucester	1435	Lydd	Kent	entertainers	REED Ken 649
Humphrey of Gloucester	1436	Canterbury	Kent	entertainers	REED Ken 64
Humphrey of Gloucester	1436	Dover	Kent	entertainers	REED Ken 330

The focus of Gloucester's entertainers may be revealing. Most often they appeared in Kent, where he was Lord Warden of the Cinque Ports, but Gloucester did not spend all his time there. He was often at Court in London. Why Kent? Kent was different from most English counties. Lacking any major secular lords, and containing several chartered towns and semi-independent liberties, much of the county was almost independent of the royal sheriffs. Further, Kent's history is marked with resistance to royal authority. The office of Lord Warden was created after the Cinque Ports sided with Simon de Montfort against Henry III in the Second Barons' War (1264–70), and in the time of Humphrey's grandfather John of Gaunt, Wat Tyler's 1381 Rising began in Kent. Only three years after Humphrey's death Kent spawned Jack Cade's rebellion.[13] In fact, Duke Humphrey may have been the first Lord Warden whose entertainer-servants travelled extensively in that problematic county. The payment of 6s 8d to Gloucester's minstrels at New Romney in 1423[14] is the first mention of a Lord Warden's performers in Kent's dramatic records. From Duke Humphrey on, entertainers of every

---

13   Patricia Hyde and Michael Zell 'Governing the County' in *Early Modern Kent* edited Michael Zell (Woodbridge: The Boydell Press, 2000) 7–21, 24–5; Maurice Powicke *The Thirteenth Century, 1216–1307* (Oxford: Clarendon Press, 1962) 187–207; P.J.P. Goldberg *Medieval England 1250–1550: A Social History* (New York: Bloomsbury, 2004) see chapter 13 for the Peasants' Revolt; Lacy Baldwin Smith *This Realm of England, 1399–1688* (Lexington, MA: D.C. Heath, 1988) 24; Wolffe *Henry VI* 232–3. Also see M. Bohna 'Armed force and civic legitimacy in Jack Cade's revolt, 1450' *English Historical Review* 118 (2003) 563–82, and Charles Ross *Richard III* (English Monarchs Series; Berkeley: University of California Press, 1981) 105–19.

14   *REED: Kent* 733.

successive Lord Warden during the reign of Henry VI performed in Kentish towns,[15] a practice continued by all subsequent Lord Wardens until 1600.[16]

That focus on Kent continues in the extensive activity of Gloucester's entertainers after Henry attained his majority. Humphrey remained Lord Warden until his fall from power and death in 1447. Yet his entertainers do occasionally appear elsewhere in the dramatic records of three other counties: Devon, Worcester, and York (TABLE 4).

TABLE 4: Tours, Performers of Humphrey, Duke of Gloucester, during Henry's Majority

Patron	Year	Place	County	Type	Source
Humphrey of Gloucester	1437	Lydd	Kent	entertainers	*REED Ken* 650
Humphrey of Gloucester	1438	Dover	Kent	entertainers	*REED Ken* 330
Humphrey of Gloucester	1438	Dover	Kent	minstrels	*REED Ken* 330
Humphrey of Gloucester	1438	Lydd	Kent	minstrels	*REED Ken* 651
Humphrey of Gloucester	1439	Exeter	Devon	minstrels	*REED Dev* 91
Humphrey of Gloucester	1439	Lydd	Kent	entertainers	*REED Ken* 651
Humphrey of Gloucester	1440	Lydd	Kent	minstrels	*REED Ken* 652
Humphrey of Gloucester	1441	Lydd	Kent	entertainers	*REED Ken* 652
Humphrey of Gloucester	1442	Canterbury	Kent	entertainers	*REED Ken* 69
Humphrey of Gloucester	1442	Hythe	Kent	minstrels	*REED Ken* 612
Humphrey of Gloucester	1443	Hythe	Kent	minstrels	*REED Ken* 612

15   *REED Kent* 63-6, 69-73, 320-33, 336-9, 612-14, 625, 647-54, 657-63, 670, 733-6, 824-5.
16   Forse 'Advertising Status' 61.

Patron	Year	Place	County	Type	Source
Humphrey of Gloucester	1443	Lydd	Kent	entertainers	REED Ken 653
Humphrey of Gloucester	1444	Hythe	Kent	entertainers	REED Ken 612
Humphrey of Gloucester	1445	Canterbury	Kent	entertainers	REED Ken 65
Humphrey of Gloucester	1445	Chartham	Kent	entertainers	REED Ken 66
Humphrey of Gloucester	1445	Lydd	Kent	entertainers	REED Ken 653
Humphrey of Gloucester	1445	New Romney	Kent	minstrels	REED Ken 735
Humphrey of Gloucester	1445	Worcester	Worcs	minstrels	REED Her 399
Humphrey of Gloucester	1446	Dover	Kent	entertainers	REED Ken 334
Humphrey of Gloucester	1446	Eastry	Kent	minstrels	REED Ken 670
Humphrey of Gloucester	1446	Lydd	Kent	minstrels	REED Ken 654
Humphrey of Gloucester	1446	York	York	entertainers	REED York 97

Henry VI's Majority

In 1437, when Henry attained his majority and appointed his own Council,[17] the presence of the King's entertainers in the provinces increased significantly. Until he was deposed in 1462, Henry's entertainers appear in provincial records 83 times from nine different counties, three or four times a year, especially from the mid-1440s on, when regional discontent and disturbances increased (TABLE 5).

---

17 Wolffe *Henry VI* 27, 87, 91.

TABLE 5: Tours by Henry's Performers during His Majority

Patron	Year	Place	County	Type	Source
King Henry VI	1439	Dover	Kent	minstrels	REED Ken 331
King Henry VI	1440	Exeter	Devon	minstrels	REED Dev 96
King Henry VI	1440	Dover	Kent	minstrels	REED Ken 332
King Henry VI	1441	Shrewsbury	Salop	minstrels	REED Shr 132
King Henry VI	1442	Cambridge	Cambs	minstrels	REED Cam 29
King Henry VI	1442	Canterbury	Kent	entertainers	REED Ken 64
King Henry VI	1442	York	York	minstrels	REED York 65
King Henry VI	1443	Cambridge	Cambs	minstrels	REED Cam 29
King Henry VI	1444	Dover	Kent	minstrels	REED Ken 334
King Henry VI	1444	Shrewsbury	Salop	minstrels	REED Shr 133
King Henry VI	1444	York	York	minstrels	REED York 65
King Henry VI	1445	Beverley	Worcs	minstrels	REED Her 399
King Henry VI	1445	Lydd	Kent	entertainers	REED Ken 653
King Henry VI	1445	Canterbury	Kent	minstrels	REED Ken 66
King Henry VI	1446	Worcester	Worcs	minstrels	REED Her 400
King Henry VI	1446	Dover	Kent	minstrels	REED Ken 334
King Henry VI	1446	Lydd	Kent	entertainers	REED Ken 654
King Henry VI	1446	Lydd	Kent	entertainers	REED Ken 654
King Henry VI	1446	Canterbury	Kent	minstrels	REED Ken 67
King Henry VI	1446	Shrewsbury	Salop	minstrels	REED Shr 135
King Henry VI	1446	York	York	minstrels	REED York 67
King Henry VI	1447	King's Lynn	Norfolk	entertainers	Malone Nor 49
King Henry VI	1447	Lydd	Kent	entertainers	REED Ken 655
King Henry VI	1447	Canterbury	Kent	minstrels	REED Ken 69
King Henry VI	1447	York	York	minstrels	REED York 70
King Henry VI	1448	Cambridge	Cambs	minstrels	REED Cam 31
King Henry VI	1448	Hythe	Kent	minstrels	REED Ken 612
King Henry VI	1448	Lydd	Kent	entertainers	REED Ken 656

Patron	Year	Place	County	Type	Source
King Henry VI	1448	Lydd	Kent	entertainers	REED Ken 656
King Henry VI	1448	Ickham	Kent	minstrels	REED Ken 70
King Henry VI	1448	New Romney	Kent	minstrels	REED Ken 736
King Henry VI	1448	Shrewsbury	Salop	minstrels	REED Shr 135
King Henry VI	1448	York	York	minstrels	REED York 72
King Henry VI	1449	Dover	Kent	minstrels	REED Ken 336
King Henry VI	1449	Shrewsbury	Salop	minstrels	REED Shr 136
King Henry VI	1449	Rye	Sussex	minstrels	REED Sus 44
King Henry VI	1449	York	York	minstrels	REED York 74
King Henry VI	1449	York	York	minstrels	REED York 76
King Henry VI	1450	Lydd	Kent	entertainers	REED Ken 657
King Henry VI	1450	Canterbury	Kent	entertainers	REED Ken 72
King Henry VI	1450	New Romney	Kent	minstrels	REED Ken 736
King Henry VI	1450	Dover	Kent	minstrels	REED Ken 336
King Henry VI	1450	Rye	Sussex	minstrels	REED Sus 44
King Henry VI	1450	York	York	minstrels	REED York 80
King Henry VI	1450	Selby Abbey	York	entertainers	Wickham Stg 332
King Henry VI	1451	Hythe	Kent	minstrels	REED Ken 613
King Henry VI	1451	Canterbury	Kent	minstrels	REED Ken 72
King Henry VI	1451	Canterbury	Kent	minstrels	REED Ken 72
King Henry VI	1451	New Romney	Kent	minstrels	REED Ken 736
King Henry VI	1451	York	York	minstrels	REED York 81
King Henry VI	1452	Dover	Kent	minstrels	REED Ken 337
King Henry VI	1452	Hythe	Kent	minstrels	REED Ken 613
King Henry VI	1452	Canterbury	Kent	entertainer	REED Ken 73
King Henry VI	1452	York	York	minstrels	REED York 81
King Henry VI	1453	Hythe	Kent	minstrels	REED Ken 614

Patron	Year	Place	County	Type	Source
King Henry VI	1453	Dover	Kent	minstrels	*REED Ken* 337
King Henry VI	1453	Lydd	Kent	entertainers	*REED Ken* 657
King Henry VI	1453	Lydd	Kent	entertainers	*REED Ken* 658
King Henry VI	1453	Canterbury	Kent	entertainers	*REED Ken* 73
King Henry VI	1453	York	York	minstrels	*REED York* 83
King Henry VI	1454	Barnstaple	Devon	minstrels	*REED Dev* 30
King Henry VI	1454	Hythe	Kent	minstrels	*REED Ken* 613
King Henry VI	1454	Lydd	Kent	entertainers	*REED Ken* 659
King Henry VI	1454	Sandwich	Kent	entertainers	*REED Ken* 824
King Henry VI	1454	Sandwich	Kent	minstrels	*REED Ken* 824
King Henry VI	1455	Canterbury	Kent	entertainers	*REED Ken* 73
King Henry VI	1455	Lydd	Kent	entertainers	*REED Ken* 859
King Henry VI	1456	Lydd	Kent	minstrels	*REED Ken* 660
King Henry VI	1456	Canterbury	Kent	entertainers	*REED Ken* 73
King Henry VI	1456	Rye	Sussex	minstrels	*REED Sus* 47
King Henry VI	1457	Cambridge	Cambs	entertainers	*REED Cam* 37
King Henry VI	1457	Dover	Kent	minstrels	*REED Ken* 338
King Henry VI	1457	Lydd	Kent	minstrels	*REED Ken* 660
King Henry VI	1457	Shrewsbury	Salop	minstrels	*REED Shr* 140
King Henry VI	1457	Rye	Sussex	minstrels	*REED Sus* 47
King Henry VI	1458	Barnstaple	Devon	minstrels	*REED Dev* 30
King Henry VI	1458	Lydd	Kent	minstrels	*REED Ken* 661
King Henry VI	1459	Cambridge	Cambs	entertainers	*REED Cam* 38
King Henry VI	1459	Canterbury	Kent	minstrels	*REED Ken* 74
King Henry VI	1459	Sandwich	Kent	minstrels	*REED Ken* 825
King Henry VI	1459	Lydd	Kent	minstrels	*REED Ken* 861
King Henry VI	1460	Shrewsbury	Salop	minstrels	*REED Shr* 144
King Henry VI	1461	Oxford	Oxford	entertainer	*REED Oxf* 17

Two counties stand out: Yorkshire with 12 appearances by Henry's entertainers, and Kent with a striking 48 appearances. Henry's government did face fiscal problems and large deficits.[18] It is possible that one reason for royal entertainers touring in Kent may have been to raise financial support. Its proximity to the Court, and the number of towns that could be visited in a short time, could have made Kent a profitable circuit for the royal entertainers.[19] That may also account for the King's entertainers performing at King's Lynn, Norfolk, in 1447.[20] Henry was in Norfolk at the time, but at Norwich; his entertainers might have earned some extra income by performing out of town. The King's entertainers' appearances in York, however, suggest another story. The King did not travel to York, so their appearances there do not correspond with a royal visit. The distance between York and the Court suggests it would not have been a profitable trip. However, the royal entertainers' visits do correspond with the years marked by the violent Percy/Neville rivalry.[21]

After Henry VI assumed personal rule in 1437 rivalries among England's magnates began to dominate the realm's politics. As early as 1440 Humphrey of Gloucester complained that he and other great magnates, like the Duke of York and Earl of Huntingdon, were excluded from decision-making.[22] By the mid-1440s rivalries had sharpened as Henry granted more and more influence and patronage to personal friends. William de la Pole, Duke of Suffolk, allied with the Beaufort Dukes of Somerset and Queen Margaret, clearly dominated the government. Popular opinion 150 years later still believed in Suffolk's dominance. To quote the last lines of Shakespeare's *Henry VI Part 1*, delivered by Suffolk: 'Margaret shall now be queen, and rule the king; | But I will rule both her, the king, and realm'.[23]

---

18 See Alex Brayson 'The English Parishes and Knight's Fees Tax of 1428' *Historical Research 89* (2016) 651–72; Ralph A. Griffiths *The Reign of Henry VI* (Stroud: Sutton, 1981) 110–11; Gerald L. Harriss *Cardinal Beaufort* (Oxford UP, 1988) 188, 277–91; Wolff *Henry VI* 43, 73–8, 229–31, 246–7, 307–9.

19 See James H. Forse 'Touring in Kent: Some Observations from Records Published to Date' *Early Theatre 22* (2019) 119–40.

20 Malone *Norfolk/Suffolk* 49.

21 See pages 170–1.

22 Wolffe *Henry VI* 153.

23 William Shakespeare *King Henry the Sixth Part 1* in *The Works of William Shakespeare* (New York: Oxford UP, 1986) 30.

Gradually, two factions within the greater nobility coalesced, one centred around William de la Pole, Duke of Suffolk, Edmund Beaufort, Duke of Somerset, and Queen Margaret, the other around Richard, Duke of York, his father-in-law Richard Neville (senior), and brother-in-law Richard Neville (junior), respectively Earls of Salisbury and Warwick.

Henry's personality, and the abuse of power by his favourites, caused royal government to be inconsistent and ineffective. Regional rivalries among the greater and lesser nobles sprang up. Various commoners in the 1440s and 1450s voiced opinions that the King was childish, and that Henry was so dominated by Suffolk and Humphrey Stafford, Duke of Buckingham, that they, not Henry, ruled the realm. Also, as Charles Ross puts it: 'Henry VI was notorious for his excessive clemency ... which did ... much to undermine the authority of the law.'[24] For example, in 1449 Henry's squire, Sir William Tailboys, a client of the Duke of Suffolk, attacked Lord Cromwell with armed retainers at Westminster as he was on his way to a Council meeting. Tailboys was remanded to the Tower and ordered to pay Lord Cromwell £3000, but was soon was released.[25]

Historian R.A. Griffiths describes the late 1440s and 1450s as witnessing a 'disintegration of public order'.[26] To give a few examples: the Duke of Buckingham was unable to stop armed conflicts among his own followers in Derbyshire. In 1448, in Bedfordshire, a brawl between the Stafford and Harcourt families resulted in the death of Richard Stafford, son and heir of Sir Humphrey. In retaliation Sir Humphrey with 200 retainers attacked and burned the Harcourts' manor.[27] Sir Humphrey and his men were pardoned, probably because Humphrey had powerful kinsmen at Court – Humphrey Stafford, Duke of Buckingham, and John Stafford, Archbishop of Canterbury.[28] In 1453, the Duke of Exeter and Baron Cromwell (both

24   Ross *Edward IV* 390.
25   *Oxford Dictionary of National Biography* online at <https://doi.org/10.1093/ref:odnb/26949>; Wolffe *Henry VI* 17–18, 222, 233–6; D.A. Morgan 'The House of Policy: the Political Role of the Late Plantagenet Household, 1422–1485' in *The English Court from the Wars of the Roses to the Civil War* edited David Starkey (London: Longman, 1987) 45.
26   R.A. Griffiths 'Local Rivalries and National Politics: The Percies, the Nevilles, and the Duke of Exeter, 1452–55' *Speculum 43* (1968) 632.
27   Christine Carpenter *The Wars of the Roses: Politics and the Constitution of England, c.1437–1509* (Cambridge UP, 1997) 126–8.
28   *ODNB* at <https://doi.org/10.1093/ref:odnb/26209>.

members of the Council) disputed the inheritance of Ampthill Manor in Bedfordshire. Exeter's retainers drove Cromwell's agents off the property. The sheriff of Bedfordshire informed the Court he could not empanel a jury to hear the case; the locals feared reprisals from one or the other disputant. When the case was called to Westminster, both Exeter and Cromwell attended with armed retainers.[29]

In short, nobles in many parts of the realm were taking the law into their own hands. Local gentry holding office as justices of the peace or royal commissioners promoted their own interests, backed up by armed retainers. Royal officers were defied. For instance, in Cumberland in 1453, Percy adherents attacked the sheriff's deputies while they were collecting royal revenues. In some counties the office of sheriff went unfilled because no one would serve, fearing the power of the magnates in those counties. The Commons at the Parliament of 1449 'complained that the king's duty to keep the peace, dispense justice and maintain the law of the land was no longer being fulfilled'.[30] Violence among the great and lesser nobles in the provinces abounded. I emphasize this political turmoil because it is within this environment of greater and lesser aristocrats asserting themselves that there occurs the burgeoning of performances by entertainers of these same aristocrats. A pattern of increased aristocratic rivalry is paralleled by a pattern of increased performances by aristocrats' performers. This phenomenon is especially evident in dramatic records from Yorkshire in the North, Devon in the South-West, and the counties of Herefordshire, Worcestershire, and Shropshire on the Welsh borders.

The North

Violent clashes were especially keen in the North. Two factions dominated political power and influence: on the one side were the Percies and Cliffords (maternally related to the Percies),[31] and on the other were the Nevilles and their adherents. Both factions had extensive holdings in Yorkshire, and the wardenships of the northern marches. The wardens' duties were to protect the border against the Scots. Hence, the wardens kept private

---

29   Payling 'The Ampthill Dispute' 881–907.
30   Griffiths 'Local Rivalries' 589–632; Carpenter *Wars of the Roses* 124–8; Wolffe *Henry VI* 116.
31   George Edward Cokayne *Complete Peerage* (London: St Catherine Press, 1913) 253.

armies at royal expense, and assumed many of the duties of the sheriffs in the northern counties.[32]

According to R.A. Griffiths, 'The city of York provided a focus for these rivalries'. York was the most important economic, religious, and governmental centre in the North. Most prominent Yorkshire families had houses within the city, and several Percy and Neville manors were nearby. The citizens of York sometimes divided loyalties between the two factions.[33] Dramatic records from York show that performances by entertainers patronized by the Percies and the Nevilles increased significantly during this period (TABLE 6).

TABLE 6: Performers of Rival Families in York and Yorkshire

Patron	Year	Place	County	Type	Source
John, Baron Neville	1448	York	Yorks	juggler	REED York 71
John, Baron Neville	1448	York	Yorks	minstrels	REED York 71
Ralph Neville, Earl of Westmorland	1446	York	Yorks	jester	REED York 66
Ralph Neville	1446	York	Yorks	minstrels	REED York 66
Ralph Neville	1448	York	Yorks	minstrels	REED York 71
Ralph Neville	1449	York	Yorks	minstrels	REED York 76
Ralph Neville	1449	York	Yorks	lutenist	REED York 75
Ralph Neville	1457	Fountains Abbey	Yorks	entertainers	Fowler 60
Richard Neville, Earl of Salisbury	1446	York	Yorks	minstrels	REED York 66
Richard Neville	1447	York	Yorks	minstrels	REED York 69
Richard Neville	1447	York	Yorks	minstrels	REED York 68
Richard Neville	1448	York	Yorks	minstrels	REED York 70
Richard Neville	1448	York	Yorks	minstrels	REED York 71
Richard Neville	1448	York	Yorks	minstrels	REED York 71
Richard Neville	1449	York	Yorks	minstrels	REED York 73

32 See R.L. Storey 'The Wardens of the Marches of England towards Scotland, 1377–1489' *English Historical Review* 72 (1957) 593–615.
33 Griffiths 'Local Rivalries' 590.

Patron	Year	Place	County	Type	Source
Richard Neville	1449	York	Yorks	minstrels	REED York 75
Richard Neville	1450	York	Yorks	minstrels	REED York 77
Robert Neville, Bishop of Durham	1446	York	Yorks	minstrels	REED York 66
Robert Neville	1447	York	Yorks	minstrels	REED York 69
Robert Neville	1449	York	Yorks	minstrels	REED York 75
Robert Neville	1449	York	Yorks	minstrels	REED York 76
Sir Alexander Neville	1449	York	Yorks	entertainer	REED York 75
Sir Thomas Neville	1447	York	Yorks	minstrels	REED York 69
Sir Thomas Neville	1447	York	Yorks	taborer	REED York 69
Sir Thomas Neville	1449	York	Yorks	minstrels	REED York 75
Henry Percy, Earl of Northumberland	1446	York	Yorks	minstrels	REED York 67
Henry Percy	1447	York	Yorks	minstrels	REED York 69
Henry Percy	1447	York	Yorks	minstrels	REED York 70
Henry Percy	1448	York	Yorks	minstrels	REED York 72
Henry Percy	1449	York	Yorks	minstrels	REED York 76
Henry Percy, Baron Poynings	1446	York	Yorks	minstrels	REED York 70
Henry Percy, Baron Poynings	1447	York	Yorks	minstrels	REED York 70
Henry Percy, Baron Poynings	1448	York	Yorks	minstrels	REED York 71
Henry Percy, Baron Poynings	1449	York	Yorks	minstrels	REED York 76
Henry Percy, Baron Poynings	1449	York	Yorks	minstrels	REED York 76
Thomas Percy, Baron Egremont	1446	York	Yorks	minstrels	REED York 67
Thomas Percy, Baron Egremont	1448	York	Yorks	minstrels	REED York 72

Patron	Year	Place	County	Type	Source
Thomas Percy, Baron Egremont	1448	York	Yorks	taborer	REED York 72
Thomas Percy, Baron Egremont	1450	York	Yorks	minstrels	REED York 77
Thomas Clifford, Baron Clifford	1446	York	Yorks	minstrels	REED York 66
Thomas Clifford	1446	York	Yorks	minstrels	REED York 67
Thomas Clifford	1447	York	Yorks	minstrels	REED York 69
Thomas Clifford	1447	York	Yorks	minstrels	REED York 69
Thomas Clifford	1448	York	Yorks	minstrels	REED York 71
Thomas Clifford	1449	York	Yorks	minstrels	REED York 75
Thomas Clifford	1449	York	Yorks	minstrels	REED York 76
Thomas Clifford	1450	York	Yorks	minstrels	REED York 77
Sir William Plumpton	1447	York	Yorks	minstrels	REED York 68
Sir William Plumpton	1448	York	Yorks	minstrels	REED York 72
Sir William Plumpton	1449	York	Yorks	minstrels	REED York 75
Sir William Plumpton	1456	Fountains Abbey	Yorks	entertainers	Lancashire 401

The available dramatic records show that, with only a few exceptions, entertainers attached to nobles named in TABLE 6 never performed anywhere other than York. The exceptions are entertainers of Ralph Neville, Earl of Westmorland (two performances in Exeter in 1430 and 1431), Richard Neville, Earl of Salisbury (two performances at King's College, Cambridge, in 1442 and 1459 and one in Worcester in 1445), and Robert Neville, Bishop of Durham (one performance in Exeter in 1439 and two in Worcester in 1439 and 1446; Worcester is an area where the Nevilles held lands and influence).[34]

---

34 REED: Cambridge 29, 40; REED: Devon 92, REED: Hereford/Worcs 399.

Along with the entertainers of the Neville family, performers patronized by allies of the Nevilles also appear in York's dramatic records. The Nevilles' most potent ally was Richard, Duke of York, who not only held lands in Yorkshire, but also held the office of JP there at various times.[35] York's minstrels appeared four times in the city of York between 1446 and 1454. There is no record of their patron's presence there at the time.[36] Minstrels patronized by William, Baron Fitzhugh, performed in York five times between 1447 and 1449; minstrels patronized by Henry, Baron Scrope of Bolton, appeared there four times between 1446 and 1448; minstrels of Robert, Baron Ogle, are listed in York records for 1447 and 1448; and minstrels patronized by Sir John Harington appear seven times in the records from 1447 to 1449. Neither Ogle nor Harington held lands in Yorkshire, but both were staunch supporters of the Nevilles.[37]

Not only did the minstrels of Henry Percy, Earl of Northumberland, now appear frequently at York, the Percy presence also was represented by entertainers of his heir Henry Percy, Baron Poynings, his younger son Thomas Percy, Baron Egremont, his cousin Baron Thomas de Clifford, and former ward, Sir William Plumpton.[38] Other entertainers patronized by allies of the Percies also performed in York. Between 1446 and 1449 performers of Sir William Maulever and three members of the Pudsay family appear in York's dramatic records. Both families had close ties to the Percies.[39] The minstrels of another Percy ally, Henry Holland, Duke of Exeter, also appeared in York four times between 1446 and 1448.[40] Though Exeter had no lands in Yorkshire, he sought the support of the Percies in his disputes over lands with Baron Cromwell, and for his resistance to Richard of York during the incapacitation of Henry VI in 1453–4.[41]

---

35 For Richard's JP offices see <https://reed.library.utoronto.ca/node/316242#details-for-offices>.

36 *REED: York* 70, 72, 73, 85, 86.

37 *REED: York* 67, 68, 70–3, 75, 77; Gillingham *Wars of the Roses,* 79, 84, 89, 142; *ODNB* at <https://doi.org/10.1093/ref:odnb/20615f>.

38 *ODNB* at <https://doi.org/10.1093/ref:odnb/22398>; Gillingham *Wars of the Roses*, 79.

39 *REED: York* 65–7, 70, 71, 75; Griffiths 'Local Rivalries', 600–2, 611–18.

40 *REED: York* 66, 69–71.

41 Anthony Pollard 'Percies, Nevilles and the Wars of the Roses' *History Today* 42:9 (Sept. 1993) 42–8; Griffiths 'Local Rivalries' 590, 593–5, 606–13; Gillingham *Wars of*

York's dramatic records reveal that the reign of Henry VI saw far more performances by visiting aristocratic entertainers than did any other reign. My spreadsheet lists a total of 274 entries of visiting performers in York, from the first instance in 1395, minstrels of King Richard II, to the last in 1623, the players of Charles, Prince of Wales.[42] After the performance by King Richard's minstrels there are no further records until 1442. From 1442 to 1454, however, there are 170 performances by visiting entertainers patronized by King Henry and by 56 peers, knights, and gentry.[43] After the appearance of entertainers attached to the Duke of York in 1454[44] there are no recorded appearances of visiting aristocratic entertainers for the next eight years. Those years correspond with the battles in the Wars of the Roses and the triumph of Edward IV over the Lancastrians. King Edward IV's entertainers appear in York's records in 1462. By that time, Henry VI, his wife Margaret, son Edward, and major Lancastrian nobles had fled to Scotland, or been killed. Edward had been anointed and crowned king, and most peers had made peace with their new monarch.[45]

Over the next 160 years, 1462 to 1623, York's dramatic records list only 110 instances of visiting entertainers.[46] Hence, in just twenty years, 1442 to 1462, the 274 performances in York by visiting aristocratic entertainers represent 60% of all performances there by visiting performers. These twenty years were when rivalries among the northern nobles were the most intense. And, I think it significant that there are almost no appearances by entertainers attached to Yorkshire's lesser nobility and gentry after the reign of Henry VI.

---

the Roses 82, 83.

42   REED: *York* 9, 482.

43   REED: *York* 5–77, 80–3, 85–7. See also Johnston 'Travelling Entertainers', forthcoming.

44   REED: *York* 85.

45   REED: *York* 94; Charles Ross *The Wars of the Roses* (London: Thames and Hudson, 1976) 55, 143; Gillingham *Wars of the Roses* 137.

46   REED: *York* 94, 144, 181, 203, 206, 214, 217, 220–1, 225–6, 234, 237, 241, 243, 245, 248, 259, 269, 273, 381, 330, 376, 382, 396–7, 403, 409, 413, 418–19, 430, 435–6, 441–2, 449, 455, 460, 462, 471, 473, 476, 479, 481–2, 486–8, 491, 494, 496, 601, 507, 517, 521–2, 524, 528, 533, 536, 538, 564, 568; McMillin and MacLean 175; Murray *Dramatic Companies* 2 411.

JAMES H. FORSE

The South-West

Peter Fleming notes that dramatic records may reveal much about local (I would add regional) politics.[47] When describing touring by aristocrats' entertainers in Warwickshire, Elza Tiner suggests that their appearances could be a way to advertise the power of their respective patrons, and that their patrons' disputes over landed properties 'may have been a possible motive for a show of power'.[48] The records from York seem to offer another example of Tiner's suggestions. And *REED* volumes from four other municipalities – two from the South-West, Exeter and Barnstaple (Devon); and two from counties on the Welsh border, Worcester and Shrewsbury (Shropshire) – also show an interesting coincidence of regional jockeying for power among the greater and lesser nobles, and an increase in performances by entertainers patronized by them.

The Courtenays were the only great family whose power-base lay in England's South-West. A Courtenay had been Earl of Devon since 1335,[49] and they held castles and substantial holdings in Devon, Cornwall, and Somerset.[50] Courtenay dominance in the area was interrupted in 1422 when the earldom passed to the eight-year-old Thomas Courtenay. Thomas was placed under the wardship of Sir John Talbot the Elder – the doughty warrior of Shakespeare's *Henry VI Part 1*. By the time Courtenay reached his majority in 1433, political dominance in the South-West was shifting towards Sir William Bonville, who controlled significant holdings in Devon and Dorset, was steward of Cornwall, and served as Commissioner of Musters and *oyer* and *terminer* in Devon and Cornwall, and also as JP in those counties.[51]

---

47 Peter Fleming 'Performance, Politics, and Culture in the Southwest of Britain, 1350–1642' *Early Theatre 6* (2003) 99.

48 Tiner 'Patrons and Travelling Companies' 37–8.

49 G.E. Cokayne *The Complete Peerage IV: Dacre to Dysart* edited Vicary Gibbs with H.A. Doubleday (London: St Catherine Press, 1916) 322–3.

50 For properties see <https://reed.library.utoronto.ca/node/315989#patrons-detail-properties> and *REED: Devon* 476.

51 Martin Cherry 'The Struggle for Power in Mid-Fifteenth-Century Devonshire' in *Patronage, the Crown and the Provinces in Later Medieval England* edited R.A. Griffiths (Gloucester: Alan Sutton, 1981) 123–5; <https://reed.library.utoronto.ca/node/315924>.

In 1440 Earl Thomas began to attack Bonville. Henry VI's Council investigated the Earl's breaches of the peace in Devon, and his misuse of his office as JP against Bonville and his adherents. In 1451, though the reasons are obscure, Earl Thomas led a large force into neighbouring Somerset and besieged Taunton Castle, tenanted by the Earl of Wiltshire's ally Sir William Bonville. At this point Richard of York, then at Ludlow, asserted his authority as Commissioner of Peace for Somerset to end the dispute.[52] Violence again broke out in 1455, when the Earl's son, Thomas junior, attacked Nicholas Radford, Sir William Bonville's lawyer. Radford was murdered, his house was sacked, and Earl Thomas seized control of Exeter. Again, as in 1451, the Duke of York intervened, this time as Lord Protector.[53]

Many of the great magnates of the realm had interests in the South-West, and dramatic records show that their performers began to appear in Devon frequently (see TABLE 7). Their appearances do not indicate they travelled there with their patrons. Though he held no lands or offices in Devon, Dorset, Cornwall, or Somerset, John Talbot, Earl of Shrewsbury, did hold the wardship of Earl Thomas Courtenay (1422–33). Richard of York held the position of Keeper of the Mines in Cornwall and Devon, and several times served as JP in Cornwall, Devon, Dorset, and neighbouring counties of Somerset and Wiltshire.[54] Humphrey Stafford, Duke of Buckingham, held property and offices in the South-West. John Holland, Earl of Huntingdon and after 1444 Duke of Exeter, held lands in Cornwall and Devon, and served several terms as JP in Devon. His son Henry Holland succeeded to both titles in 1447, and also served as JP in Devon and in Cornwall. Richard Beauchamp, Earl of Warwick, served several terms as JP in Cornwall, Devon, and nearby Gloucestershire.[55] Edmund Beaufort, Earl of Dorset, held lands in Dorset and Somerset, and frequently served as JP in both counties.[56] Walter, Baron Hungerford, held lands in Cornwall, Devon, Dorset, Wiltshire, Worcestershire, and at various times served as JP in Devon, Cornwall, and

---

52 Wolffe *Henry VI* 251–2; Gillingham *Wars of the Roses*, 71–2; Cherry 'Struggle for Power' 131.
53 Wolffe *Henry VI* 298; Gillingham *Wars of the Roses*, 94–7; Cherry 'Struggle for Power' 135–8.
54 <https://reed.library.utoronto.ca/node/316242#details-for-offices>; *REED: Devon* 525.
55 *REED: Devon* 468, 484, 493, 520–1.
56 <https://reed.library.utoronto.ca/node/315933>.

Wiltshire.[57] William Bourchier, Baron FitzWarin, held Brampton Castle and Tawstock Court in Devon, and lands in Devon, Cornwall, and Wiltshire, and at various times was Commissioner of Musters in Devon and Cornwall.[58] Entertainers of all these lords now appear in Devon's dramatic records.

TABLE 7: Performers of Patrons in Records from
Exeter and Barnstaple, 1422–62

Patron	Year	Place	County	Type	Source
John Stafford, *later* Archbp of Canterbury	1439	Exeter	Devon	entertainers	*REED Dev* 96
Archbp John Stafford	1440	Exeter	Devon	entertainers	*REED Dev* 96
James, Baron Berkeley	1428	Exeter	Devon	entertainers	*REED Dev* 90
James Berkeley	1429	Exeter	Devon	entertainers	*REED Dev* 91
Robert Neville, Bishop of Durham	1439	Exeter	Devon	minstrels	*REED Dev* 96
Edmund Lacey, Bishop of Exeter	1439	Exeter	Devon	minstrels	*REED Dev* 96
John Hals, Bishop of Exeter	1426	Exeter	Devon	jester	*REED Dev* 88
Henry Beaufort, Bishop of Winchester	1429	Exeter	Devon	jester	*REED Dev* 91
Bishop Henry Beaufort	1434	Exeter	Devon	jester	*REED Dev* 94
Bishop Henry Beaufort	1434	Exeter	Devon	jester	*REED Dev* 95
Bishop Henry Beaufort	1432	Exeter	Devon	minstrels	*REED Dev* 93
William, Baron Botreaux	1427	Exeter	Devon	minstrels	*REED Dev* 90

57 <https://reed.library.utoronto.ca/node/316108>.
58 <https://reed.library.utoronto.ca/node/315939>; Ross *Wars of the Roses* 144.

Patron	Year	Place	County	Type	Source
William Botreaux	1429	Exeter	Devon	minstrels	REED Dev 91
William Botreaux	1430	Exeter	Devon	minstrels	REED Dev 92
William Botreaux	1432	Exeter	Devon	minstrels	REED Dev 93
William Botreaux	1433	Exeter	Devon	minstrels	REED Dev 94
William Botreaux	1434	Exeter	Devon	minstrels	REED Dev 94
Nicholas, Baron Carew	1432	Exeter	Devon	minstrels	REED Dev 93
Nicholas Carew	1439	Exeter	Devon	minstrels	REED Dev 96
Anne Talbot, Countess of Devon	1428	Exeter	Devon	minstrels	REED Dev 90
Sir Giles Daubeney	1433	Exeter	Devon	entertainers	REED Dev 94
John of Lancaster, Duke of Bedford	1433	Exeter	Devon	entertainers	REED Dev 94
John, Duke of Bedford	1433	Exeter	Devon	minstrels	REED Dev 94
John, Duke of Bedford	1434	Exeter	Devon	minstrels	REED Dev 95
John, Duke of Bedford	1433	Exeter	Devon	taborer	REED Dev 94
Humphrey Stafford, Duke of Buckingham	1426	Exeter	Devon	minstrels	REED Dev 89
Humphrey, Duke of Buckingham	1447	Exeter	Devon	minstrels	REED Dev 98
Thomas Beaufort, Duke of Exeter	1423	Exeter	Devon	minstrels	REED Dev 87
Thomas, Duke of Exeter	1424	Exeter	Devon	minstrels	REED Dev 88
Thomas, Duke of Exeter	1425	Exeter	Devon	minstrels	REED Dev 88
Thomas, Duke of Exeter	1425	Exeter	Devon	minstrels	REED Dev 88
Thomas, Duke of Exeter	1426	Exeter	Devon	minstrels	REED Dev 88

Patron	Year	Place	County	Type	Source
John Holland, 2nd Duke of Exeter	1425	Exeter	Devon	minstrels	REED Dev 88
John, Duke of Exeter	1427	Exeter	Devon	minstrels	REED Dev 90
John, Duke of Exeter	1428	Exeter	Devon	minstrels	REED Dev 90
John, Duke of Exeter	1429	Exeter	Devon	minstrels	REED Dev 91
John, Duke of Exeter	1431	Exeter	Devon	minstrels	REED Dev 92
John, Duke of Exeter	1432	Exeter	Devon	minstrels	REED Dev 93
John, Duke of Exeter	1434	Exeter	Devon	minstrels	REED Dev 95
John, Duke of Exeter	1438	Exeter	Devon	minstrels	REED Dev 95
John, Duke of Exeter	1439	Exeter	Devon	trumpeter	REED Dev 96
Henry Holland, Duke of Exeter	1456	Exeter	Devon	minstrels	REED Dev 99
Humphrey, Duke of Gloucester	1430	Exeter	Devon	entertainers	REED Dev 92
Humphrey of Gloucester	1433	Exeter	Devon	entertainers	REED Dev 94
Humphrey of Gloucester	1432	Exeter	Devon	minstrels	REED Dev 93
Humphrey of Gloucester	1439	Exeter	Devon	minstrels	REED Dev 96
Edmund Beaufort, Duke of Somerset	1427	Exeter	Devon	minstrels	REED Dev 90
William de la Pole, Duke of Suffolk	1447	Exeter	Devon	minstrels	REED Dev 98
Richard, Duke of York	1432	Exeter	Devon	minstrels	REED Dev 93

Patron	Year	Place	County	Type	Source
Richard, Duke of York	1433	Exeter	Devon	minstrels	*REED Dev* 94
Thomas Courtenay, Earl Devon	1428	Exeter	Devon	minstrels	*REED Dev* 90
Thomas Courtenay, Earl of Devon	1429	Exeter	Devon	minstrels	*REED Dev* 91
Thomas, Earl of Devon	1430	Exeter	Devon	minstrels	*REED Dev* 92
Thomas, Earl of Devon	1431	Exeter	Devon	minstrels	*REED Dev* 92
Thomas, Earl of Devon	1432	Exeter	Devon	minstrels	*REED Dev* 93
Henry Percy, Earl of Northumberland	1428	Exeter	Devon	minstrels	*REED Dev* 90
Thomas Montagu, Earl of Salisbury	1427	Exeter	Devon	minstrels	*REED Dev* 89
John Talbot, Earl of Shrewsbury	1428	Exeter	Devon	minstrels	*REED Dev* 90
John, Earl of Shrewsbury	1429	Exeter	Devon	minstrels	*REED Dev* 91
John, Earl of Shrewsbury	1431	Exeter	Devon	minstrels	*REED Dev* 92
Richard Beauchamp, Earl of Warwick	1425	Exeter	Devon	minstrels	*REED Dev* 88
Richard, Earl of Warwick	1427	Exeter	Devon	minstrels	*REED Dev* 89
Richard, Earl of Warwick	1428	Exeter	Devon	minstrels	*REED Dev* 90
Richard, Earl of Warwick	1429	Exeter	Devon	minstrels	*REED Dev* 91
Richard, Earl of Warwick	1431	Exeter	Devon	minstrels	*REED Dev* 92
Richard, Earl of Warwick	1433	Exeter	Devon	minstrels	*REED Dev* 94

Patron	Year	Place	County	Type	Source
Ralph Neville, Earl of Westmorland	1430	Exeter	Devon	minstrels	REED Dev 92
Ralph, Earl of Westmorland	1431	Exeter	Devon	minstrels	REED Dev 92
Mr John Copplestone	1433	Exeter	Devon	entertainers	REED Dev 94
Mr John Copplestone	1433	Exeter	Devon	entertainers	REED Dev 94
Mr John Copplestone	1433	Exeter	Devon	minstrels	REED Dev 94
Mr John Copplestone	1433	Exeter	Devon	minstrels	REED Dev 94
Walter, Baron Hungerford	1427	Exeter	Devon	minstrels	REED Dev 90
Walter Hungerford	1428	Exeter	Devon	minstrels	REED Dev 90
Walter Hungerford	1429	Exeter	Devon	minstrels	REED Dev 91
Walter Hungerford	1430	Exeter	Devon	minstrels	REED Dev 92
Walter Hungerford	1431	Exeter	Devon	minstrels	REED Dev 92
Walter Hungerford	1433	Exeter	Devon	minstrels	REED Dev 93
King Henry VI	1425	Exeter	Devon	minstrels	REED Dev 88
King Henry VI	1426	Exeter	Devon	minstrels	REED Dev 88
King Henry VI	1428	Exeter	Devon	minstrels	REED Dev 90
King Henry VI	1440	Exeter	Devon	minstrels	REED Dev 96
Sir Maurice Berkley (d.1460) or Maurice (d.1464)	1432	Exeter	Devon	entertainers	REED Dev 93
Sir William Bodrugan	1432	Exeter	Devon	minstrels	REED Dev 93
Sir William Bonville	1432	Exeter	Devon	entertainers	REED Dev 93
Sir Philip Courtenay	1432	Exeter	Devon	minstrels	REED Dev 94

Patron	Year	Place	County	Type	Source
Sir Philip Courtenay	1433	Exeter	Devon	minstrels	REED Dev 94
Sir Philip Courtenay	1438	Exeter	Devon	minstrels	REED Dev 95
Sir Giles Daubeney	1433	Exeter	Devon	minstrels	REED Dev 94
Sir William Holland	1459	Exeter	Devon	trumpeter	REED Dev 101
Sir Hugh Lutrell	1428	Exeter	Devon	minstrels	REED Dev 90
Sir Thomas Rempston	1439	Exeter	Devon	musician	REED Dev 96
Lady Harington (Margaret Hill, wife of William Harington)	1428	Exeter	Devon	minstrels	REED Dev 90
Queen Catherine of Valois (m. Henry V)	1432	Exeter	Devon	jester	REED Dev 93
John Scrope, Baron Scrope	1431	Exeter	Devon	minstrel	REED Dev 93
John de la Zouche, Baron Zouche	1431	Exeter	Devon	entertainers	REED Dev 82
John Holland, Duke of Exeter	1435	Barnstaple	Devon	minstrels	REED Dev 30
Henry Holland, Duke of Exeter	1454	Barnstaple	Devon	minstrels	REED Dev 30
Henry Holland, Duke of Exeter	1458	Barnstaple	Devon	minstrels	REED Dev 30
Thomas Courtenay, Earl of Devon	1454	Barnstaple	Devon	minstrels	REED Dev 30
William Bourchier, Baron FitzWarin	1454	Barnstaple	Devon	minstrels	REED Dev 30
William Bourchier	1456	Barnstaple	Devon	minstrels	REED Dev 30
William Bourchier	1461	Barnstaple	Devon	minstrels	REED Dev 30
King Henry VI	1454	Barnstaple	Devon	minstrels	REED Dev 30

Patron	Year	Place	County	Type	Source
Thomas Bourchier, Archbishop of Canterbury	1455	Barnstaple	Devon	minstrels	REED Dev 30
King Henry VI	1458	Barnstaple	Devon	minstrels	REED Dev 30
George Neville, Archbishop of York	1461	Barnstaple	Devon	minstrels	REED Dev 31
John Tuchet, Baron Audley (d.1490)	1461	Barnstaple	Devon	minstrels	REED Dev 31

Unlike at York, the appearances of these entertainers do not reflect rivalries among their patrons in the South-West. Rather, they may have helped to remind locals of the various interests and influences in the area of their respective patrons. With the exception of a single performance in Launceston, Cornwall, by entertainers of Viscount Beaumont in 1447, and 14 performances by other entertainers between 1435 and 1462 in Barnstaple,[59] most touring entertainers performed in Exeter.

The appearance of aristocrats' entertainers in Barnstaple, and especially Exeter, makes sense economically for the entertainers and, probably, politically for their patrons. Exeter, with a population of over 2,000, was the chief city not only for Devon but also for Dorset and Cornwall. A cathedral city, Exeter served the Crown as an administrative centre, and was a busy market town, a centre for Devon's wool trade.[60] Sally-Beth MacLean calls Exeter the 'provincial capital of the Southwest', noting that the city also was a hub for major roads leading south to Dartmoor and Plymouth, west to Cornwall, and north to Bristol, Gloucester, Worcester, and Shrewsbury.[61] Barnstaple was 'the busiest market town in Devon' and, like Exeter, a centre for Devon's wool trade. It was also a significant port for trade with Ireland.[62] In terms of earnings both towns offered good opportunities for entertainers. At the same time, their presence 'advertised' the power and status of their patrons, especially to the important local gentry.

59 REED: Dorset/Cornwall 485.
60 REED: Devon xv–xvii.
61 Sally-Beth MacLean 'At the End of the Road: An Overview of Southwestern Touring Circuits' Early Theatre 6 (2003) 18, 19.
62 MacLean 'Overview' 19; REED: Devon xii–xiii.

Dramatic records from Exeter during the reign of Henry VI do not match the pattern in York, when performances in the city by aristocratic entertainers seem to spike at the height of the Percy–Neville disturbances. The entertainers of the chief protagonists in Devon's power struggle do not appear to be very active at the height of their hostilities. Earl Thomas's minstrels only show up in Exeter's records five times, in 1428, 1429, 1430, and 1432, and Bonville's minstrels only appear once in Exeter's records, in 1432.[63] There also are few appearances by other entertainers during the violence of 1440s: one by entertainers of King Henry and one by entertainers of John Stafford, Bishop of Bath and Wells, both in 1440; and in 1447, one each for the entertainers of Humphrey Stafford, Duke of Buckingham, and of William de la Pole, Duke of Suffolk. Only one appearance occurs in the 1450s: in 1456 the minstrels of Henry Holland, Duke of Exeter, performed in Exeter. After that year the next entry does not appear in Exeter's records until 1490, a gap of twenty-five years.[64]

Yet Exeter's dramatic records do reveal a pattern. Most appearances by patronized entertainers correspond with the minorities of both Earl Thomas Courtenay and King Henry. King Henry's entertainers may have been touring more frequently, since entertainments are likely to have been less frequent at Court during the minority government. Courtney's minstrels performed in Exeter in 1428, 1429, 1430, and 1431.[65] By 1428 Courtenay was approaching the end of his minority, and it is possible that this is a company of entertainers newly created for his impending majority household. The last recorded performance by an Earl of Devon's entertainers before Earl Thomas was by his grandfather's minstrels in 1419.[66] Courtenay's minority also may account for performances in Exeter by minstrels patronized by his guardian, Sir John Talbot, in 1428, 1429, and 1431. Talbot held neither lands nor offices in the South-West, and during those years was fighting in France. Why his minstrels travelled to Devon is unknown, but their appearance does coincide with the waning years of his guardianship of the young Earl.[67]

It is also during Earl Thomas's minority in the 1420s and 1430s that suddenly the entertainers of several members of the South-West's

---

63   *REED: Devon* 90–3.
64   *REED: Devon* 96, 98, 99, 110.
65   *REED: Devon* 90–2.
66   *REED: Devon* 86.
67   *REED: Devon* 90–2; *ODNB* at <https://doi.org/10.1093/ref:odnb/26932>.

lesser lords and gentry appear in Exeter's records (see TABLE 7). Their performances may well reflect the political uncertainties in the South-West, as these lesser aristocrats sought to demonstrate their presence and status within the South-West's power structure.

It is not necessary to give details of all the local aristocrats and upper gentry; two examples will serve. Exeter's records note performances by entertainers of Earl Thomas' cousin, Sir Philip Courtenay, twice in 1433, the year in which Earl Thomas reached his majority, and again in 1438.[68] Sir Philip was the head of the cadet branch of the Courtenays, with substantial holdings in Devon, Somerset, and Cornwall. His role in the politics of the South-West is evidenced by several terms as JP in Devon and Cornwall, and as commissioner of muster, of array, and *oyer* and *terminer*.[69] His relationship with his cousin was hostile; in 1455, when Earl Thomas seized the city of Exeter, he also laid siege to Sir Philip at Powderham Castle.[70] Sir William, Baron Botreaux, serves as another example. His minstrels appear in Exeter's records in 1427, 1428, 1429, 1430, 1432, 1433, and 1434,[71] for the most part during Earl Thomas's minority. Though Botreaux's power base was in Cornwall, he was very active in the politics of Devon, Dorset, Wiltshire, and Somerset, serving several times as JP and commissioner of array, muster, and *oyer* and *terminer* in those counties.[72]

Entertainers of several other members of the South-West's lesser nobles and gentry appear in Exeter's records. None appear anywhere else in England's dramatic records, and their entertainers disappear after Henry's reign. Between 1426 and 1439 Exeter's records include performances by entertainers patronized by: Barons Nicholas Carew, James Berkeley, and William Zouche, Sirs Giles Daubeney, Hugh Luttrell, William Bodrugan, Maurice Berkeley, and Thomas Remptson, Mr. John Hals, and Mr. John

---

68 *REED: Devon* 94.
69 For Courtenay see <https://reed.library.utoronto.ca/node/315988>.
70 See Nicholas Orme 'Representation & Rebellion in the Later Middle Ages' in *Historical Atlas of South-West England* edited Roger Kain and William Ravenhill (University of Exeter Press, 1999) 141–4; Wolffe *Henry VI* 254; Gillingham *Wars of the Roses* 71.
71 *REED: Devon* 90–4.
72 See <https://reed.library.utoronto.ca/node/315923#birth-death-info>. On his death at second Battle of St. Albans, see W.H. Rogers *The Ancient Sepulchral Effigies and Monumental and Memorial Sculpture of Devon* (Exeter: William Pollard, 1877) 389.

PEERS AND PERFORMERS IN THE REIGN OF HENRY VI

Copplestone. All were active in Devonshire politics.[73] Given the fluidity of politics in the South-West during Earl Thomas's minority, is it mere coincidence that all these performances occur in the 'provincial capital of the Southwest' when local aristocrats were jockeying among themselves for power and influence?[74]

Like the dramatic records of York, the dramatic records of Exeter reveal an increase in the appearance of aristocrats' performers during the reign of Henry VI. For the sixty years between 1361 – the performance of the trumpeters of Prince Edward (the Black Prince) – and 1420, the last appearance of entertainers before the reign of Henry VI, Exeter's records show 60 such appearances.[75] In the forty years 1422 to 1462 there are 82.[76] For a period of 262 years – from 1361 to 1625 – Exeter's records list a total 315 performances by visiting performers.[77] Hence, the 82 performances in Exeter during Henry's reign account for over a quarter of all such appearances.

There is no mention of aristocratic performers in Barnstaple until 1435, when the minstrels of John Holland, Earl of Huntingdon, were paid 40 pence.[78] Whether the Earl was present in the town is not known, but the year does coincide with his appointment as Lord Admiral of England, Aquitaine, and Ireland. As such the port of Barnstaple, with its connections to Ireland, fell under his purview. The only great magnates whose entertainers performed there were those of Earl Thomas Courtenay; Henry Holland, Duke of Exeter; and King Henry. Courtenay's minstrels played Barnstaple only once, in 1454. Those of Duke Henry appeared thrice, in 1454, 1458, and 1462; and the King's minstrels twice, in 1454 and 1458. There is no indication their patrons were in the town at the time. Yet the year 1454 does coincide with Richard of York's appointment as Lord Protector, as the York–Neville and the royal factions jockeyed for power, and in 1458 that rivalry was heating up again. Also appearing in Barnstaple were single performances

---

73 *REED: Devon* 82, 88, 91–4; for Carew see <https://reed.library.utoronto.ca/node/315985> and the biography of his father Nicholas, <www.historyofparliamentonline.org/volume/1386–1421/member/carew-nicholas-1356–1432>.
74 MacLean 'Overview' 19; *REED: Devon* xii–xiii.
75 *REED: Devon* 70, 72, 75, 77–86, 91.
76 *REED: Devon* 87–98.
77 *REED: Devon* 70, 251.
78 *REED: Devon* 30.

159

by the minstrels of Thomas Bourchier, Archbishop of Canterbury (1455), and George Neville, Bishop of Exeter (1461). Though there seems no clear reason for the appearance of Archbishop Bourchier's minstrels in Barnstaple, the event does coincide with his elevation to the see of Canterbury and his time as Lord Chancellor. The appearance of Bishop Neville's entertainers has a clearer connection with local matters. It coincides with the year in which Neville became Bishop of Exeter, and may have been in residence there.[79]

Along with appearing in Barnstaple in 1454, the King's minstrels were fairly active elsewhere too. In that year his minstrels also performed in Hythe and Sandwich (Kent). King Henry's minstrels performed again in Barnstaple in 1458, another year in which they were also active in Kent and Sussex. Again, they were not accompanying their patron. King Henry and Queen Margaret had withdrawn the Court to the Midlands.[80] The Duke of Exeter probably had nothing to do with the visit of his minstrels to Barnstaple in 1462. On the wrong side at the Battle of Towton in 1461, Exeter was then a fugitive. The minstrels may have been there at the behest of his wife Anne, sister to the new King Edward IV; despite Exeter's attainder, she was granted his goods and possessions for life. Alternatively, the minstrels may have been there on their own, since they now lacked an active patron.

Entertainers of two lesser nobles also appear in Barnstaple's records: the minstrels of John Tuchet, Baron Audley, in 1461, and of William Bourchier, Baron FitzWarin, in 1455, 1456, 1461, and 1462.[81] In 1461 Baron Audley served on commissions of array and *oyer* and *terminer* and as JP in Dorset, Somerset, and Wiltshire, so his minstrels may well have been accompanying him while on these duties. William Bourchier was brother to Archbishop Thomas Bourchier, as well as Henry, Viscount Bourchier. William possessed substantial holdings in Devon, Cornwall, and Somerset, and often served as JP in Devon and on commissions of muster, array, and *oyer* and *terminer* in Devon, Cornwall, and Somerset.[82] Performances by his minstrels in Barnstaple coincide with his exercise of those duties.

---

79 *REED: Devon* 30, 31; for Bourchier see *ODNB* at <https://doi.org/10.1093/ref:odnb/2993>; for Neville see *ODNB* at <https://doi.org/10.1093/ref:odnb/19934> and <https://reed.library.utoronto.ca/node/316210>.

80 Wolffe *Henry VI* 285, 300–19; *REED: Kent 2*: 612, 613, 824; *REED Sussex* 47.

81 *REED: Devon* 30, 31.

82 For Bourchier see *ODNB* at <https://doi.org/10.1093/ref:odnb/50242> and <https://reed.library.utoronto.ca/node/315939>.

Besides reflecting the possible interests of their patrons, these entertainers may have performed at Barnstaple because of the violence in and around Exeter in the 1440s and 1450s. It does seem telling that Barnstaple hosted no entertainers until violence broke out around Exeter. As was the case in York, after the reign of Henry VI there were very few performances by the entertainers of lesser nobles and gentry in either Exeter or Barnstaple.

The Welsh Borders

Another area that saw some increase in travelling entertainers was in counties clustered about the Welsh borders. Some of England's greatest magnates held lands there. By the middle of Henry VI's reign the majority of lordships in the Welsh Marches were held by Richard, Duke of York; Humphrey Stafford, Duke of Buckingham; and Richard Beauchamp and later Richard Neville, Earls of Warwick.[83] York held several lordships in Wales, Shropshire, Worcestershire, and Herefordshire, and was JP several times in Shropshire, Worcestershire, and Herefordshire. Buckingham held lordships in those same counties, and was lieutenant for the Marches of Wales (1443–51). He served as JP in Shropshire, Herefordshire, and Gloucestershire. Richard Beauchamp, Earl of Warwick, was hereditary sheriff of Worcestershire, where he served several years as JP as well as in Shropshire and Herefordshire. His successor as Earl of Warwick, Richard Neville, also was hereditary Sheriff of Worcestershire and served as JP in Worcestershire, Herefordshire, and Somerset.[84]

The Talbot Earls of Shrewsbury – John senior (died at the Battle of Carillon, France, 1453) and John junior (died at the Battle of Northampton, 1460) – were the only magnates whose main base was in counties bordering Wales, mostly in Herefordshire and Shropshire. They held Goodrich Castle (Herefordshire) and Blackmere Castle (Shropshire). The Talbots possessed

---

83 Wolffe *Henry VI* 118–19; Ross *Edward IV* 194.

84 Ailsa Herebert 'Herefordshire, 1413–61: Some Aspects of Society and Public Order' in *Patronage, the Crown, and the Provinces in Later Medieval England* edited R.A. Griffiths (Gloucester: Sutton, 181) 105: *ODNB* at <https://doi.org/10.1093/ref:odnb/1838>; Gillingham *Wars of the Roses* 65, 74; *REED: Devon* 520–1, 525. See also <https://reed.library.utoronto.ca/node/316242>; <https://reed.library.utoronto.ca/node/315839>; and <https://reed.library.utoronto.ca/node/316208>.

other extensive holdings in Shropshire, and served as Justices of the Peace in Shropshire, Herefordshire, and Gloucestershire.[85]

Since all these magnates, except the Talbots, were absentee lords, their deputies looked after their interests in local affairs,[86] but another way they maintained a presence was, as mentioned above, by holding local offices in those counties. In some ways the Talbots also were absentee landlords. Sir John senior was frequently away fighting in France in the Hundred Years War, and Sir John junior spent much time at Court as part of Queen Margaret's and Somerset's faction.[87]

As in the North, South-West, and Kent, the counties on the Welsh Border were prone to local disturbances.[88] In Gloucestershire a disputed family inheritance among descendants of Thomas, Baron Berkeley (d.1417), continued off and on for thirty years. Twice, his heir, James, Baron Berkeley, had Berkeley Castle and its attached manors seized by his cousins, and he, his son, and his wife were seized and imprisoned by them.[89] Herefordshire also saw its share of local violence. In 1452 Richard of York's client, Sir Walter Devereux, seized the city of Hereford and raised troops to support York's attempts to force King Henry to reform his government. By Easter 1456 Devereux and Sir William Herbert had again seized the city. The two sought revenge for the murder of Herbert's kinsman Walter Vaughan. Devereux and Herbert jailed Hereford's mayor, freed prisoners from the jails, and coerced local justices of the peace into condemning six Hereford citizens to death whom they believed had participated in Vaughan's murder. Later, in August 1456, acting for the Duke of York, Devereux raised a force of 2,000 men, marched into Wales, and seized Carmarthen Castle from Edmund Tudor.[90]

Given the interests of England's great magnates in the Marches of Wales, one might expect to see many appearances throughout those counties by their entertainers. However, the dramatic records for Wales and the

---

85 See <https://reed.library.utoronto.ca/node/316340> and <https://reed.library.utoronto.ca/node/316344>; Gillingham, *Wars of the Roses* 74, 114.
86 Wolffe *Henry VI* 119.
87 Wolffe *Henry VI* 55–6, 153–4, 166, 211, 262–3, 270, 281, 303, 306, 310, 322.
88 Herebert 'Herefordshire' 105; Wolffe *Henry VI* 118–19.
89 *ODNB* at <https://doi.org/10.1093/ref:odnb/50214> and <https://doi.org/10.1093/ref:odnb/56573>.
90 Herebert 'Herefordshire' 106–7, Wolffe *Henry VI* 257, 303–4; Ross *Edward IV* 391.

bordering counties show few instances of such performances. Records from Wales and the counties of Cheshire, Gloucestershire, Herefordshire, and Somerset list none. There are, however, 19 such performances in Worcester, and 42 in Shrewsbury, Shropshire (TABLe 8).

TABLE 8: Performers of Patrons Appearing in Records from Shrewsbury and Worcester

Patron	Year	Place	County	Type	Source
James Tuchet, Baron Audley (d.1459)	1452	Shrewsbury	Salop	entertainers	*REED Shr* 138
Henry Grey, Earl of Tankerville	1445	Shrewsbury	Salop	entertainers	*REED Shr* 133
Henry, Earl of Tankerville	1446	Shrewsbury	Salop	entertainers	*REED Shr* 135
Henry, Earl of Tankerville	1447	Shrewsbury	Salop	entertainers	*REED Shr* 135
Jasper Tudor, Earl of Pembroke	1457	Shrewsbury	Salop	minstrels	*REED Shr* 140
Humphrey Stafford, Duke of Buckingham	1442	Shrewsbury	Salop	entertainers	*REED Shr* 132
H., Duke of Buckingham	1447	Shrewsbury	Salop	entertainers	*REED Shr* 135
H., Duke of Buckingham	1450	Shrewsbury	Salop	entertainers	*REED Shr* 136
H., Duke of Buckingham	1451	Shrewsbury	Salop	entertainers	*REED Shr* 138
H., Duke of Buckingham	1452	Shrewsbury	Salop	entertainers	*REED Shr* 138
H., Duke of Buckingham	1436	Shrewsbury	Salop	entertainers	*REED Shr* 131
H., Duke of Buckingham	1438	Shrewsbury	Salop	entertainers	*REED Shr* 131

Patron	Year	Place	County	Type	Source
H., Duke of Buckingham	1457	Shrewsbury	Salop	minstrels	*REED Shr* 139
Henry Holland, Duke of Exeter (d.1475)	1452	Shrewsbury	Salop	minstrels	*REED Shr* 139
Henry, Duke of Exeter	1457	Shrewsbury	Salop	minstrels	*REED Shr* 141
Humphrey, Duke of Gloucester	1426	Shrewsbury	Salop	entertainers	*REED Shr* 130
Humphrey, Duke of Gloucester	1427	Shrewsbury	Salop	entertainers	*REED Shr* 130
William de la Pole, Duke of Suffolk	1445	Shrewsbury	Salop	entertainers	*REED Shr* 134
Richard, Duke of York	1445	Shrewsbury	Salop	entertainers	*REED Shr* 133
Richard, Duke of York	1450	Shrewsbury	Salop	entertainers	*REED Shr* 136
Richard, Duke of York	1457	Shrewsbury	Salop	entertainers	*REED Shr* 137
Richard, Duke of York	1446	Shrewsbury	Salop	minstrels	*REED Shr* 135
Richard, Duke of York	1451	Shrewsbury	Salop	minstrels	*REED Shr* 138
Richard, Duke of York	1457	Shrewsbury	Salop	minstrels	*REED Shr* 141
William FitzAlan, Earl of Arundel	1444	Shrewsbury	Salop	entertainers	*REED Shr* 132
William, Earl of Arundel	1445	Shrewsbury	Salop	entertainers	*REED Shr* 133
William, Earl of Arundel	1447	Shrewsbury	Salop	entertainers	*REED Shr* 135

Patron	Year	Place	County	Type	Source
William, Earl of Arundel	1450	Shrewsbury	Salop	minstrels	*REED Shr* 137
William, Earl of Arundel	1450	Shrewsbury	Salop	minstrels	*REED Shr* 137
John Talbot senior, Earl of Shrewsbury	1426	Shrewsbury	Salop	entertainers	*REED Shr* 130
John, Earl of Shrewsbury	1443	Shrewsbury	Salop	entertainers	*REED Shr* 132
John, Earl of Shrewsbury	1444	Shrewsbury	Salop	entertainers	*REED Shr* 133
John, Earl of Shrewsbury	1445	Shrewsbury	Salop	entertainers	*REED Shr* 133
John, Earl of Shrewsbury	1450	Shrewsbury	Salop	entertainers	*REED Shr* 137
John, Earl of Shrewsbury	1446	Shrewsbury	Salop	minstrels	*REED Shr* 135
John, Earl of Shrewsbury	1450	Shrewsbury	Salop	minstrels	*REED Shr* 137
John, Earl of Shrewsbury	1451	Shrewsbury	Salop	minstrels	*REED Shr* 137
John, Earl of Shrewsbury	1451	Shrewsbury	Salop	minstrels	*REED Shr* 137
John Earl of Shrewsbury	1452	Shrewsbury	Salop	minstrels	*REED Shr* 139
John, Earl of Shrewsbury	1453	Shrewsbury	Salop	minstrels	*REED Shr* 139
John Talbot junior, later Earl of Shrewsbury	1446	Shrewsbury	Salop	minstrels	*REED Shr* 134
John Talbot junior	1450	Shrewsbury	Salop	minstrels	*REED Shr* 137
John Talbot junior	1457	Shrewsbury	Salop	minstrels	*REED Shr* 140

Patron	Year	Place	County	Type	Source
John Talbot junior	1458	Shrewsbury	Salop	minstrels	REED Shr 140
John Grey, Baron Grey of Codnor	1426	Shrewsbury	Salop	entertainers	REED Shr 130
Richard Grey, Baron Grey of Powis	1457	Shrewsbury	Salop	minstrels	REED Shr 140
Richard, Baron Grey of Powis	1457	Shrewsbury	Salop	minstrels	REED Shr 140
King Henry VI	1446	Shrewsbury	Salop	minstrels	REED Shr 135
King Henry VI	1457	Shrewsbury	Salop	minstrels	REED Shr 140
King Henry VI	1460	Shrewsbury	Salop	minstrels	REED Shr 144
King Henry VI	1441	Shrewsbury	Salop	minstrels	REED Shr 132
King Henry VI	1444	Shrewsbury	Salop	minstrels	REED Shr 133
King Henry VI	1448	Shrewsbury	Salop	minstrels	REED Shr 135
King Henry VI	1449	Shrewsbury	Salop	minstrels	REED Shr 136
Prince Edward 'of Westminster'	1457	Shrewsbury	Salop	minstrels	REED Shr 140
Prince Edward	1458	Shrewsbury	Salop	minstrels	REED Shr 141
Edmund, Baron Hungerford	1447	Worcester	Worcs	minstrels	REED Her 400
Edmund Hungerford	1448	Worcester	Worcs	minstrels	REED Her 400
Robert Neville, Bishop of Durham	1446	Worcester	Worcs	minstrels	REED Her 399
Cecily Neville, Duchess of Warwick	1447	Worcester	Worcs	entertainers	REED Her 400

Patron	Year	Place	County	Type	Source
Humphrey Stafford, Duke of Buckingham	1441	Worcester	Worcs	entertainers	*REED Her* 399
H., Duke of Buckingham	1445	Worcester	Worcs	entertainers	*REED Her* 399
H., Duke of Buckingham	1451	Worcester	Worcs	entertainers	*REED Her* 400
Henry Holland, Duke of Exeter	1445	Worcester	Worcs	minstrels	*REED Her* 399
Henry, Duke of Exeter	1451	Worcester	Worcs	minstrels	*REED Her* 401
Humphrey, Duke of Gloucester	1445	Worcester	Worcs	minstrels	*REED Her* 399
William de la Pole, 1st Duke of Suffolk	1445	Worcester	Worcs	minstrels	*REED Her* 399
William, Duke of Suffolk	1446	Worcester	Worcs	minstrels	*REED Her* 400
Richard, Duke of York	1446	Worcester	Worcs	minstrels	*REED Her* 399
William FitzAlan, Earl of Arundel	1447	Worcester	Worcs	minstrels	*REED Her* 400
Richard Neville, Earl of Salisbury	1445	Worcester	Worcs	minstrels	*REED Her* 399
Henry Beauchamp, Earl of Warwick	1445	Worcester	Worcs	minstrels	*REED Her* 399
Richard Neville, Earl of Warwick	1451	Worcester	Worcs	entertainers	*REED Her* 400
King Henry VI	1446	Worcester	Worcs	minstrels	*REED Her* 400

Patron	Year	Place	County	Type	Source
Sir Roland Leynthale	1446	Worcester	Worcs	harper	REED Her 400
Sir Walter Devereux	1447	Worcester	Worcs	minstrels	REED Her 400
Sir Walter Devereux	1447	Worcester	Worcs	minstrels	REED Her 400
Sir William Lucy	1451	Worcester	Worcs	minstrels	REED Her 400

Both Worcester and Shrewsbury make sense as performance sites for entertainers and their patrons. By late medieval standards, Worcester was large with perhaps as many as 8,000 inhabitants. A cathedral city, it contained the shrines of Saints Wulstan and Oswald, making it a pilgrimage site. The city had a thriving cloth industry and trading ties to France, Germany, the Low Countries, and Spain.[91] Shrewsbury, only nine miles from the Welsh border, was the centre for royal government in Shropshire and the adjoining Welsh counties. It contained a busy market, with a major castle, a population of perhaps 2,000, and an important pilgrimage site at the shrine of St. Winifred.[92] All in all, Worcester and Shrewsbury offered entertainers and their patrons a larger exposure to important local populations than most other towns on the Welsh marches.

Entertainers of the Talbot Earls clearly dominate the dramatic records of Shrewsbury. Between 1426 and 1458 entertainers of John Talbot senior and John Talbot junior appear 18 times.[93] Minstrels of Richard of York appear at Shrewsbury six times between 1446 and 1457, and once in Worcester in 1446. Entertainers of Sir Walter Devereux, one of York's most trusted agents, appeared in Worcester in 1547.[94] Not surprisingly, entertainers of one of York's chief rivals at Court, Humphrey Stafford, Duke of Buckingham, also performed eight times in Shrewsbury between 1436 and 1457, and thrice in Worcester between 1441 and 1451.[95] With their extensive Welsh holdings,

91 See <www.francisfrith.com/uk/worcester/history>.
92 'Historical Background' in REED: Shropshire 2 359–66, 369–72.
93 REED: Shropshire 1 129, 130, 132–5, 137, 139–40.
94 REED: Shropshire 1 131, 135–8, 141; REED: Hereford/Worcs 399, 400.
95 REED: Shropshire 1 131–2, 135–6, 138–9; REED Hereford/Worcs 399, 400.

both York and Buckingham had much reason to promote themselves in these borderland counties. Between 1444 and 1450 the minstrels of William FitzAlan, Earl of Arundel, made five appearances in Shrewsbury and one in Worcester. FitzAlan did have lands in Shropshire, and served as JP and Commissioner of array and *oyer* and *terminer*, as well as a Commissioner of *oyer* and *terminer* in neighbouring Herefordshire. Arundel's mother was a Berkeley, and the dates for his entertainers fall within the period in which Baron James Berkeley was feuding with his cousins.[96] King Henry's entertainers performed in Shrewsbury five times between 1441 and 1449, and, as the Lancaster–York rivalry erupted into open warfare, again in 1457 and 1460 (see TABLE 5). Entertainers under the name of Henry's heir, Prince Edward, further represented the royal 'presence' in Shropshire in 1457 and 1458.[97] Neither the King, the Queen, nor the Prince travelled to Shropshire in those years. Whatever their reasons, it seems doubtful that these royal entertainers were travelling so far from Court simply to earn extra money.

Overall, dramatic records for Worcester contain 116 entries recording performances by visiting performers over 288 years – from the first in 1337 (minstrels of Henry, Earl of Lancaster), to the last in 1625 (players of Lord Dudley).[98] Between 1441 and 1457[99] there are 19 such appearances. Hence 16% of all performances by visiting aristocratic entertainers over 288 years occurred during the reign of Henry VI. For Shrewsbury the percentage is about the same. Shrewsbury's records list 292 such performances over 236 years – from the first in 1388 (minstrels of the Earl of Arundel) to the last in 1624 (the King's Men).[100] During Henry's reign there are 46 such performances, accounting for over 15% of all performances. Though patterns are less striking than in York, Exeter, and Barnstaple, still, as in those areas, appearances by entertainers employed by lesser aristocracy and gentry almost disappear from the dramatic records of Worcester and Shrewsbury after the reign of Henry VI.

---

96 *REED: Shropshire 1* 132, 133, 135, 137; *REED: Hereford/Worcs* 400; <https://reed.library.utoronto.ca/node/316072>.

97 *REED: Shropshire 1* 132–3, 135, 140–1, 144.

98 *REED: Hereford/Worcs* 396, 455.

99 *REED: Hereford/Worcs* 399, 400.

100 *REED: Shropshire 1* 127, 144.

Lancastrian and Yorkist

Given the breakdown of royal authority throughout the kingdom after Henry VI attained his majority, the increase of royal entertainers touring the provinces may seem surprising. The city of York's records mention performances by the royal minstrels every year (save 1445) from 1444 to 1453 (see TABLE 5). The royal minstrels were not travelling there with the king, although their presence would have signalled his authority.[101] It seems unlikely that his entertainers travelled that far from Court solely for extra pay. And it also may be that performances at York in 1447, 1448, and 1449 by minstrels patronized by three of Henry's favourites[102] – William de la Pole, Duke of Suffolk; Sir William Tailboys, Henry's squire; and Viscount John Beaumont, Constable of England[103] – also may have served to advertise the royal government's presence. None of these lords possessed holdings in Yorkshire, and performances by Tailboys's and Beaumont's entertainers appear nowhere else in provincial records.

It also is interesting that coincident to the coalescence of the great magnates into a Lancastrian faction – headed by the Dukes of Suffolk and Somerset and Queen Margaret – and a Yorkist faction – headed by the Duke of York and the Earls of Salisbury and Warwick – activity by their respective entertainers seems to have increased in the provinces (TABLE 9).

---

101   *REED: York* 65, 67, 70, 72, 74, 76, 80, 81, 83. Wolffe's Appendix gives Henry's itineraries year-by-year from 1536 to 1561. The only year that Henry visited York when his minstrels had appeared there was 1448, but the date of payment to his minstrels was 24 June (*REED: York* 72), whereas Henry was at York 3 months later, 20–23 September and 13–15 October (Wolffe *Henry VI* 367).

102   *REED: York* 69–72, 76.

103   Wolffe *Henry VI* 102, 104, 107, 114–16, 131, 189, 222; *ODNB* at <https://doi.org/10.1093/ref:odnb/26949>.

TABLE 9: Performances by Principal Leaders of the Lancastrian and Yorkist Factions

Patron	Year	Place	County	Type	Source
Lancastrian Faction					
William de la Pole, Duke of Suffolk	1416	King's Lynn	Norfolk	entertainers	Malone Nor 49
William, Duke of Suffolk	1440	Dover	Kent	minstrels	*REED Ken* 332
William, Duke of Suffolk	1445	Great Yarmouth	Norfolk	entertainers	Malone Nor 11
William, Duke of Suffolk	1445	King's Lynn	Norfolk	entertainers	Malone Nor 48
William, Duke of Suffolk	1445	Shrewsb'y	Salop	entertainers	*REED Shr* 124
William, Duke of Suffolk	1445	Worcester	Worcs	minstrels	*REED Her* 399
William, Duke of Suffolk	1446	Worcester	Worcs	minstrels	*REED Her* 400
William, Duke of Suffolk	1447	King's Lynn	Norfolk	entertainers	Malone Nor 49
William, Duke of Suffolk	1447	Exeter	Devon	minstrels	*REED Dev* 98
William, Duke of Suffolk	1447	York	York	minstrels	*REED York* 72
William, Duke of Suffolk	1448	Chartham	Kent	entertainers	*REED Ken* 71
William, Duke of Suffolk	1448	York	York	minstrels	*REED York* 72
William, Duke of Suffolk	1448	York	York	minstrels	*REED York* 72
William, Duke of Suffolk	1449	York	York	minstrels	*REED York* 76
Edmund Beaufort, Duke of Somerset	1427	Exeter	Devon	minstrels	*REED Dev* 40

Patron	Year	Place	County	Type	Source
Edmund, D. of Somerset	1435	Dover	Kent	minstrels	REED Ken 331
Edmund, D. of Somerset	1445	Chartham	Kent	minstrels	REED Ken 66
Edmund, D. of Somerset	1446	Canterbury	Kent	minstrels	REED Ken 59
Edmund, D. of Somerset	1446	York	York	minstrels	REED York 67
Edmund D of Somerset	1447	King's Lynn	Norfolk	entertainers	Malone Nor 49
Edmund D of Somerset	1447	Eastry	Kent	minstrels	REED Ken 69
Edmund, D. of Somerset	1447	Canterbury	Kent	entertainers	REED Ken 69
Edmund, D. of Somerset	1448	Canterbury	Kent	entertainers	REED Ken 71
Edmund, D. of Somerset	1449	Canterbury	Kent	minstrels	REED Ken 71
Edmund, D. of Somerset	1449	Rye	Sussex	minstrels	REED Sus 44
Edmund, D. of Somerset	1453	Dover	Kent	minstrels	REED Ken 337
Edmund, D. of Somerset	1454	Sandwich	Kent	entertainers	REED Ken 824
Edmund, D. of Somerset	1454	Sandwich	Kent	entertainers	REED Ken 824
Queen Margaret of Anjou	1452	Cambridge	Cambs	entertainers	REED Cam 30
Margaret of Anjou	1452	Canterbury	Kent	entertainers	REED Ken 73
Margaret of Anjou	1453	Canterbury	Kent	entertainers	REED Ken 73
Margaret of Anjou	1455	Canterbury	Kent	entertainers	REED Ken 73

Patron	Year	Place	County	Type	Source
Margaret of Anjou	1456	Canterbury	Kent	entertainers	REED Ken 73
Prince Edward, son of Henry VI	1457	Shrewsb'y	Salop	minstrels	REED Shr 140
Prince Edward	1458	Shrewsb'y	Salop	minstrels	REED Shr 141
Yorkist Faction					
Richard, Duke of York	1427	Cambridge	Cambs	minstrels	REED Cam 225
Richard, Duke of York	1432	Exeter	Devon	minstrels	REED Dev 93
Richard, Duke of York	1433	Exeter	Devon	minstrels	REED Dev 94
Richard, Duke of York	1433	Dover	Kent	minstrels	REED Ken 327
Richard, Duke of York	1445	Shrewsb'y	Salop	entertainers	REED Shr 133
Richard, Duke of York	1446	Shrewsb'y	Salop	minstrels	REED Shr 135
Richard, Duke of York	1446	Worcester	Worcs	minstrels	REED Her 395
Richard, Duke of York	1446	York	York	minstrels	REED York 86
Richard, Duke of York	1447	York	York	minstrels	REED York 70
Richard, Duke of York	1448	York	York	minstrels	REED York 72
Richard, Duke of York	1449	York	York	minstrels	REED York 73
Richard, Duke of York	1450	Selby Abbey	York	entertainers	Wickham *Stg* 332
Richard, Duke of York	1450	Shrewsb'y	Salop	entertainers	REED Shr 136

Patron	Year	Place	County	Type	Source
Richard, Duke of York	1451	Shrewsb'y	Salop	minstrels	*REED Shr* 138
Richard, Duke of York	1454	Rye	Sussex	minstrels	*REED Sus* 45
Richard, Duke of York	1454	York	York	minstrels	*REED York* 85
Richard, Duke of York	1457	Cambridge	Cambs	entertainers	*REED Cam* 39
Richard, Duke of York	1457	Shrewsb'y	Salop	entertainers	*REED Shr* 137
Richard, Duke of York	1457	Cambridge	Cambs	jester	*REED Cam* 37
Richard, Duke of York	1457	Rye	Sussex	minstrels	*REED Sus* 46
Richard, Duke of York	1457	Cambridge	Cambs	piper	*REED Cam* 37
Richard, Duke of York	1458	Rye	Sussex	entertainers	*REED Sus* 46
Richard Neville, Earl of Warwick	1451	Worcester	Worcs	Minstrels	*REED Her* 400
Richard, Earl of Warwick	1454	Rye	Sussex	minstrels	*REED Sus* 45
Richard, Earl of Warwick	1458	Rye	Sussex	minstrels	*REED Sus* 47
Richard, Earl of Warwick	1459	Sandwich	Kent	minstrels	*REED Ken* 825
Richard, Earl of Warwick	1460	Rye	Sussex	minstrels	*REED Sus* 48
Richard, Earl of Warwick	1461	Lydd	Kent	entertainers	*REED Ken* 662
Richard, Earl of Warwick	1461	Rye	Sussex	minstrels	*REED Sus* 48

William de la Pole, Duke of Suffolk, became heavily involved in the French campaigns after 1416. That year also marks the first appearance of his performers in provincial records. Their next appearance is not until 1440, and it is only after 1445, the year he negotiated the marriage between Henry VI and Margaret of Anjou, and became a favourite of the King and his new Queen,[104] that his performers show up regularly in provincial records. Performances of the Duke's entertainers in Norfolk correspond to a time he and his clients there were meddling in local affairs and usurping rights traditionally held by the Duke of Norfolk.[105] The last recorded performances by Suffolk's entertainers, in York (1447–9) correspond not only to the almost out-of-control Percy–Neville disputes, but also to the first appearances in York by performers of his chief rival, Richard of York. Performers attached to Edmund Beaufort, Duke of Somerset, first appear in 1427, when he began his military career in France. Yet it is only after 1444, when he replaced Richard of York as Lieutenant in France, and clearly enjoyed the favour of the King and Queen,[106] that his entertainers start to appear frequently in provincial records, especially in Kent.

Though there are few references in provincial records to Queen Margaret's and Prince Edward's entertainers, it seems significant that their appearances also coincide with crucial times. The Queen's performers appear in the two years in which she was pregnant, accompanied the King on progresses, and was delivered of Henry's son and heir. Henry suffered his first mental breakdown during these years, and Margaret went on progress alone in an attempt to gain support to be named as Regent.[107] They next appear in the years that included the first battle at St. Albans (1455), when the Yorkist faction achieved temporary ascendancy by gaining custody of the King and Queen, then again after Margaret regained custody of Henry, and clearly asserted herself as head of government. The two appearances of Prince Edward's performers at Shrewsbury in 1457 and 1458 may well have

---

104 Wolffe *Henry VI* 55, 66, 79, 102–8, 111–12, 116, 123–4, 180–5; Gillingham *Wars of the Roses* 62, 63.
105 Wolffe *Henry VI* 121–3; Gillingham, *Wars of the Roses* 56–8.
106 Wolffe *Henry VI* 38, 153, 163–4, 192–5, 203–8, 211, 254, 273; *ODNB* at <https://doi.org/10.1093/ref:odnb/1855>.
107 Wolffe *Henry VI* 259, 275, 277; Gillingham *Wars of the Roses*, 81; A.L Rowse *Bosworth Field and the Wars of the Roses* (Ware: Wordsworth, 1998) 130–2.

been associated with his status as heir apparent in the Welsh Marches – one of Richard of York's primary sources of support.[108]

Richard of York's entertainers first appear in the records in 1427, shortly after he was knighted and inherited large holdings in the Welsh border area from his uncle, the Earl of March. They next appear in 1432–3, the years in which he assumed his majority and joined the campaigns in France. No dramatic records mention his performers again until 1445, when he was relieved of his Lieutenancy in France and returned to England.[109] It is from 1445 on that York's entertainers appear in provincial records almost every year until 1458. Of those appearances, 68% (13 out of a total of 19), are in Yorkshire, Shropshire, and Worcestershire – areas where York possessed extensive holdings and support,[110] and where he was rallying support against his rivals at Court.[111]

Since provincial notices of the entertainers of the Earls of Westmorland and Salisbury – allies of Richard of York – already have been discussed in connection with the aristocratic rivalries in the North (see TABLE 6), they are omitted in TABLE 9. But taking TABLES 6 and 9 together, the data suggest that whatever the reasons, appearances in the provinces by entertainers attached to the leaders of the Lancaster and York factions do seem to parallel the growing rivalry of those factions during the 1440s and 1450s.

That pattern seems to hold for the aristocracy in general once Henry assumed personal rule. During his minority (1422–36) there are twenty-nine peers and knights whose entertainers appear in provincial records. After Henry reached his majority in 1437, there are more than sixty new peers and knights whose entertainers appear in the dramatic records (TABLE 10).

108 Wolffe *Henry VI* 302–22; Gillingham *Wars of the Roses* 99–102.
109 Wolffe *Henry VI* 35–7, 44, 89, 121, 151–5, 160, 164–7, 220, 240–2; Gillingham *Wars of the Roses* 56, 65–72.
110 Gillingham *Wars of the Roses* 65–6.
111 R.A. Griffiths 'Duke Richard of York's Intentions in 1450 and the Origins of the Wars of the Roses' *Journal of Medieval History* 1 (1975) 187–209; Gillingham *Wars of the Roses* 72–4; Wolffe *Henry VI* 253–4.

TABLE 10: Performers of Patrons Appearing in
Provincial Records only after 1437

Patron	Year	Place	County	Type	Source
John Kemp, Archbishop of Canterbury	1453	Dover	Kent	entertainers	REED Ken 337
John Stafford, Archbishop of Canterbury	1444	Exeter	Devon	entertainers	REED Ken 65
Thomas Bourchier, Archbishop of Canterbury	1454	Lydd	Kent	minstrels	REED Ken 658
Richard Talbot Abp Dublin	1447	Chartham	Kent	minstrels	REED Ken 68
George Neville, Abp York	1461	Barnstaple	Devon	minstrels	REED Dev 31
Edward Neville, Baron Abergavenny	1454	Sandwich	Kent	entertainers	REED Ken 824
James Tuchet, Baron Audley	1452	Shrewsbury	Salop	minstrels	REED Shr 138
John, Baron Bourchier	1444	Chartham	Kent	minstrels	REED Ken 65
Thomas, Baron Browne	1454	Sandwich	Kent	entertainers	REED Ken 827
Thomas, Baron Clifford	1446	York	York	minstrels	REED York 66
Reynold, Baron Cobham	1444	Dover	Kent	minstrels	REED Ken 334
Richard Fiennes, Baron Dacre	1454	Rye	Sussex	minstrels	REED Sus 45
John, Baron Darcy	1449	York	York	minstrels	REED York 75
Thomas Percy, Baron Egremont	1446	York	York	minstrels	REED York 67

Patron	Year	Place	County	Type	Source
Sir Walter Devereux, Baron Ferrers	1447	Worcester	Worcs	minstrels	*REED Her* 400
William, Baron Fitzhugh	1447	York	York	minstrels	*REED Shr* 140
William Bourchier, Baron FitzWarin	1454	Barnstaple	Devon	minstrels	*REED Dev* 30
Richard, Baron Grey of Powis	1457	Shrewsbury	Salop	minstrels	*REED Shr* 140
Ralph, Baron Greystoke	1446	York	York	minstrels	*REED York* 66
William, Baron Harington	1447	York	York	minstrels	*REED York* 70
Edmund, Baron Hungerford	1447	Worcester	Worcs	minstrels	*REED Her* 400
John, Baron Neville	1448	York	York	juggler	*REED York* 71
Robert, Baron Ogle	1447	York	York	entertainers	*REED York* 68
James Fiennes. Baron Saye & Sele	1446	Lydd	Kent	entertainers	*REED Ken* 654
William Fiennes, Baron Saye & Sele	1454	Rye	Sussex	minstrels	*REED Sus* 45
Robert Neville, Bishop of Durham	1439	Exeter	Devon	minstrels	*REED Dev* 97
Henry, Baron Scrope	1442	Dover	Kent	minstrels	Murray 2 211
Lionel, Baron Welles	1446	York	York	minstrels	*REED York* 66

Patron	Year	Place	County	Type	Source
Henry Grey, Count Tankerville (Fr. title)	1445	Shrewsbury	Salop	minstrels	*REED Shr* 133
William FitzAlan, Earl of Arundel	1444	Shrewsbury	Salop	entertainers	*REED Shr* 132
Henry Bourchier, Earl of Essex	1444	Dover	Kent	entertainers	*REED Ken* 334
Edmund Grey, Earl of Kent	1447	York	York	entertainers	*REED York* 69
Jasper Tudor, Earl of Pembroke	1457	Shrewsbury	Salop	minstrels	*REED Shr* 140
Richard Neville, Earl of Salisbury	1442	Cambridge	Cambs	minstrels	*REED Cam* 29
Richard Woodville, Earl Rivers	1454	Sandwich	Kent	minstrels	*REED Ken* 824
Sir Edward Beetham	1449	York	York	minstrels	*REED York* 76
Sir William Bowes	1446	York	York	minstrels	*REED York* 67
Sir Thomas Brews	1454	Mettingham	Suffolk	minstrels	Lancashire 377
Sir Henry Brounflete	1447	York	York	minstrels	*REED York* 69
Sir Thomas Browne	1454	Sandwich	Kent	minstrels	*REED Ken* 824
Sir John Butler	1449	York	York	minstrels	*REED York* 75
Sir Thomas Chaworth	1447	York	York	minstrels	*REED York* 69
Sir Robert Clifton	1450	Mettingham	Suffolk	minstrels	Lancashire 379

Patron	Year	Place	County	Type	Source
Sir William Eure	1448	York	York	minstrels	*REED York* 71
Sir John Harrington	1447	York	York	minstrels	*REED York* 69
Sir Alexander Iden	1454	Sandwich	Kent	entertainers	*REED Ken* 824
Sir William Lumley	1446	York	York	minstrels	*REED York* 66
Sir William Mauleverer	1446	York	York	minstrels	*REED York* 67
Sir Thomas Metham	1446	York	York	minstrels	*REED York* 67
Sir Richard Musgrove	1446	York	York	minstrels	*REED York* 67
Sir Thomas Neville	1447	York	York	minstrels	*REED York* 75
Sir Alexander Neville	1449	York	York	entertainers	*REED York* 75
Sir John Pennington	1446	York	York	minstrels	*REED York* 67
Sir William Plumpton	1447	York	York	minstrels	*REED York* 68
Sir Thomas Pudsay	1447	York	York	minstrels	*REED York* 70
Sir Nicholas Radclyffe	1449	York	York	entertainers	*REED York* 73
Sir Thomas Rampston	1449	York	York	minstrels	*REED York* 75
Sir Robert Roos	1446	York	York	minstrels	*REED York* 66
Sir John Savage	1446	York	York	minstrels	*REED York* 66
Sir John Savile	1450	York	York	minstrels	*REED York* 77
Sir Robert Ughtred	1446	York	York	minstrels	*REED York* 66

PEERS AND PERFORMERS IN THE REIGN OF HENRY VI

Patron	Year	Place	County	Type	Source
Sir Robert Waterton	1447	York	York	jester	REED York 69
Sir Hugh Willoughby	1446	York	York	minstrels	REED York 66
John, Viscount Beaumont	1447	Launceston	Cornwall	minstrels	REED Dor 495

During Henry's minority, excluding the King's entertainers, 147 performances by aristocrats' entertainers appear in provincial records. After 1437 the number swells to 414 performances. In other words, almost three-quarters of all the aristocrats and almost three-quarters of all performances by their entertainers occurred only after Henry assumed personal rule. After Edward IV took the throne, those numbers rapidly declined.

I suggest that the lopsided percentage does reflect the breakdown in royal authority when English nobles were flaunting their powers vis-à-vis one another, and thumbing their noses at the Crown. Like entertainers attached to the Nevilles and Percies (see TABLE 6), most entertainers, whether attached to the great magnates or to lesser nobles and gentry, performed most often in regions where their patrons possessed substantial holdings and influence. For instance, of the 26 performances by entertainers of John Talbot the Elder and the Younger, Earls of Shrewsbury between 1426 and 1458, 18 were held in Shrewsbury.[112] Performances by entertainers patronized by Sir William Botreaux and William Bourchier, Baron FitzWarin, only appear in records from Devon, which were close to their major holdings.

The Lords Spiritual

Is it just coincidence that there also was a sharp increase during Henry's reign in the appearance of entertainers attached to the Lords Spiritual? Performers patronized by bishops rarely appear in provincial records. Of the more than 9,000 instances of provincial performances (covering the years 1277 through 1625), episcopal performers appear only 101 times – the first in 1338 when the minstrels of Bishop Wulstan de Bransford of

---

112 REED: Devon 90–2; REED: Kent 327, 333; REED: Shropshire 120, 132–3, 135, 137, 139.

Worcester performed at Worcester, the last in 1623 when the trumpeters of George Abbot, Archbishop of Canterbury, performed at Balliol College, Oxford.[113] One half of those 100 performances fall within the reign of Henry VI (see TABLE 11). Dramatic records list several appearances between 1426 and 1464 (the date when Henry VI was shut up in the Tower) by the entertainers of three successive archbishops of Canterbury – John Stafford (d.1452), Cardinal John Kemp (d.1454), and Thomas Bourchier (d.1486). In total, 25 performances are attributed to entertainers of these archbishops. Only 7 occurred at Canterbury, and only one other was directly connected to the Archbishop's residence at Chartham in the neighbourhood. Records do not specify locations in Canterbury for the 7 performances there, making it seem likely these were public performances for the townsfolk. Other prelates whose entertainers appear in provincial records are the Archbishop of York, George Neville (d.1476); the Bishop of Durham, Robert Neville (d.1457); the Bishop of Exeter, Edmund Lacey (d.1439); and the Bishop of Winchester, Cardinal Henry Beaufort (d.1447).

TABLE 11: Episcopal Performers 1426–64

Patron	Year	Place	County	Type	Source
John Stafford, Archbishop of Canterbury	1444	Canterbury	Kent	entertainers	*REED Ken* 65
Archbp John Stafford	1446	Canterbury	Kent	entertainers	*REED Ken* 66
Archbp John Stafford	1446	Canterbury	Kent	entertainers	*REED Ken* 69
Archbp John Stafford	1448	Canterbury	Kent	entertainers	*REED Ken* 70
Archbp John Stafford	1449	Canterbury	Kent	entertainers	*REED Ken* 71
Archbp John Stafford	1449	Canterbury	Kent	entertainers	*REED Ken* 71
Archbp John Stafford	1446	Chartham	Kent	entertainers	*REED Ken* 67

---

113 *REED: Hereford/Worcs* 397; *REED: Oxford* 452.

Patron	Year	Place	County	Type	Source
Archbp John Stafford	1451	Dover	Kent	entertainers	REED Ken 336
Archbp John Stafford	1439	Exeter	Devon	entertainers	REED Dev 96
Archbp John Stafford	1440	Exeter	Devon	entertainers	REED Dev 96
Archbp John Stafford	1448	Hythe	Kent	entertainers	REED Ken 612
Archbp John Stafford	1447	King's Lynn	Norfolk	entertainers	Malone Nor 49
Archbp John Stafford	1447	King's Lynn	Norfolk	entertainers	Malone Nor 49
Archbp John Stafford	1449	Lydd	Kent	entertainers	REED Ken 855
Archbp John Stafford	1450–2	Lydd	Kent	entertainers	REED Ken 856
Archbp John Stafford	1449	New Romney	Kent	entertainers	REED Ken 736
Cardinal John Kemp, Archbp of Canterbury	1453	Dover	Kent	entertainers	REED Ken 337
Cardinal John Kemp, Archbp of Canterbury	1453	Rye	Sussex	entertainers	REED Sus 45
Thomas Bourchier, Archbp of Canterbury	1455	Barnstaple	Devon	minstrels	REED Dev 30
Archbp Thomas Bourchier	1455	Canterbury	Kent	minstrels	REED Ken 738
Archbp Thomas Bourchier	1456	Hythe	Kent	minstrels	REED Ken 614
Archbp Thomas Bourchier	1454	Lydd	Kent	minstrels	REED Ken 658
Archbp Thomas Bourchier	1460	Lydd	Kent	minstrels	REED Ken 662

Patron	Year	Place	County	Type	Source
Archbp Thomas Bourchier	1464	Lydd	Kent	minstrels	REED Ken 658
Archbp Thomas Bourchier	1465	Lydd	Kent	minstrels	REED Ken 664
George Neville, Archbp of York	1461	Barnstaple	Devon	minstrels	REED Dev 31
Archbp George Neville	1464	Canterbury	Kent	minstrels	REED Ken 74
Robert Neville, Bishop of Durham	1439	Exeter	Devon	minstrels	REED Dev 96
Bishop Robert Neville	1446	Worcester	Worcs	minstrels	REED Her 399
Bishop Robert Neville	1446	York	York	minstrels	REED York 66
Bishop Robert Neville	1447	York	York	minstrels	REED York 69
Bishop Robert Neville	1449	York	York	minstrels	REED York 75
Bishop Robert Neville	1449	York	York	minstrels	REED York 76
Edmund Lacey, Bishop of Exeter	1439	Exeter	Devon	minstrels	REED Dev 96
Cardinal Henry Beaufort, Bishop of Winchester	1429	Exeter	Devon	jester	REED Dev 91
Cardinal Beaufort	1434	Exeter	Devon	jester	REED Dev 94
Cardinal Beaufort	1434	Exeter	Devon	jester	REED Dev 95
Cardinal Beaufort	1445	Canterbury	Kent	minstrels	REED Ken 66
Cardinal Beaufort	1445	Canterbury	Kent	minstrels	REED Ken 67
Cardinal Beaufort	1446	Canterbury	Kent	minstrels	REED Ken 69
Cardinal Beaufort	1429	Dover	Kent	minstrels	REED Ken 323
Cardinal Beaufort	1429	Dover	Kent	minstrels	REED Ken 324
Cardinal Beaufort	1431	Dover	Kent	minstrels	REED Ken 326

Patron	Year	Place	County	Type	Source
Cardinal Beaufort	1432	Dover	Kent	minstrels	REED Ken 326
Cardinal Beaufort	1438	Dover	Kent	minstrels	REED Ken 330
Cardinal Beaufort	1439	Dover	Kent	minstrels	REED Ken 331
Cardinal Beaufort	1440	Dover	Kent	minstrels	REED Ken 331
Cardinal Beaufort	1444	Dover	Kent	minstrels	REED Ken 334
Cardinal Beaufort	1444	Eastry	Kent	minstrels	REED Ken 65
Cardinal Beaufort	1432	Exeter	Devon	minstrels	REED Dev 93
Cardinal Beaufort	1448	Chartham	Kent	harper	REED Ken 68

This increased activity by episcopal performers corresponds to a period when the bishops were more closely tied to the aristocracy than to the King. In the North the Percies and the Nevilles secured powerful dioceses for kinsmen, William Percy as Bishop of Carlisle and Robert Neville as Bishop of Durham.[114] John Stafford, kinsman of the Duke of Buckingham and protégé of Cardinal Henry Beaufort, was first appointed Bishop of Bath and Wells in 1425 and then Archbishop of Canterbury in 1443.[115] R.J. Knecht points out: 'Under Henry VI bishops were recommended not so much by the king as by the lords who dominated his council'.[116] Richard Beauchamp, kinsman to Richard Beauchamp, Earl of Warwick, became Bishop of Hereford in 1448, and was translated to the see of Salisbury in 1450.[117] After the Yorkist faction gained control of the Council during Henry's first mental breakdown in 1453, bishoprics fell to those with ties to the Duke of York and the Nevilles. When Queen Margaret gained dominance in 1556, her personal chancellor, Lawrence Booth, was named to the vacant see of Durham.[118] Knecht further points out that when armed hostilities broke out between the Lancastrians and Yorkists some bishops chose sides. Archbishop Bourchier of Canterbury

---

114 Wolffe *Henry VI* 268, 326 note 60.
115 *ODNB* at <https://doi.org/10.1093/ref:odnb/26209>.
116 R.J. Knecht 'The Episcopate and the Wars of the Roses' *University of Birmingham Historical Review* 8 (1957–8) 110; Ross *Wars of the Roses* 158.
117 *ODNB* at <https://doi.org/10.1093/ref:odnb/1859>.
118 Knecht 'The Episcopate' 111; Wolffe *Henry VI* 308.

and Bishop George Neville of Exeter tended to favour the Yorkist faction;[119] Bishops William Percy of Carlisle and John Hals of Coventry supported Henry and Queen Margaret. As Knecht puts it: 'In 1461 the episcopate was as divided in its allegiance as the aristocracy which had helped to establish it'.[120] This burgeoning appearance of episcopal entertainers under Henry VI coincides tellingly with the period when bishops were asserting their own power and interests, since the King seemed unable to control the lay nobles.[121]

The performances by entertainers attached to the archbishops of Canterbury are a good example. Almost 65% (24 out of 37) of all appearances by entertainers patronized by archbishops of Canterbury occurred during the reign of Henry VI.[122] Most of these appearances were in Kent, where the only other magnate of consequence was whoever served as the Lord Warden of the Cinque Ports. Each of these archbishops was involved in balancing on the see-saw of power between Lancaster and York between 1454 and 1462.

The Reign of Edward IV

To further emphasize the amount of touring during the reign of Henry VI, it must again be noted that touring by aristocratic performers declined after Edward IV seized the throne. During Edward's twenty-two-year reign (1461–83) the number of provincial accounts recording aristocrats' performers drops from 563 during Henry's reign to about 405 – over 150 fewer appearances. However, about 227 of those records (over 56%) name performers whose patrons were members of the royal family: Edward IV; his Queen, Elizabeth Woodville; his two sons Edward and Richard; his mother Cecily Neville, dowager Duchess of York; and his brothers George, Duke of Clarence, and Richard, Duke of Gloucester.[123]

---

119   Knecht 'The Episcopate' 110–11.
120   Knecht 'The Episcopate' 111; Ross *Wars of the Roses* 158; Wolffe *Henry VI* 326.
121   Knecht 'The Episcopate' 111.
122   The other archbishops were: Simon Islip (d. 1366), *REED Kent 1* 48; William Wittlesey (d. 1374), *REED: Kent* 57; John Morton (d. 1500), *REED: Kent* 384, 756–7, *REED: Devon* 214, *REED: Sussex* 68–9; William Warham (d.1532), *REED: Kent* 839; George Abbot (d.1633), *REED: Oxford* 52.
123   Sources: REED: *Cambridge* 45–6, 49–50, 52, 54–5, 57, 62–3; *REED: Dorset/Cornwall* 443, 493; *REED: Devon* 32–6; *REED: Kent* 75–82, 342, 344–6, 348, 350–6, 358–65, 38,

Bearing those facts in mind, the comparison between touring activity in the reigns of Henry VI and Edward IV becomes more striking. Under Henry VI, excluding royal patrons, the entertainers of 129 nobles appear in 563 provincial records. Under Edward IV, again excluding royal patrons, the numbers shrink to the entertainers of 36 nobles in 178 provincial records.[124] Even that number is somewhat misleading. It is inflated by 111 records naming only two patrons: 34 naming entertainers of Richard Neville 'the King Maker', and 77 naming entertainers of William FitzAlan, Earl of Arundel.[125] Both lords were closely tied to Edward IV. When the records of performances by entertainers of these two great and favoured lords are subtracted, there are only 67 provincial records mentioning performances by the entertainers of 34 aristocratic patrons. Those patrons mostly were great magnates such as the Dukes of Buckingham, Exeter, Norfolk, and Suffolk, and the Earls of Essex, Kent, and Northumberland. Entertainers attached to lesser nobles and gentry virtually disappear from the dramatic records.

It does not seem to be the deaths of aristocrats in the Wars of the Roses that accounts for this sharp decline of aristocratic entertainers in provincial records under Edward IV and beyond. As John Gillingham notes, 'although many nobles were killed, their families were not extinguished, the old nobility was not exterminated'. The percentage of families whose direct male line died out is no different in the last half of the 1400s than it had been throughout the 1300s and first half of the 1400s. Most aristocratic titles

616–18, 620, 627, 668–71, 739–44, 828–9; *REED: Hereford/Worcs* 401, 405; *REED Inns of Court* 77; *REED: Oxford* 17, 21, 25; *REED: Shropshire* 148–50, 152–3; *REED Somerset 1* 25, 41; *REED: Sussex* 49–53, 60; *REED: York* 94; *Malone Norfolk/Suffolk* 208; Wickham *Early English Stages* 332. See also Forse 'Advertising Status' Appendix: TABLES 4 and 5, 77–81.

124 Sources: *REED: Cambridge* 43–6, 50: *REED: Devon* 30–6; *REED: Dorset/Cornwall* 405, 463, 492; *REED: Kent* 74, 84, 264, 335, 339–46, 349, 350–2, 354–7, 359–67, 374, 376, 615, 619–20, 658, 662–7, 669–71, 738–44, 825–30; *REED: Oxford* 30; *REED: Shropshire* 145, 155; *REED Sussex* 48–9, 51–5; Lancashire *Dramatic Texts* 376–7; Wickham *Early English Stages* 332.

125 *REED: Cambridge* 44–5, 50: *REED: Devon* 31–2; *REED: Dorset/Cornwall* 492; *REED: Hereford/Worcs* 405; *REED: Kent* 74, 339–46, 348, 350–2, 354–5, 357, 359–60, 362–7, 615, 617–20, 662–3, 665–7, 669–71, 738–44, 825–30; *REED Sussex*, 48–9, 51–5.

survived through sons and other male kin of the nobles who perished in the Wars of the Roses.[126]

Rather, it almost seems that the decline may be because Edward IV's nobles were keeping a lower profile. Perhaps for good reason – Edward gave his nobles many examples of how harsh he would be with those he discovered, or suspected, of challenging his rule. In 1478 Edward even executed his own brother, George, Duke of Clarence, when convinced Clarence was plotting against him and his heirs.[127]

Conclusions

Charles Ross points out that late medieval England was 'a strongly hierarchical society which judged a man's – and a king's – importance by the size and splendour of his entourage'.[128] Entertainers wearing livery, or bearing a patent from a privileged patron, showing up at a location and then performing before the gentry and commons, no doubt helped to display that 'splendour'. Jeffrey Leininger, though looking at sixteenth-century examples, points out that the entertainers of an aristocratic patron 'symbolized a patron's influence in a particular region or town; receiving a company meant receiving the patron behind the company'.[129] Many other scholars suggest that at least by the time of Henry VIII touring performers probably served the political purposes of their patrons, in one way or another advertising their agendas, statuses, and legitimacy, sometimes also serving as couriers and 'intelligencers', carrying messages and bringing back titbits of information about people and events in the provinces.[130]

---

126   Gillingham *Wars of the Roses* 5, 14.
127   Ross *Edward IV* 122–3, 172, 182–3, 191–2, 240–3; Gillingham *Wars of the Roses* 135, 207.
128   Charles Ross *Richard III* (Berkeley: University of California Press, 1983) 148.
129   Jeffrey Leininger 'Evangelical "Enterluders": Patronage and Playing in Reformation England' *Reformation and Renaissance Review* 4:1 (2002) 64.
130   See Sally-Beth MacLean 'The Politics of Patronage: Dramatic Records in Robert Dudley's Household Books' *Shakespeare Quarterly* 44:2 (1993) 175–82; Elza C. Tiner 'Patrons and Travelling Companies in Warwickshire' *Early Theatre* 4 (2001) 35–52; Alan Somerset, '"How chances it they travel:" Provincial Touring, Playing Places, and the King's Men' *Shakespeare Survey* 47 (1994) 45–60; Mary A. Blackstone 'Patrons and Elizabethan Dramatic Companies' *The Elizabethan Theatre* 10 edited C.E. McGee (Papers given at the Tenth International Conference on Elizabethan Theatre, University of Waterloo, July 1983) 112–32; Peter Greenfield 'Touring' in *A New History of Early English Drama* edited John Cox and David Kastan (New York:

What entertainers and actors presented apparently mattered little to provincial record-keepers. In records to date there are fewer than thirty titles or descriptions of plays and very few details about any other kind of performance.[131] Yet the *patrons* of these entertainers certainly did matter to provincial record-keepers. Out of over 9,000 references to all types of entertainers in the dramatic records, most are identified by a patron's name and/or status. Fewer than 550, only 6%, are unnamed.

It must be remembered that aristocratic entertainers in the 1400s were not the semi-independent acting companies playing in London and the provinces of Elizabeth's reign. Those companies, though considered servants of their respective patrons, earned their living by performing.[132] In contrast, entertainers in the 1400s truly were members of their patrons' households, although at least in the case of consorts of musicians, it seems to have been normal for entertainers to tour when they were not required by their patron. Nonetheless, whether sent there by their patron, or travelling to augment their income, performances in a community by an aristocrat's liveried entertainers still promoted the patron's public image, at least, as mentioned above, within the written records of that community. It would have been beneficial to both parties if patrons encouraged their entertainers to travel to locales in which those patrons held particular interests. Whatever the reasons for their travel, it seems logical that

    Columbia University Press, 1977) 251–68; Scott McMillin and Sally-Beth MacLean *The Queen's Men and their Plays* (Cambridge UP, 1998) 1–17; Paul W. White *Theatre and Reformation: Protestantism, Patronage, and Playing in Tudor England* (Cambridge UP, 1993); Greg Walker *Plays of Persuasion. Drama and Politics at the Court of Henry VIII* (Cambridge UP, 1991); James H. Forse 'Getting Your Name Out There: Travelling Acting Companies and Aristocratic Prestige in Tudor England' *Quidditas 25–26* (2006) 116–17 at <http://humanities.byu.edu/rmmra>; Forse 'Advertising Status' 61–86.

131 See *REED: Cumberland/Westmorland/Gloucester* 185, 187, 309; *REED: Bristol* 66, 111, 114–16, 119, 143; *REED: Hereford/Worcs* 376–7, *REED: Lincolnshire* 355; *REED: Norwich* 24; Lancashire *Dramatic Texts* 363; Murray *Dramatic Companies 2* 288; Siobhan Keenan *Travelling Players in Shakespeare's England* (London: Palgrave Macmillan, 2002) 72–3.

132 See Peter Meredith 'The Professional Travelling Players of the 15th Century: Myth or Reality?' *European Medieval Drama 2* (1998) edited Sydney Higgins (Turnhout: Brepols, 1998) 21–34; Forse 'Getting Your Name Out There' 127–33.

travelling entertainers probably did errands and brought back information to their respective patrons.

Data from the surviving records suggests a significant increase in provincial performances by the entertainers of the nobility in the reign of Henry VI. It seems likely that this was in some way connected to the troubled state of the country and the inability of the King to control the rivalries among his nobles that led to what we call the Wars of the Roses. The nature of that connection is not easily discernible. Could it be that it was during Henry's reign that aristocrats first began to use touring entertainers as a means to advertise their power and status? If so, could it also be that some of those political purposes ascribed to the entertainers of the Tudors may in fact pre-date the Tudors? While these questions cannot be answered definitively, they may prompt us to explore further the political implications of touring performance at this period.

Bowling Green State University

'THAT GAM ME THOGHT WAS GOOD!':
Structuring Games into Medieval English Plays

Philip Butterworth

Game and Play; Games in Plays

It is well known to medieval theatre scholars that the medieval word *game* was used, in one of its senses, somewhat interchangeably with the medieval term *play*.[1] There is considerable evidence of the interchangeability of these terms in the prologues and epilogues of plays, where the terms of reference for the presentation are established and reinforced.[2] Additionally, in the synonymous relationship between *game* and *play* there are many references to 'game players', 'game places', and 'game books'.[3]

However, even though some (theatrical) plays are recorded as *games*, the word *game* predominantly, both in the Middle Ages and today, possesses non-theatrical meanings, which determine the focus of this work. In this article I propose to examine the structural relationship between games

---

1 *Promptorium Parvulorum sive Clericorum* edited A.L. Mayhew *EETS ES 102* (1908) col. 186: '**Game**, pley: *lud*us, *-di*: *locus, -ci*'; Richard Huloet *Abecedarivm Anglico Latinvm* (London: Gulielmi Riddel, 1552): 'Game. locus. ci, *Ludus. di. Vide* in Playes'. See the extended discussion in V.A. Kolve *The Play Called Corpus Christi* (Stanford UP, 1966) Chapter 2, 8–32.

2 *Non-Cycle Plays and Fragments* edited Norman Davis *EETS SS 1* (1970) 90 lines 7 and 16, 93 line 111, 115 line 8, 118 lines 3 and 5, 123 lines 4, 6, 24, and 30; *The N-Town Play* edited Stephen Spector 2 vols *EETS SS 11* and *12* (1991) *1* 6 line 47, 21 lines 517, 519, 520, 526; Henry Medwall *Fulgens and Lucres* in Alan Nelson *The Plays of Henry Medwall* (Cambridge: D.S. Brewer, 1980) 33, 35, 88–9 (*play*), 87, 88 (*game*); *The Castle of Perseverance* in *The Macro Plays* edited Mark Eccles *EETS 262* (1969) 111 line 3645; *Records of Plays and Payers in Norfolk and Suffolk 1330–1642* edited David Galloway and John Wasson (Malone Society Collections 11; Oxford UP, 1980/1) 141 (*game booke*), 142, 185 (*games, gamyng, playe*), 186 (*game*).

3 *REED: Cambridge* edited Alan H. Nelson, 2 vols (Toronto UP, 1989) *1* 544; J. Charles Cox *Churchwardens' Accounts: From the Fourteenth Century to the Close of the Seventeenth Century* (London: Methuen, 1913) 275; *Norfolk and Suffolk* edited Galloway and Wasson, 11, 12, 13, 14, 16, 132, 141, 143; *REED: Norwich 1540–1642* edited David Galloway (Toronto UP, 1984) 9; *REED: Sussex* edited Cameron Louis (Toronto UP, 2000) 54, 55; for others of the same and similar examples, see Kolve *Play Called Corpus Christi* 15–16; James Stokes 'The Beccles Game Place and Local Drama in Early North-East Suffolk' *Medieval English Theatre 39* (2018) 77–102.

that are ostensibly non-theatrical, and their absorption into fifteenth- and sixteenth-century English plays. Thus, following the modern practice, I shall refer to theatrical plays as *plays* and non-theatrical games as *games*.

The word *game* has most frequently referred to non-theatrical activities conducted by both adults and children. The activity termed *play*, when formalized as theatre, requires onlookers. Games, however, do not normally require external witnesses, although they may have them, and participants in games may, at times, also be spectators. This may be because of the nature of the game, that individuals are 'counted out' for whatever reason (usually concerned with the purpose and structure of the game); or they may deliberately 'opt out' as permitted by the rules of the game. Thus, they become observers within the game rather than participants in it. Similarly, personages in plays, depending on theatrical intentions and presentational conventions, may be required to withdraw, retire, or leave the action of the play and, like participants in games, stand around as observers of the action.[4] This practice and resulting convention is accepted by personages and spectators alike.

I have written elsewhere of the necessity for theatre to engage in the process of 'agreed pretence':[5] that is, a voluntary agreement between the instigators of the theatre and its witnesses to the effect that an activity called *theatre* is about to be played. Such an agreement is generally a tacit one established by those who put on the play and confirmed by the continued voluntary contribution of the spectators. All concerned agree that the pretence should take place and the witnesses volunteer their engagement

---

4   Julius Caesar Scaliger *Poetices Libri Septem* ([Lyons]: Antonium Vincentium, 1561) 34 gives an interesting account of this practice: for a citation and translation see Edmond Malone *An Historical Account of the Rise and Progress of the English Stage, and of the Economy and Usages of our Ancient Theatres* (Basel: Tourneisen, 1800) 34–5. Also Lewis [Luigi] Riccoboni *An Historical and Critical Account of the Theatres in Europe. viz. The Italian, Spanish, French, English, Dutch, Flemish, and German Theatres* (London: T. Waller and R. Dodsley, 1741) 118 note; Philip Butterworth 'Comings and Goings: English Medieval Staging Conventions' *Early Drama, Art, and Music 21:1* (1998) 25–34; Philip Butterworth *Staging Conventions in Medieval English Theatre* (Cambridge UP, 2014) 83–4, 211.

5   Butterworth *Staging Conventions* Introduction; Philip Butterworth 'Magic Through Sound: Illusion, Deception and Agreed Pretence' *Medieval English Theatre 21* (1999) 52–65; Philip Butterworth *Magic on the Early English Stage* (Cambridge UP, 2005) 1–2; *European Theatre Performance Practice, 1400–1580* edited Philip Butterworth and Katie Normington (Farnham: Ashgate, 2014) 347–67.

with it. 'Agreed pretence' determines, consolidates, and confirms the rules of the activity called *theatre*. These rules are axiomatic and integral to the developing action. However, not only is this process critical to the enactment of theatre and its purpose, it is also central to the operation of non-theatrical games. Johan Huizinga (here using *play* in its non-theatrical sense) reinforces this concept in respect of games:

> These rules in their turn are a very important factor in the play-concept. All play has its rules. They determine what 'holds' in the temporary world circumscribed by the play. The rules of a game are absolutely binding ... Indeed, as soon as the rules are transgressed the whole play-world collapses. The game is over. The umpire's whistle breaks the spell and sets 'real' life going again.[6]

The structural frameworks of games are clearly demonstrated in children's games which may, or may not, imitate structures of adult games.[7]

Both the non-theatrical game and the theatrical play begin when they are named and invitations are issued to play or watch them. In game invitations this may take the form of 'Who wants to play ...?' or 'What shall we do next?', whereas equivalent play invitations may begin with the proclamation of banns followed by subsequent requests in prologues. Such invitations to witness plays may exist inside or outside the narrative of the play.

Such distinctions between *game* and *play* serve to focus those occasions when medieval plays include representations of non-theatrical games as part of their developing action. This article investigates the theatrical relevance of selected games that appear in identified medieval plays, and that contribute to the plays' purpose, action, and structural value.

The Buffeting of Christ and the Game of *Abobbed*

One popular occurrence of a game sequence occurs in plays enacting the 'Buffeting' of Christ during the Passion. In Play 21 of the Towneley Plays, the *Coliphizacio* ('Buffeting'), *2 Tortor* invites Jesus to be seated, saying: 'Com,

---

6 J. Huizinga *Homo Ludens: A Study of the Play-Element in Culture* translated R.F.C. Hull (London: Routledge & Kegan Paul, 1949) 11.

7 I am excluding modern computer games from this analysis although some of them might be capable of contributing similar criteria to the discussion. The kinds of games with which I am concerned are physical and social ones, and not of the virtual or solitary kind.

PHILIP BUTTERWORTH

syr, and syt downe ... Youre sete is arayde'. This invitation turns out to be a sadistic prelude to the buffeting. When Jesus is seated, Froward declares:

Froward	Here a vayll haue I fon;	
	I trow it will last.	
1 Tortor.	Bryng it hyder, good son.	
	That is it that I ast.	*asked for*
Froward	How shuld it be bon?	*bound*
2 Tortor	Abowte his head cast.	
1 Tortor	Yei, and when it is well won,	
	Knyt a knot fast,	*tie a knot tightly*
	I red.	
Froward	Is it weyll?	
2 Tortor	Yei, knaue.[8]	

lines 560–9

Thus Jesus is blindfolded, and *1 Tortor* says: 'Now sen he is blynfeld, | I fall to begyn' (lines 573–4) and strikes Jesus 'on his crowne' (see line 525). *1 Tortor* and *2 Tortor* now compete to see which of them can deliver the most vicious blows. The two torturers alternate and synchronize the timing of their blows until *2 Tortor* asks of Jesus 'Who smote the last?' and *1 Tortor* asks 'Was it I?' (line 597). Froward's assessment is that Jesus does not know which of the torturers struck him.[9]

The Buffeting sequence also occurs in the York Bowyers and Flecchers pageant, *Christ before Annas and Caiaphas* (Play 29), where Christ is similarly invited to sit on a stool with a cloth covering his head:

III Miles	Sertis, will ye sitte, and sone schall ye see
	Howe we schall play popse for þe pages prowe.
IV Miles	Late see, who stertis for a stole?
	For I haue here a hatir [*cloth*] to hyde hym.
I Miles	Lo, here is one full fitte for a foole,
	Go gete it, and sette þe beside hym.[10]

lines 354–9

---

8   *The Towneley Plays* edited Martin Stevens and A.C. Cawley, 2 vols *EETS SS 13* and *SS 14* (1994) *1* 267.
9   *Towneley Plays 1* 268, line 599.
10 *The York Play: A Critical Edition of the York Corpus Christi Play as recorded in British Library Additional MS 35290* edited Richard Beadle, 2 vols *EETS SS 23* and *SS 24* (2009) *1* 253.

In this play, the name of this game is *popse*.[11] The *OED* defines *pop* as 'A blow, a knock, a punch; a slight rap or tap', and the *MED pop(pe)* as 'A blow, stroke, buffet',[12] so the word appears to refer to a game of blows. The first four blows are delivered by *III Miles*:

III Miles	Playes faire in feere: and þer is one, and þer is – ij;	
	And I schall fande to feste it with a faire flappe –	
	And ther is – iiij; and there is iiij.	
	Say nowe, with an nevill happe,	
	Who negheth þe nowe? Not o worde, no!	
IV Miles	Dose noddill on hym with neffes,[13] that he noght nappe.	*fists*
I Miles	Nay, now to nappe is no nede,	
	Wassaille! Wassaylle! I warande hym wakende.	
II Miles	Ȝa, and bot he bettir bourdis can b[e]de	
	Such buffettis schall he be takande.	
III Miles	*Prophet[iz]a*, to be oute of debate,	
	[Q]uis te percussit, man? Rede, giffe þou may.	

lines 362–73

The Fourth Soldier incites the others to hit Christ with their fists and the exclamations, 'Wassaille! Wassaylle! I warande hym wakende' by the First Soldier indicate additional blows delivered on the words 'Wassaille!' and 'Wassaylle!', ironically to prevent Christ from dropping into unconsciousness. The normal meaning of *wassaile* is as a celebratory salutation – 'Good Health!'[14] Like the equivalent scene in the Towneley *Coliphizacio*, the York Christ is taunted with the question '*Prophet[iz]a*, to be oute of debate, *[Q]uis te percussit*, man? Rede, giffe þou may'. Here, the playwrights are adapting the Vulgate 'Prophesy unto us, O Christ! Who is he that struck thee?'[15]

---

11 An understandable misreading of the manuscript by Lucy Toulmin Smith in her edition of the York Play led to the creation of the ghost word *papse*; *York Plays* (Oxford: Clarendon Press, 1885) 267. The *MED* therefore records *papse* as 'some kind of game involving buffets'. Beadle *York Play* reads it correctly as *popse*. Thanks to Meg Twycross for drawing my attention to this.

12 *OED* sv *pop n.1*; *MED* sv *pop(pe)*.

13 'Hit him on the head with your fists'. See Beadle *York Play 2* 249 note to line 367.

14 *MED* sv *wassail* n.(a) 'also *fig.* & *iron.* a sharp or sudden blow', citing this passage.

15 Luke 22:64 *prophetiza quis est qui te percussit*; Matthew 26:68: *prophetiza nobis Christe quis est qui te percussit*.

PHILIP BUTTERWORTH

In the N. Town *Trial before Annas and Cayphas* (Play 29), the same sequence is initiated by an explicit stage direction:

Here þei xal bete Jesus about þe hed and þe body, and spyttyn in his face, and pullyn hym down, and settyn hym on a stol, and castyn a cloth ouyr his face; and þe fyrst xal seyn:[16]

In this play the Torturers are referred to as *Primus, Secundus, Tercius*, and *Quartus Judeus*. Because the forthcoming sequence requires Jesus to guess which of the four Jews struck him, *Primus Judeus* warns 'A, felawys, beware what ʒe do to þis man, | For he prophecye weyl kan' (line 182). This painful twist on the word *prophesy* is intended to indicate that Jesus will be very good at guessing who hits him.[17] Whereupon, *Secundus Judeus*, as he strikes Jesus, says: 'þat xal be asayd be þis batte' (*that will be tested by this blow*: 183). Immediately after the blow *Secundus Judeus* asks Jesus, 'What, þu Jesus, ho ʒaff þe þat?' (184). After the next blow *Tercius Judeus* asks, 'Ho was þat?' (187).

Quartus Judeus then ups the ante by declaring 'now wole I a newe game begynne' (188). This seems effectively a variant on the same game, but with added rules, designed to disorientate the victim even more. *Quartus Judeus* says: 'Whele and pylle, whele and pylle, | Comyth to halle hoso wylle – Ho was þat?' (190–2). These lines suggest that Jesus is now on his feet and that, still blindfolded, he is spun round on the word 'whele'. The *MED* defines *whēlen* as 'To turn about an axis, revolve;– used in fig. context; also, turn oneself about, wheel around'.[18] The action of spinning a player round three times occurs in some children's games as a means of disorientating the player prior to the main part of the game.[19] The word *pylle* probably implies that after being spun, instead of being struck on the head Jesus

---

16 Spector *N-Town Play 1* 302, sd at line 180; *2* 507, note to sd.
17 See Kolve *Play Called Corpus Christi* 185.
18 *MED* sv *whēlen* v. *(2)* (a); also early references in *OED* sv *wheel* 2. a. 'To turn (something) on or as on a wheel; to cause to revolve about an axis; to rotate'.
19 William Hawkins in his *Apollo Shroving Composed for the Schollars of the Free-schoole of Hadleigh in Suffolke* (London: Robert Mylbourne, 1627) 51 outlines a variant game of Blindman's Buff involving two people, Lauriger and Ludio, where Ludio is blindfolded and tied by the wrists. Lauriger says: 'So, you are tyed, now I must turne you about thrice'. See also Iona and Peter Opie *Children's Games in Street and Playground* (Oxford: Clarendon Press, 1969; reprinted 1970) 117.

has his hair forcefully pulled. Both the *MED* and the *OED* variously offer definitions of *pyll*, *pile*, and *pull* as referring to the pulling or pulling out of hair.[20] Representations of the Instruments of the Passion sometimes include images of a hand holding a hank of hair, suggesting that this was a common tradition.[21] The rhyme 'Whele and pylle, whele and pylle | Comyth to halle hoso wylle' given to this action sounds convincingly like a traditional chant from an existing game, although it could have been tailor-made for the scene.

In representing the buffeting as a game, the sequences in the Towneley Plays, the York Play, and the N. Town Plays are following a long-established tradition. The episode was called a *game* well before dramatization of the episode, starting with the hint in the gospel account in Luke 22:63: *Et viri qui tenebant illum inludebant ei* ('And the men that held him mocked him'). Although the Douai-Rheims Bible translates *inludebant* as 'mocked', the primary meaning is 'played with'.[22] The gospel account continues with what appears to be the description of a game, even though it is not named as such: *et velaverunt eum et percutiebant faciem eius et interrogabant eum dicentes prophetiza quis est qui te percussit* ('And they blindfolded him and

---

20 *MED* sv *pilen* v. (1) 6. (a) 'To remove the hair from (an animal); remove (hair); also of hair: fall out; *piled awei*, fallen out; (b) ppl. *piled*, deprived of hair, without hair, bald; shaven, tonsured; also mangy; also, as a term of abuse'; *MED* sv *dēpilen* v. 'To deprive of hair, depilate'. Also *OED* sv *pile* and *pull*.

21 Aspects of such a tradition may be seen in two manuscript illuminations depicting the Man of Sorrows and the Instruments of the Passion in Willem Vrelant 'Man of Sorrows with the Instruments of the Passion' from the Arenberg Hours (Flemish, Bruges) c.1460–1465; Los Angeles: J. Paul Getty Museum MS Ludwig IX 8 fol. 234. Here, in the overall image, are smaller images of the Instruments of the Passion and the heads and faces of significant personages at the Crucifixion. Among the smaller images is a hand holding a hank of hair presumably pulled from Christ. The same sort of depiction is contained in Master of Edward IV 'Man of Sorrows with Instruments of the Passion' from a Dutch Book of Hours (Utrecht), c.1495–1505. see New York: Pierpont Morgan Library MS G 5, fol. 59ᵛ. Another tradition refers to the pulling out of Christ's beard as accounted for in Isaiah 50:6. I am grateful to Meg Twycross for pointing me towards these examples as a means of supporting my reading of the word *pylle*.

22 *DMLBS*: From Lewis and Short: inludo – *to play at* or *with any thing*, *to sport with*, *amuse one's self with* (syn. colludo; cf. ludificor). *To make sport* or *game of*, *to jest*, *mock*, or *jeer at*, *to ridicule* (class).

smote his face. And they asked him saying: Prophesy: Who is it that struck thee?').[23]

Stevens and Cawley in their edition of the *Towneley Plays* write of this sequence as 'an ancient game known as Hot Cockles' in which a blindfolded player is struck, and invited to guess who delivered the blow.[24] It is unclear just how 'ancient' this is, for the earliest written reference to the game by this name appears to be in Sir Philip Sydney's *The Countess of Pembroke's Arcadia* (1593): 'As for the rest, howe shepeheardes spend their daies, | At blowe point, hotcocles, or els at keeles'.[25] Sidney does not describe the game, but a later account, from *Francis Willughby's Book of Games* (1660s), explains:

> **Hockcockles**, is when one stoopes downe & lays his head in anothers lap, that hoodwinks him, and his hand spread upon his breech, which one of the rest strikes with the palme of his hand as hard as hee can. If hee can tel who struck him, hee is free & hee that struck must ly downe.[26]

---

23 Luke 22:64 *prophetiza quis est qui te percussit*; Matthew 26:68: *prophetiza nobis Christe quis est qui te percussit* . Mark 14:65 merely gives *prophetiza*. This scene is only in the Synoptic Gospels, each of which gives varying details. John 18:22 merely says that 'one of the Priests servants' gave him a slap. For translations see *The Vulgate Bible, Volume 6 The New Testament, Douay-Rheims Translation* edited Angela M. Kinney (Dumbarton Oaks Medieval Library 21; Cambridge MA: Harvard UP, 2013).

24 Stevens and Cawley *Towneley Plays 2* 561 note 498; see also A.C. Cawley and Martin Stevens 'The Towneley *Processus Talentorum*: a Survey and Interpretation' *Leeds Studies in English NS* 17 (1986) 95–130, at 124; in the prologue of *The Retvrne From Pernassvs*, Momus, in an apologetic description of the play about to be performed, declares 'It's a Christmas toy indede, as good a conceite as slauging [*sloughing*] hotcockles, or blinde-man buffe': Anon *The Retvrne From Pernassvs: or The Scourge of Simony* (London: G[eorge] Eld for John Wright, 1606) sig. A2ᵛ; Thomas Hawkins *The Origin of The English Drama* 3 vols (Oxford: Clarendon Press, 1773) *3* 204 note: 'Sloughing hotcockles is a sport, still retained among children. The diversion is of long standing, having been in use with the ancients'. See also A.C. Cawley *The Wakefield Pageants in the Towneley Cycle* (Manchester UP, 1958; reprinted 1971) 121 note 344.

25 Sir Philip Sidney *The Covntesse of Pembrokes Arcadia* (London: William Ponsonbie, 1593) sig. V4ʳ.

26 *Francis Willughby's Book of Games: A Seventeenth-Century Treatise on Sports, Games and Pastimes* edited and introduction David Cram, Jeffrey L. Forgeng, and Dorothy Johnston (Aldershot: Ashgate, 2003) 190. A later variant is described by Joseph

This echoes Randle Cotgrave's 1611 definition of *A bouchon*, 'Groueling; lying with his teeth downeward; or, couched vpon his face; as he is that lyes down at the play called Hot-cockles'.[27] Given these descriptions by Willughby and Cotgrave, a more accurate version of the game absorbed into the buffeting scenes is the game of *Abobbed*.

The *MED* does not record the name 'Hot Cockles' but it does articulate the process of the game of *Abobbed*, under the verb *bobben*, as '1.(a) To strike (a blindfolded person) in cruel jest; (b) to strike or beat (sb.). 2.(a) To deride or insult (sb.); (b) to fool or deceive (sb.)'.[28] The two definitions indicate the overlap between the action of striking and the deception caused by the blindfold. One of the *MED* sources of this definition comes

---

Strutt *Glig Gamena Angel-Ðeod, or The Sports and Pastimes of the People of England* (London: T. Bensley, 1801) 293. See Barry Sanders, 'Who's Afraid of Jesus Christ?: Games in the *Coliphizacio*' *Comparative Drama* 2:2 (Summer 1968) 94–9; John Denham *Certain Verses Written By severall of the Authors Friends; to be Reprinted with the Second Edition of Gondibert* (London: no pub., 1653) 23; William Stearns Davis *Life on a Medieval Barony: A Picture of a Typical Feudal Community in the Thirteenth Century* (New York and London: Harper, 1923) 52; Alice Bertha Gomme *The Traditional Games of England, Scotland, and Ireland* 2 vols (London: David Nutt, 1894, 1898) *1* 229; Opie *Children's Games in Street and Playground* 293.

27 Randle Cotgrave *A Dictionarie of the French and English Tongves* (London: Adam Islip, 1611) sv *Bouchon*.

28 For 'bobbiden Crist', see *A Tretise of Miraclis Pleyinge* edited Clifford Davidson (EDAM Monograph Series 19; Kalamazoo: Medieval Institute Publications, Western Michigan University, 1993; revised 2011) 97; *Mary Magdalen* in *The Late Medieval Religious Plays of Bodleian MSS Digby 133 and E Museo 160* edited Donald C. Baker, John L. Murphy, and Louis B. Hall Jr *EETS OS 283* (1982) 53, line 863; Thomas Elyot *The Boke named the Gouernour* (London: Thomas Berthelet, 1531) sig. Cvii[r]: 'And if any man hapned by longe sittynge to slepe / or by any other countenance to shewe him selfe to be weary / he was sodaynly bobbed on the face by the seruantes of Nero'; Robert Armin *Foole Vpon Foole, or Six sortes of Sottes* (London: William Ferbrand, 1600) sig. D1[v]: 'but the fellow belaboured the foole cunningly and got the fooles head under his arme and bob'd his nose'; *The first Book of the Works of Mr Francis Rabelais* translated Sir Thomas Urquhart, 2 vols (London: Richard Baddeley, 1653) *1* 95 'At bob and hit'; 97 'at bobbing, or the flirt on the nose'. When I was at primary school in the 1950s, wordplay formed much of our playful culture, as demonstrated by the following tongue-twister: 'If your Bob doesn't give our Bob that bob that your Bob owes our Bob then our Bob'll give your Bob a bob on't nose'. This, of course, plays with three meanings of *bob*. Other than a person's name and the process of striking something or someone, a *bob* was the slang term for a shilling which had the monetary value of 5p but the physical size of a 10p coin.

from Towneley Play 24, the *Processus Talentorum* ('Play of the Dice'), when *2 Tortor* declares:

> The play, in fayth, it was to rowne,
> That he shuld lay his hede downe
> And sone I bobyd hym on the crowne –
> That gam me thoght was good![29]
>
> lines 148–51

The game, combining blindfolding and striking, is further referenced in the *MED* by the name of *Abobbed*, which it defines as: 'The game of blindman's buff [see first quot.]; **pleien** ~; *fig.* to fool or delude a helpless person'. As with Hot Cockles, one of our later explanations of what this game involves is found in Willughby's *Book of Games*:

> **A Foole Who Bobed Thee**. One blinds his fellow hoolding 2 of his fingers upon his eyes. Another gives him a boxe of the eare and askes him, A Foole, Who Bob'd Thee … This is like Hockcockles but that he that is blinded stands up right.[30]

This coincides well with the description in the fourteenth-century 'Charter of the Abbey of the Holy Ghost' of the treatment of the Buffeting as the game *Abobbed*:

> And þenne wente boyes and harlotes and spitten on his face, and hudden [*hid*] his eʒen wiþ a cloþ and smiten him on þe croune and pleyeden wiþ him abobbeþ as þei wold ha don wiþ a fol, and beden him telle hem who smot him last.[31]

---

29   *Towneley Plays 1* 313.
30   *Willughby's Book of Games* 194, 244.
31   From 'The Charter of the Abbey of the Holy Ghost' (anonymous, second half of fourteenth century) in *Yorkshire Writers: Richard Rolle of Hampole, an English Father of the Church and his Followers* edited C. Horstman (London: Swan Sonnenschein, 1895) 358. The Soldiers in the York *Christ before Annas and Caiaphas* also suggest that the *popse* game is a suitable treatment for a *fol* ('fool'): *York Play 1* 253, line 358. It was generally accepted that by dressing Christ in white, which took place in the next episode, before Herod, he was being identified as a fool. This was then extended to other episodes: see e.g. *A Talkyng of þe Loue of God: Edited from MS. Vernon (Bodleian 3938) and Collated with MS. Simeon (Brit. Mus. Add 22283)* edited M. Salvina Westra (The Hague: Martinus Nijhoff, 1950) 46–8: 'And bi foren þe princes. buffeteden. & scornden. & blyndfellede þyn eʒen. pleieden a Bobbeþ. & maden þe heor fool'.

Owst translates an account of *Abobbed* from MS Bodley 649 fol. 82ʳ (c.1420) which adds further details to this account:

> A common game in use nowadays is that which the soldiers played with Christ at his Passion: it is called the *bobbid* game. In this game one of the company will be *blindfold* and set in a prone position; then those standing by will hit him on the head and say –
>
> *A bobbid, a bobbid, a biliried:* [corrected to *a byrlyryhode* in margin] *Smyte not her, bot thu smyte a gode!*
>
> And as often as the former may fail to guess correctly and *rede amys*, he has to play a fresh game. And so, until *he rede him that smote him*, he will be *blindfold stille and hold in* for the post of player.[32]

The *MED* translates *abobbed* as: 'The game of blind-man's buff'. This can be misleading for modern readers as the quotations used to illustrate the word do not coincide with the game we know as 'Blind Man's Buff', which the *OED* defines as '**1.** A game in which one player is blindfolded, and tries to catch and identify any one of the others, who, on their part, push him about, and make sport with him'.[33] The definition is repeated by many modern scholars: Owst refers to 'abobbid (i.e. Blindman's Buff)',[34] though he later modifies this to 'a well-known medieval variant of Blindman's Buff, known as *Qui fery?* or Hot Cockles'.[35] Rosemary Woolf also states in her *English Mystery Plays*: 'More importantly the blindfolding of Christ with the question, "Prophesy who smote thee?", led to the recurring ironic elaboration that the men were pretending to play a game of blind man's buff'.[36]

---

32   G.R. Owst *Literature and Pulpit in Medieval England* (Oxford: Blackwell, 1933; revised 1966) 510.
33   See Gomme *Traditional Games 1* 37, 223, 229–30; Opie *Children's Games* 117–20.
34   Owst *Literature and Pulpit* 373.
35   Owst *Literature and Pulpit* 510; *Qui fery?* [who struck?]: Edward B. Taylor 'The History of Games' *The Popular Science Monthly* 15 (New York: Appleton, May to October, 1879) 225–37, at 226; *Francis Willughby's Book of Games* 190, 194, 244, 265; see also *handikruppen* in the *Scottish National Dictionary* (*SND*) at <https://dsl.ac.uk/our-publications/scottish-national-dictionary/>; Gomme *Traditional Games* 188–9.
36   Rosemary Woolf *The English Mystery Plays* (London: Routledge & Kegan Paul, 1972) 254.

Willughby's 1660s explanation confirms modern expectations, talking of 'Blind Man's Buffe' as a game in which 'one of the biggest must bee hoodwinked, with a cloth or something tied before his eyes. All the rest ... run about him, clapping their hands. Hee runs after them and whoever hee catches ... must be hoodwinked' (190). But the name itself suggests hitting (*buff/buffet*), and early variants of the game may have included something closer to *abobbed*, since the *OED* cites a reference from 1629 which already compares the game with the Buffeting of the Passion: 'Others make him [Christ] no better then their Pastime, at no more discreet a Sport, then Childs, or Fooles Blind-man-Buffet: Prophecie vnto us, who is he that smote thee?'[37] John Baret in his *Aluearie* of 1574 provides a fuller account of potential violence in what he calls 'the Hoodwinke play, or hoodmanblind, in some places called blindmanbuf':

Puerilis lusus, vbi obstructis pileo tæniaue luminibus, fugientes tantisper exquirit, pulsatus interim, dum prehenderit aliquem.

A boys' game, where one with eyes covered by a cap or band searches for those who run away, being struck meanwhile, as he catches anyone.[38]

However, it seems that in general in Blind-Man's Buff the blindfolded figure seeks out other players, to catch and identify them, while the action of *Abobbed* and Hot Cockles requires the blindfolded person to be stationary, or relatively so, in order to receive the strikes. In *Abobbed*, the roles of striker and struck are swapped over when the blindfolded person has guessed the identity of the last striker.

In *Abobbed* the blindfolded person is also required to identify and name the person who last struck him/her with a soft, padded object. This is the pivotal point of the game which defines its name and purpose. In

---

37 *OED* sv *Blind Man's Buff*; citing J. Gaule *Practique Theories Christs Predict.* 231.

38 John Baret *An Aluearie or Triple Dictionarie, in Englishe, Latin, and French* (London: Henry Denham, 1574) sv *Hoodwinke* (Entry 566); John Higgins *The Nomenclator, or Remembrancer of Adrianus Iunius* (London: Ralph Newberie and Henry Denham, 1585) 298 sv *Myinda* 'The play called hoodman blind, blind bob, or blindman buffe'; John Florio *Qveen Anna's New World of Words, or Dictionarie of the* Italian *and* English tongues (London: Edward Blount and William Barret, 1611) sv *Minda*, 'the play, blind-hob, or blind-mans-buffe, or hood-man-blind'; *OED* sv *hoodman-blind* 'An old name for BLIND-MAN'S-BUFF'.

Fig. 1: 'Dick Coming Up Full Bounce'. This game has elsewhere in England been known as 'Hi Jimmy Knacker' and 'Hey Cockalorum'. *Boy's Own Annual 22* (1899–1900) 656.

children's games, generally, there are mechanisms and devices for expressing such guesses. For instance, in some games a player will hold up a previously named or numbered finger, which is unseen by a blindfolded or unsighted player, which then has to be guessed.[39] Fig. 1 illustrates a game, surviving into the mid-twentieth century, which includes such guesses.[40] Deliberate attempts are apparently made by those striking the

---

39 Gomme *Traditional Games 1* 229; Opie *Children's Games* 295–301.
40 When I was in the Cubs we played a game called 'Dick Coming Up Full Bounce'. This game has elsewhere in England been known as 'Hi Jimmy Knacker' and 'Hey Cockalorum' (Fig. 1). The game consisted of two teams (two 'sixes' in the Cubs) in which one set of players jumped astride the other team who presented a line of backs. The intention was to get all the members of the jumping team sitting astride the backs of the other team. Jumping team members took a long run-up before they leaped onto the backs of the opposing team and in the process shouted 'Dick Coming up Full Bounce'. When settled, the lead jumper held up a finger and the lead

blindfolded person to disguise the nature of the strike, particularly if all the players know each other.

Modern confusion over the identity of these games arises partly because the central figure in all cases is blindfolded, and partly because of our uncertainty about the shifting variants of medieval games.[41] For ourselves, as far as the action of the *Buffeting* plays is concerned, the principal purpose of distinguishing between the games hinges on whether the blindfolded person is struck (Hot Cockles, *Abobbed*, perhaps Blind Man's Buff); and whether he/she is stationary (Hot Cockles, *Abobbed*) or required to seek out other players (Blindman's Buff, Hoodman Blind, Hide and Seek). But it is not clear that medieval and early modern commentators were concerned with these distinctions. John Florio certainly collapses them in his definition of the Italian game *A mosca cièca*: 'a game where one is hoodwinkt and who being hit must guesse who did it, as we say at hote cockles, or hoodman blinde'.[42]

Another game, 'Frog in the Middle', where a stationary player is also taunted by other players, looks initially like *Abobbed*. But whereas in *Abobbed* the striker has to be identified by the stationary player, the stationary player in Frog in the Middle has to catch hold of the other taunting players without moving from the spot. This illustrates the fact that these apparently insignificant differences in games are often key structural components in defining the purpose and fascination to be enjoyed by the

---

'back', who was inevitably looking at the floor, had to guess which one. In our case, the fingers were named 'Dick, Prick, Talamanca, Jack, and Little Tom'. If the named finger was guessed correctly then the teams swapped over. Otherwise, another round took place using the same roles; for similar finger counting and names see Iona and Peter Opie *Childrens' Games* 255–6, 294–301 at 297. FIG. 1 shows boys in the bending team with their heads held up. This could be quite dangerous so they had to ensure that their heads were tucked under the bottom of the person in front. There is an account of this game at <www.georgemainwaring.co.uk/artwork/dick-prick-calamanca-jack-little-tom/>.

41 Randle Cotgrave confirms these shifting uncertainties by combining many different games in some of his definitions: *Dictionarie* sv *Savate* 'also the play called Bob and hit, or Hodman blind'; *Savatier* 'also, the play called Hodman blind'; *Clignemusset* 'The childish play called Hodman blind, Harrie-racket, or, are you all hid'; *Capifou* 'A play which is not much unlike our Harry-racket, or Hidmen-blind'.

42 *Qveen Anna's New World of Words* sv *A mosca cièca* (page 26).

players. Such confusion tends to occur as a result of interpreting unclear or ambiguous visual sources.[43]

The game of *Abobbed* has been absorbed into the structure of the Towneley *Coliphizacio*, the York *Christ before Annas and Caiaphas*, and the same play in the N. Town Plays, and because of this assimilation we may be left with the impression that *Abobbed* or Hot Cockles was always a vicious and punitive game. However, the game when played non-theatrically was not in itself sadistic, although it could be played with the simulation of vicious intent. Interestingly, this seems to be acknowledged in Willughby's inclusion of the description of 'A Foole Who Bobed Thee' in a section of his manuscript which he headed 'Tricks to Abuse and Hurt One Another' (192). But then, as now, it appears that the object used to strike the blindfolded person was usually made of soft material such as cloth or sacking and was not intended to seriously hurt or injure the blindfolded person.[44] Players of the game may be seen to wind themselves up into simulated frenzy as they build up to the strike but the resultant impact upon the blindfolded person is only a soft one. A useful analogy might be one where a player viciously strikes the blindfolded player with a blown-up balloon or bladder.

Certainly, this is the impression to be derived from MS Bodley 264, where two marginal images (fol. 130^{r-v}) separately depict young men and young women playing what we take to be *Abobbed* (FIGS 2 and 3).[45]

These images are composite, presenting at once the main contributory features of the game, which do not actually all occur at the same moment. In each image there are four players: one person is blindfolded, one is about to strike, another is preparing the cloth with which to strike and the fourth player holds up a number of fingers and seemingly asks the blindfolded player: 'How many fingers do I hold up?' On fol. 130^r the blindfolded player is seen to reply by holding up the number of fingers guessed (compare FIG.

---

43   See Lilian M.C. Randall 'Games and the Passion in Pucelle's Hours of Jeanne D'Évreux' *Speculum* 47:2 (April 1972) 246–57; Richard H. Randall 'Frog in the Middle' *Metropolitan Museum of Art Bulletin* NS 16:10 (June 1958) 269–75; Iona and Peter Opie *Children's Games* 121, 293–4.

44   Compare 'Stroke the Baby' in Iona and Peter Opie *Children's Games* 292–4.

45   Bodleian Library MS Bodley 264, 'The Romance of Alexander', fols 130^r and 130^v. In his *Glig Gamena Angel-Ðeod, or The Sports and Pastimes of the People of England* (London: T. Bensley, 1801) PLATE 34, Joseph Strutt copies these images but identifies them as showing 'Hoodman Blind'. See also Strutt *Sports and Pastimes* 292–3; Opie *Children's Games* 294–301 at 297.

PHILIP BUTTERWORTH

FIGS 2 and 3: Young Men and Women play at *Abobbed*.
Oxford: Bodleian Library MS Bodley 264 fol. 130^{r-v}.
Creative Commons Licence CC-BY-NC 4.0.

1). One of the players may be seen preparing to strike the blindfolded player violently, but in effect the blow makes only soft contact. This discrepancy is very suitable for a theatrical purpose, when it needs to appear that the blindfolded player is hit very hard. The difference between hard intent and soft impact is important in turning this game into theatre of the kind illustrated in the Towneley, York, and N. Town pageants. It is the use of what we think of as harmless playfulness to stage vicious cruelty that gives these plays their intensity.

Dicing Games

Rules are essential to the playing of all games. William Horman advises the reader of his *Vulgaria* (1519) to 'Kepe and obbey the lawe of the game'.[46] Such rules are necessary in order to direct the purpose of the game and release the value and enjoyment to its participants. Acceptance and enactment of the rules of the game are equivalent to the necessary 'agreed pretence' when theatre takes place. If the rules of the game are broken, or manipulated to such an extent that they become contorted, then the purpose and value of the existing game becomes unachievable. Different stances may be taken to rules of the game: the rules may be acknowledged, observed, and adhered to; or they may be responded to indifferently or ignored; further, they may be challenged, perverted, or flouted. Flouting of rules may be extended into cheating.[47] Motives for these different responses provide significant opportunities for theatrical development.

However, when a game is woven into a play it often operates within the new framework by breaking or modifying previously understood rules of the game in order to promote the narrative and structural development of the play. The original purpose of the game is changed in order to support the purpose of the play. This is the case in the Towneley *Processus Talentorum* ('Play of the Dice') where Pilate masterfully trumps the implicitly agreed rules of the game when he and the Torturers dice for

---

46 William Horman *Vulgaria uiri doctissimi Guil. Hormani Caesariburgensis* (London: Richard Pynson, 1519) 282.

47 Huizinga makes a distinction between the 'cheat' and the 'spoil-sport': 'The player who trespasses against the rules or ignores them is a 'spoil-sport'. The spoil-sport is not the same as the false player, the cheat; for the latter pretends to be playing the game and, on the face of it, still acknowledges the magic circle'. The 'magic circle', in Huizinga's terms, is the name given to one of the 'temporary worlds within the ordinary world, dedicated to the performance of an act apart': Huizinga *Homo Ludens* 10; for further articulation of Huizinga's 'magic circle' see *Games and Gaming in Medieval Literature* edited Serina Patterson (Basingstoke: Palgrave Macmillan, 2015) 9–10.

Christ's gown.[48] Initially, Pilate has no intention of releasing the gown to the torturers, and he declares ownership of it by snatching it and declaring: 'That appentys [*belongs*] vnto me – mafa! art thou mad? | I ment that no mytyng shuld mell hym of this' ('I meant that no knave should meddle with this'; lines 264–5). Attempts to cut up the gown so that it might be shared are unsuccessful because the garment lacks appropriate seams by which it can be divided.[49] Thus, Pilate demands that the gown be left in one piece (300). He forcefully suggests that they should decide ownership of the gown by drawing lots (312). The Torturers suspect Pilate's motives and overturn his proposal with the suggestion that they play at dice for the gown.[50] Three dice are involved and it is agreed that the highest score should win the gown (325–7). In a prolonged sequence *3 Tortor* throws the highest score, and by the agreed rules has won the gown. Pilate is furious, demands that the gown be delivered up to him, and threatens the Torturer into agreeing (364–71). Having initially been ready to dice for the gown the Torturers then, in a rapid moral conversion, denounce at length the practice of dicing (378–429). While this might be seen as comic hypocrisy, to modern understanding and sensibilities such an instant reversal of attitude could seem somewhat theatrically gawky and ill-considered. However, within a structural framework deliberately constructed as a didactic one, with an overt teaching aim, the instantaneous volte-face is perfectly appropriate.

In the play the rules of the game are established and not apparently broken during the playing of it. Pilate's manipulation of the situation exists outside the rules of the game. For his purpose, the game is simply a means to an end which then becomes the pretext for bullying and blackmailing the

---

48 Kinney *The Vulgate Bible The New Testament Douay-Rheims Translation* Matthew: 27:36; Mark: 15:24; Luke: 23:34; John: 19:24; Stevens and Cawley *Towneley Plays 1* 309–22.

49 For further discussion of the significance of the 'seamless garment', see Theresa Coletti 'Theology and Politics in the Towneley Play of the Talents' in *Medievalia et Humanistica NS 9* (1979) 111–26; Mendel G. Frampton 'The *Processus Talentorum* (Towneley XXIV)' *Publications of the Modern Language Association* 59:3 (1944) 646–54.

50 The same problem and its solution is differently arrived at in the *Passio Domini* of the *Cornish Ordinalia*. Here, the four executioners have four dice one of which clearly looks different from the others. They do not play at dice for the gown, but the four are divided between the four executioners and the one who receives the differently looking die receives the gown; Edwin Norris *The Ancient Cornish Drama* 2 vols (Oxford UP, 1859) *1* 446–9.

Tortores into releasing the gown into his possession. Thus, the game of dice is transformed into a theatrical device to serve and condition the structure of the play where the technical details of the game become subservient to the developing narrative.

Although the dice throws of 13, 8, 7, and 15 are precise in the narrative of the Towneley *Play of the Dice*, enabling the spectator's understanding and appreciation of the outcome of the game, it is unlikely that members of an audience would be able to read the numbers – whether the play was played indoors or outdoors and whether or not conscious staging permitted spectators to see the dice themselves. Consequently, it would have been irrelevant which numbers actually came up on the dice in performance. This is true of all games of dice incorporated into plays: the important numbers are those that are declared to have been thrown. These recorded numbers permit one of the Torturers to win the gown and Pilate subsequently to commandeer it. Whether there is any additional significance to the declared numbers is unclear. Or indeed, whether any cheating has gone on. Presumably, all the players would have been capable of cheating in order to win the gown but the audience is not offered any terms of reference which might suggest that cheating is taking place.

One way of interpreting the permutations of thrown dice numbers related to the element of chance in dice games. Dice could be used as a means of predicting fortune. A fifteenth-century manuscript commonplace book contains the poem 'Fortune in Life told by the Casting of Dice'. The stanzas of the poem each focus on different dice scores with three dice. Two examples – '6/6/6' and '5/4/5' are given below:

> [þou þat hast y-cast tre syses here]
> Schall haue 30wr dessyer ye same 3er,
> How 30w stabyll and ware nowt,
> For 3e shall haue after 30wr thowt.
>
> lines 666–9

> Synke, cater, synke, 3e haue on the dysse;
> I cownsell 30w be war and wysse,
> Trost non erdely thyng that may be,
> For the wor[l]d ys but a vanite.[51]
>
> lines 545–8

---

51 *A Common-place Book of the Fifteenth Century, Containing A Religious Play and Poetry, Legal Forms, and Local Accounts* edited Lucy Toulmin Smith (London: Trübner, 1886) 15–18.

In the tenth century Archdeacon Wibold at Noyon, France, in his *Ludus Regularis* assembled a system which interpreted thrown dice numbers in such a way as to promote and instruct clerics in virtuous living.[52] This was a way of circumventing canon law that forbade dicing by turning the activity into a pleasurable one for the purpose of clerical instruction. But since the game played in the Towneley *Processus Talentorum* is a straightforward one where 'whoso has most' (325) determines the outcome, coded monastic values attached to the thrown numbers as determined by a tenth-century manuscript seem somewhat remote and unnecessary to the didactic purpose of the play.[53]

Dicing for Christ's gown is also played out in the Chester Ironmongers' pageant of the Passion, lines 65–148.[54] As in the equivalent Towneley pageant, the game, or the pretence of it, is played with three dice. Again, like the Towneley scene, the rolled numbers are unlikely to have been seen by the spectators. Indeed, there should be no theatrical need to expect an audience to have seen the numbers. The Ironmongers are likely to have played on the floor of their carriage since *Tertius Judeus* says 'Yea, nowe I read that wee | sytt downe, as mote I thee' (lines 117–18). The implication is that the four Jews sit sprawled or cross-legged and roll the dice between them. The progress of the scene does not depend upon visual recognition of the numbers by the spectators. The spoken narrative is sufficient, with individual speeches that refer to the numbers thrown by three of the Jews. They tell the audience the denomination of the rolled numbers, and within the context of the played scene and its agreed pretence there is no need to confirm or question the results.

---

52   The following attributions are cited by Wibold that may be attached to the scores of 13, 8, 7, and 15 as scored by Pilate and the *Tortores*. 13: 1.6.6. (Wisdom), 2.5.6. (Virginity), 3.4.6. (Mortification), 3.5.5. ((Innocence), 4.4.5. (Concern); 8: 1.1.6. ((Temperance), 1.2.5. (Mercy), 1.3.4. (Foresight), 2.2.4. (Sobriety), 2.3.3. (Cleverness); 7: 1.1.5. (Prudence), 1.3.3. (Fear), 2.2.3. (Joy); 15: 3.6.6. (Exomologesis), 4.5.6. (Longing), 5.5.5. (Cheerfulness): Richard Pulskamp and Daniel Otero *Wibold's Ludus Regularis, a 10th Century Board Game – Virtues – Outcomes* at <www.maa.org/book/export/html/430411>.

53   For an analysis and discussion of the possible relevance of the numbers thrown in this pageant, see Michael Olmert 'The Towneley *Processus Talentorum*: Dicing Toward Jerusalem' *Florilegium* 5 (1983) 157–77.

54   *The Chester Mystery Cycle* edited R.M. Lumiansky and David Mills 2 vols *EETS SS 4* and *SS 9* (1974 and 1986) 306–10.

The numbers thrown in this sequence are puzzling and do not appear to match any known game of dice in the fifteenth and sixteenth centuries.[55] *Primus Judeus* is the first to roll the dice and he scores an unspecified total (lines 121–4). *Secundus Judeus* throws what he declares to be 'dubletts', which conventionally refers to two dice of the same number (line 130). Here it may refer to all three dice showing the same number – but this is unclear. *Tertius Judeus* tells *Secundus Judeus* that he 'fayles' and that his throw of 'cator-traye' (4 and 3) beats his 'dubletts' (line 133). The audience is not given the rules of the game in order to understand the significance of this assertion. There is no mention of what the third die achieves. *Quartus Judeus* scores five ('synnce' or 'synke'; lines 143, 147) and this appears to be the winning score, for *Primus Judeus* acknowledges 'well wonne yt thou hasse' (line 146). How the total of five is made up by the three dice is unstated.[56]

These scores make no clear reference to a third die, and they appear to exist either as randomly selected or as belonging to a game unknown to us. Since the value of the throw by *Primus Judeus* is not declared, the audience is not in a position to know of the significance of his roll. The only indication offered to the audience is from *Secundus Judeus* when he says 'noe parte hasse thou therin' (line 126), thus suggesting a weak score. Unless the game is one unknown to us which contemporaries would be expected to

---

55   For some of the known games, see Anon *The [In]terlude of youth* (London: J. King for John Waley, 1557) sig. Ci^r: 'Syrl can teche you to play at the dice | At the quenes game and at the Iryshe | The Treygobet and the hasarde also | And many oþer games mo'; Cotgrave *Dictionarie* sv *Renette*: f. 'A game at Tables of some resemblance with our Doublets, or Queens Game'; *OED* sv *doublet* 'An old game at tables or backgammon'. See also Charles Cotton *The Compleat Gamester: or, Instructions how to play at Billiards, Trucks, Bowls, and Chess. Together with all manner of usual and most Gentile Games either on Cards or Dice. To which is added, The Arts and Mysteries of Riding, Racing, Archery, and Cock-Fighting* (London: A.M. for R. Cutler, 1674) 154–5: for the Hazzard game 168–73; *MED* sv *trei~go bet*, 'three go best', the name of a dice game'.

56   *MED* sv *cink* (1) Also *sink(e* [OF]. 'In the game of dice or hazard: the five on a die; a throw that turns up a five [inferior only to a six].' See Matthew Sergi 'Dice at Chester's Passion' in *The Chester Cycle in Context, 1555–1575: Religion, Drama, and the Impact of Change* edited Jessica Dell, David Klausner, and Helen Ostovich (Farnham: Ashgate, 2012) 65–77: Sergi makes a careful examination of the game played, its structure, sequence, and timing. He does this through a naturalistic interpretation of the scene although at various points he warns against the adoption and use of naturalistic criteria. Thus, there is something of a self-conscious tension in the declaration to avoid naturalistic principles.

recognize, as far as the audience is concerned there are no discernible rules to the game although the Jews play as if there are rules.[57]

Playing dice in the moral interlude *Nice Wanton* operates in a more complicated fashion and for a quite different purpose.[58] Here, dicing is selected by the author as the perfect means of symbolizing and expressing debauchery. Within these terms of reference, cheating at dice is thus permissible and necessary in promoting the purpose and structure of the play. The game being played here is not one, as in the Towneley *Processus Talentorum*, where the winner is the player who rolls the highest score. Here, it appears to be the game called 'Hazard' where two dice are thrown together. On first encounter, the rules of the game seem quite complicated. However, in this game the winner is not determined by the highest score but by rolling a particular combination of numbers.[59]

57 This condition is reminiscent of the spoof comedy game, 'Mornington Crescent' as played in the BBC Radio 4 programme, 'I'm Sorry I Haven't a Clue'. Here, the players improvise verbal journeys on the London Underground by naming stations as if they are logically connected. Sometimes the selected stations are known ones and sometimes they are fictional ones. The game is played with all apparent seriousness and ends when, having taken a circuitous route, one of the players declares *Mornington Crescent* – the climax of the game. This declaration is random, without reason but played in such a way as to appear to have consisted of a series of brilliant and clever moves according to ever moveable fictional rules. The audience is also aware of this pretence and it too pretends that it knows the rules of the game. The game exemplifies the sub-title of the programme: *An Antidote to Panel Games*.
58 Anon *A Preaty Interlude called, Nice wanton* (London: John Kyng, 1560) sigs Aiiii^r–Bi^v.
59 With minor variations the rules of the game are as follows: the game consists of two rounds. The first one is called the *Main* and the subsequent ones called the *Chance*. The game is initiated by a player throwing a *Main* and the resultant number must fall within the range from 5 to 9. *Main* numbers are thus 5, 6, 7, 8, or 9. Then, in turn, each player rolls the two dice as a *Chance*. If the player rolls the same number as the *Main* then he wins or *nicks*. If he throws a 2 or a 3 (outside of the *Main* range), he loses or *throws out* or *outs*. If he delivers an 11 or 12 (again outside the *Main* range) the result depends on the following changeable circumstances: if the *Main* has been a 5 or a 9 then the player *throws out* with both an 11 and a 12. If the *Main* has been a 6 or an 8 and the player rolls an 11 then he *throws out* but if he rolls a 12 he *nicks*. If the *Main* has been rolled as a 7 then the player *nicks* with an 11 but *throws out* with a 12. If the player neither *nicks* nor *throws out* then the number rolled is called the *chance* and the player throws the dice again. If he throws the same number as the *Chance*, he wins; if he rolls the same number as the *Main* then he loses – unlike his first roll; if he throws neither then he keeps rolling until he rolls one or the other whereby he wins with the *Chance* or loses with the *Main*; see Cotton *The Compleat Gamester* 168–73.

STRUCTURING GAMES INTO MEDIEVAL ENGLISH PLAYS

Given that Hazard was an existing and recognizable game, adherence to the rules of the game would seem to be critical to audience perception of its relevance to the narrative and structure of the play. Any divergence from the normal rules of the game would need to be justified by the developing narrative and/or signals to spectators through performance. The game of Hazard (*hasard*) is defined by the *MED* as 'A game of chance played with dice'.[60] In spite of the game's apparently complicated rules it appears to have been popular, addictive, and fertile territory for gambling and cheating. Hence it is the game of choice for Iniquity, the Vice, in *Nice Wanton*. The debauched game of Hazard played in the play promotes the corrupting influence of Iniquity upon Dalila. Their agreed connivance to cheat Dalila's brother, Ismael, provides the perfect vehicle to develop the structure of the play. If, as suggested above, an audience does not see, or is not permitted to see, the actual rolled numbers, as distinct from the numbers required by the narrative, then the means by which cheating is to take place within the narrative needs to be demonstrated to the spectators. In order to cheat Ismael, two sets of dice need to be used by Iniquity and Dalila; the audience needs to know of this, but not Ismael.[61] When the corrupted dice are thrown they need to add up to 5 so that Dalila can win. She only throws once in the game. If the spots on the dice were to be seen by the audience then an arrangement would need to take place whereby one of the dice is marked with 2s only and the other with 3s only. These 'rigged' numbers would not be necessary if the spectators were not permitted to see the actual rolled numbers.

As far as the narrative is concerned, the game may thus be played with alternate use of clean dice and cheating ones. Ismael and Iniquity play with the clean dice and Dalila plays with the corrupted dice. Dalila says to Iniquity, 'Mayster Iniquitie, by your leaue | I wyll play a crowne or two here by your sleue' (sig. Aiiij[v] lines 2–3). This is the point at which Dalila places

---

60 It can also be a term for the player: 'A player at hazard, gambler'; 'a trickster, rascal' and 'cheat'.

61 Informative exposés of cheating practices occur in Gilbert Walker (attrib.) *A manifest detection of the moste vyle and detestable vse of Diceplay, and other practices lyke the same* (London: Abraham Vele, c.1555); *Cony-Catchers and Bawdy Baskets* edited and introduced Gāmini Salgāldo (Harmondsworth: Penguin, 1972) 27–57; *Rogues Vagabonds & Sturdy Beggars: A New Gallery of Tudor and Early Stuart Rogue Literature* edited Arthur F. Kinney (Amherst: University of Massachusetts Press, 1990) 61–84.

her money next to Iniquity's sleeve and one of two potential points at which she might surreptitiously pick up the false die released from his sleeve. The surreptitiousness is necessary to deceive Ismael but not the audience, which needs to have the terms of reference of cheating displayed to it. The other point at which she might receive the doctored dice is when she asks Iniquity to 'gyue me your hand' (sig. Aiiij^v line 27) and the dice are exchanged. Ismail throws a 7 and Iniquity rolls an 11, leaving Ismael to exclaim 'Do ye nycke vs be knaue your noly [*curse your head*]' (sig. Bi^r line 1). Thus Ismael loses.[62] Within the rules of the game if the 'main' throw is a 7 and the 'chance' roll is an 11, then he who rolls the 11 *nicks*, i.e. wins. This is followed by Dalila's win with a throw of 5, and a falling out between her and Iniquity when he finds she has tried to cheat him too by concealing her winnings.

Cock-Fighting

In some games, simply winning is a perfectly adequate reward. In others, winning is rewarded with a prize which may well have provided the motivation to take part in the game. Prizes can take many different forms. In Henry Medwall's *Fulgens and Lucres* the two personages A and B enter into a 'boyes game' to win the approval of Lucres's maid, Joan.[63] A and B think that she is the prize. They compete first by singing, then by wrestling, and finally by taking part in a game that they call *farte prycke in cule*. The basis of this game is the game of 'Cock-Fighting', as it was named and understood in the nineteenth century and later (see FIGS 4 and 5).

The game also appears under the names 'Skiver the Goose', 'Knee and Toe Wrestle', and 'Trussed Fowls'. One late-nineteenth-century glossary defines 'Skiver the Goose' as 'a boys' game. Two persons are trussed somewhat like fowls: they then hop about on their "hunkers", each trying to upset the other'.[64] Another describes the game's action more fully:

---

62 For two carefully considered production editions of the play see *English Moral Interludes* edited and introduced Glynne Wickham (London: Dent, 1976); *Nice Wanton, A PLS Performance Text* edited David Parry and Kathy Pearl (Toronto: Poculi Ludque Societas, 1978).

63 Henry Medwall *Fulgens and Lucres* (Henry E. Huntington Facsimile Reprints; New York: George D. Smith, 1920) sigs di^v–diii^v, at di^v; *The Plays of Henry Medwall* edited Alan H. Nelson (Cambridge: D.S. Brewer, 1980) 58, line 1106.

64 William Hugh Patterson *A Glossary of Words and Phrases used in Antrim and Down* (London: Trübner for the English Dialect Society, 1880); Gomme also refers to the

Trussed Fowls. Two boys having seated themselves on the floor, are trussed by their playmates; that is to say, each boy has his wrists tied together with a handkerchief, and his legs secured just above the ancles with another; his arms are then passed over his knees, and a broomstick is pushed over one arm, under both knees, and out again over the other arm. The 'trussed fowls' are now carried into the centre of the room and placed opposite each other, with their toes just touching. The fun now begins; as each fowl endeavours, with the aid of his toes to turn his antagonist over on his back or side, and the one who can succeed in doing this wins the game. It frequently happens that both players turn over together, to the great amusement of the spectators. On board ship these comical encounters frequently take place between the boys, who are trussed by their elder shipmates.[65]

The basic game of 'Cock-Fighting' consists of a contest between two players who each squat with a stick held behind their knees which is long enough to accept the player's crooked elbows underneath it. The hands of the players may then be simply clasped in front of the knees or they may be tied at the wrists. The players are then lifted by others into a position where

---

game as 'Shiver the Goose' in *Traditional Games 2* 192. For 'Knee and Toe Wrestle' see Jessie H. Bancroft *Games for the Playground, Home, School and Gymnasium* (New York: Macmillan, 1909) 246.

65   *Every Boy's Book; A Complete Encyclopædia of Sports and Amusements* edited Edmund Routledge (London: George Routledge, 1868) 40; see Twycross, Jones, and Fletcher cited at note 68 for images of 'Norwegian Cockfighting' on the SS Norman Castle 103; see also *The Boy's Own Paper 31* (London: Boy's Own Paper Office, 1908–9) 649 (FIG. 6); Dorothy Canfield and others *What Shall We Do Now? Over Five Hundred Games and Pastimes* (New York: Stokes, 1907; revised reprint 1922) 37: 'The Trussed Fowls. In this contest two boys are first trussed. Trussing consists of firmly tying wrists and ankles, bringing the elbows down below the knees and slipping a stick along over one elbow, under both knees and over the other elbow, as in the picture. The game is for the two fowls to be placed opposite each other with their feet just touching, and for each then to strive to roll the other over with his toes'; for analogous activity see John Mactaggart *The Scottish Gallovidian Encyclopedia, or, The Original, Antiquated, and Natural Curiosities of the South of Scotland* (London: printed for the author, 1824) 155: 'CURRCUDDY or KIRRCUDDY – A singular, rustic dance, now common to be seen danced on the stages of theatre by buffoons. The dancers *curr* or sit down on their hams, with their hands joined beneath their thighs, and so they hop about, and go through various evolutions'; also *Dictionaries of the Scots Language* (*DSL*) sv *Harry Hurcheon* <https://dsl.ac.uk/entry/snd/harry_hurcheon>.

Fig. 4: 'Cock-Fighting' as played by school boys. Leaf probably taken from an unidentified boys' magazine c.1908.

the squatting players each touch the other player's toes with their toes.[66] From this point, the object of the game is to push over the opponent (Fig. 6). As with similar contests of balance and strength,[67] the effort involved

---

66   The players were clearly intended to face each other at the start of the encounter and not sit back to back as suggested by Alan Nelson in *The Plays of Henry Medwall* 184.

67   Bancroft *Games for the Playground* 245-8; other games are also known of as 'cockfighting' when fighting while hopping or fighting on piggyback: Opie *Children's Games* 214-19.

in pushing over one's opponent is such that both players may lose their balance and roll over, leaving the game without a winner.

However, an elaboration of the game of 'Cock-Fighting' takes place here in *farte prycke in cule* with the addition of another stick, the *prycke*, which is held by the hands and projects forwards as a 'spear' that is intended to strike the opponent's bottom after toppling. The only way that the players can achieve their objectives is by hopping in their trussed state to align themselves for the final thrust. The game as it features in *Fulgens and Lucres* has been investigated previously by Peter Meredith and Meg Twycross and later examined by Alan J. Fletcher, who cites a 1602 version from Ireland, later given the name of 'Skiver the Goose'. These were followed by a third article by Meg Twycross, Malcolm Jones, and Alan Fletcher, providing contemporary and other images.[68]

Meredith outlined the basic problems of realizing the game in practice as dictated by attempts to deliver the text as it is written. His

A TRUSSED FOWL

FIG. 5: 'A Trussed Fowl' from Dorothy Canfield and Others *What Shall We Do Now? Over Five Hundred Games and Pastimes* (New York: Stokes, 1907) 37.

---

68   Peter Meredith with an interpolation from Meg Twycross '"Farte Pryke in Cule" and Cock-Fighting' *Medieval English Theatre* 6:1 (1984) 30–9; Alan J. Fletcher '"Farte Prycke in Cule": A Late-Elizabethan Analogue' *Medieval English Theatre* 8:2 (1986) 132–9; Meg Twycross with Malcolm Jones & Alan Fletcher '"Farte Prycke in Cule": The Pictures' *Medieval English Theatre* 23 (2001) 100–21. Here, the authors present some splendid contemporary misericord examples of the games.

PHILIP BUTTERWORTH

FIG. 6: 'Water Sports – The Seaside Regatta' *The Boy's Own Paper 31*
(London: Boy's Own Paper Office, 1908–9) 649.

discussion is illuminated with reference to Rudyard Kipling's description of 'Cock-Fighting' by schoolboys.[69] Twycross added a further description of her experience in constructing the mechanism of the game, again following

---

69 See Rudyard Kipling *The Complete Stalky & Co.* edited Isabel Quigly (Oxford UP, 1987) 126–8; *Fulgens and Lucres by mayster henry medwall* edited Peter Meredith *Leeds Studies in English* (Leeds: School of English, University of Leeds, 1981).

the script, in her production of the play. She concentrates on the physical ability of the players to reproduce the demands of the text. Her rehearsal experiments with the logistical requirements of the text confront the discomfort experienced by the players in creating the game. Similarly, she is also concerned about the relative unpredictability of the players' ability to control their balance in order to achieve the required outcome of the game. The means by which the forward-thrusting 'spear' is to be secured and manipulated is a focus of concern.

Both Meredith and Twycross initially stick as closely to the text as they can. (Apart from Kipling's description, this was the only evidence they had, and even that was not available when Twycross staged the scene.) The staging problems they identify arise out of this intention. However, both offer alternative sequential arrangements to those determined by the text as dictated by practical feasibility. In guiding these concerns the purpose of the game within the play's structure needs to be kept uppermost. The non-theatrical game of 'Cock-Fighting' is absorbed into the play and changed in its purpose and structural function in order to present a comic mock-joust conditioned by the needs of the play.

When the game is played as 'Cock-Fighting' in a non-theatrical context the contest is paramount. Ostensibly, the so-called 'joust' between A and B is also of great importance in deciding the suitability of the contestants as suitors to Joan. However, within the comic purpose of the scene the augmented and encumbered game is designed to fail in the purpose of resolving the winner of Joan's affection. Such is the silliness of its choice as a mock contest. Thus, the buffoonish mock joust of the game is itself subjugated to a farcical routine to serve the purpose of the play by providing content for the sub-plot. The failure of the contest is quickly overridden when Joan overcomes and abandons both A and B as directed by an explicit stage direction: *Et vtroq[ue] flagellato recedit ancilla* ('And having beaten them both the maid withdraws').

Although the non-theatrical game of 'Cock-Fighting' is straightforward in its aim, it appears to become more complicated in the game of *farte prycke in cule* if the text of *Fulgens and Lucres* is interpreted literally, or indeed, embellished. The combatants' accoutrements are described with some exaggeration as if they are taking part in a real joust. In fact, all that is needed are two sticks each and something to bind the wrists.[70] Glynne Wickham embellished the required gear as a 'broom and mop as spears, sauce-pans as helmets, the lids as shields and dish-cloths as slings or harnesses for the lances'.[71] None of these items are stipulated as requirements in the text. Similarly, Twycross employed brooms as 'spears'. Again, there is no textual requirement for these items. It seems that Meredith, Twycross, and Wickham had initially interpreted the need for 'spears' as objects of length that project forwards from the hands and trail between the player's legs. Twycross acknowledges that her choice of brooms arose 'because I was thinking of hobby-horses and liked the tail effect'.[72] The adoption of brooms as 'spears' appears to have complicated the action in Twycross's production. Shorter sticks as 'spears' are recorded in the description, originally identified by Fletcher, in 'Bodley's Visit to Lecale, County of Down, A.D. 1602–3':

> *Inter indices et pollices utriusque manus bacillum quoddam, longitudinis fere unius pedis, ab anteriori parte acutum, tenebant. Et isto modo locantur duo illi – alter ex opposito alterius, per distantiam unius ulnae. His ita dispositis incipiunt congredi; et quisque per se, junctis pedibus, adversarium subvertere conatur; subversus enim nunquam se potest recuperare, sed podicem praebet, perjungendum cum dicto bacillo.*[73]

> Between forefinger and thumb of each hand they held a certain small stick of about a foot in length and sharpened at the further end. These two servants are placed in the following way: one faces the other at about an ell's distance. When these things have been arranged, the two start to approach each other, and tacklng with his feet, each tries to topple his opponent; for once thrown over he can never recover himself, but he offers his backside to be prodded with the small stick previously mentioned.

70 These sticks need to be thin ones for Meg Twycross writes of the difficulties of holding the sticks behind the knees: 'I should however point out that this posture is extremely uncomfortable and can become actively painful if kept up for any length of time': Meredith/Twycross 'Farte Pryke in Cule' 37.
71 Wickham *English Moral Interludes* 71 note.
72 Meredith/Twycross 'Farte prycke in Cule' 38.
73 'Bodley's Visit to Lecale, County of Down, A.D. 1602–3' *Ulster Journal of Archaeology First Series* 2 (1854) 73–95; as quoted in Fletcher '"Farte Prycke in Cule"' 135–7.

The Irish account provides understanding of the way in which 'spears' could be used in *farte prycke in cule*. Clearly, this 'spear' is not long enough to pass between the legs of the players and appears to be much more controllable than a long stick or broom handle. It fits well into B's instructions to Joan on the order of preparation: 'Go to, bynd me fyrst', then 'So, lo, now, geve me my spere' and finally 'put me a staffe thorow here – then am I all redy' (1185–8). The nineteenth-century editor of Bodley's manuscript, who refers to the game in his own day as 'Skiver the Goose', commented that 'As now generally practised, the pointed stick [spear] is properly dispensed with'.[74] The game described, but not named, by Bodley is the same activity as *farte prycke in cule*, and when practised as 'Skiver the Goose' without 'the pointed stick' is the same game as 'Cock-Fighting'.

Conclusion

Even though the games selected above have been termed 'non-theatrical games', because of their original purposes, it is clear that each of them already possesses inherent theatrical qualities that make it an attractive choice for overt theatrical use. The composition of the original games is such that their structures, while maintaining their former identity and rules, are sufficiently malleable to be incorporated into the host play. It is the purpose of these games that changes, to promote that of the play. These absorbed games, or 'intrusions' as Tom Pettitt refers to them, are examples of his term *interaxionality*, which refers to actions borrowed or shared between theatrical events:

> Like intertextuality, interaxionality covers a wide range of relationships between what might be termed the 'recipient' or 'host work', into which material is intruded, and the 'donor' forms contributing those intrusive materials, and it is precisely in both conglomerating this variety of processes, and bringing out the similarities and differences between them, that the concept of intertextuality, and hence interaxionality, may ultimately have the greatest value.[75]

---

74   'Bodley's Visit to Lecale' note at 94.
75   Tom Pettitt 'Performing Intrusions: Interaction and Intertextuality in Medieval English Theatre' in *Medieval Theatre Performance: Actors, Dancers, Automata and their Audiences* edited Philip Butterworth and Katie Normington (Cambridge: D.S. Brewer, 2017) 52–75.

I put stress upon the 'absorption' of these games into plays rather than their 'intrusion', since they are presumably assimilated into the creation of the play by the author and do not invade an existing play. The two terms imply different processes of creation.

In the case of *Abobbed*, the biblical narrative supplies the content and action of the game for the *Buffeting* of the Towneley Plays, the N. Town pageant of *The Trial before Annas and Cayphas* and the York Play *Christ before Annas and Caiaphas*. The game is also referred to in the Towneley *Processus Talentorum*. Hitherto, there has been an unacknowledged blurring between *Abobbed* and other games that involve a central player who is blindfolded. While all such games are malleable, modified by region and chronology, this discussion has attempted to clarify the significant distinctions between the games of *Abobbed*, Hot Cockles, Blind Man's Buff, and Hoodman Blind.

In each of the dice games outlined above, the declared denomination of the thrown dice is determined by the spoken and performed narrative. This is deliberately constructed to relay meaning and significance to the spectators, whether this be an actual and known game, or an invented one that is previously unknown to the audience. The same conditions of chance that operate in normal dice games exist onstage: the numbers thrown could not be guaranteed to be the same as those determined by the play's narrative. The significance of the game's intention must be delivered by dialogue and the quality of the players' performance.

Although the name *farte prycke in cule* does not appear to be recorded elsewhere, Bodley's account plainly seems to describe the same game. It appears to be a variant, or perhaps the origin, of the game later going by the names of 'Skiver the Goose' and 'Cock-Fighting'. The game was clearly designed to create a good deal of enjoyment for spectators, as recorded in Bodley's Irish eye-witness account:

> *Quod fecit nos ita ridere per unam horam, ut lacrymae ex oculis nostris distillarunt; et uxor Philippi coqui rideat etiam, et ipsa lixa, quae fuerunt ambo presentes. Dixisses tonsorum aliquem chirurgum fuisse ibi, ad quem omnes monstrabant dentes.*

> This made us laugh for a whole hour so much that the tears streamed from our eyes; and the wife of Phillip the cook laughed and the kitchen maid too, who were both present. You would have said that

some barber-surgeon were there to whom everyone was showing their teeth.[76]

The uncontrollable laughter created here is an indicator of the inherent theatrical quality produced by the protagonists' ineffectual mastery of their movement in order to win the game. The opponents' apparent ineffectiveness in controlling their movement through the physical limitations placed upon them creates ridiculous action that amounts to a form of slapstick. Despite their best efforts, one or both of the opponents cannot succeed and it is their apparently incompetent struggle that creates the infectious laughter. It is knowledge of these likely spectator responses that Medwall could seemingly rely upon in absorbing the game into *Fulgens and Lucres*.

University of Leeds

---

76 'Bodley's Visit to Lecale' 94, as cited in Fletcher "'Fart Pryke in Cule'" 137.

FEMINISM, THEATRE, AND HISTORICAL FICTION:
Anna of Cleves in 2021

Elisabeth Dutton

As theatres cautiously reopened in Autumn 2021, post-lockdown, across the country, tickets went on sale for Hilary Mantel's dramatization of her novel *The Mirror and the Light*, playing at London's Gielgud Theatre from September. The final volume of Mantel's Thomas Cromwell trilogy perhaps demonstrates most clearly the novelist's unique capacity to write historical figures who feel familiar, to reveal the past as challengingly continuous with the present. For Mantel, her novels tell history as political, for 'There is no life without politics'.[1] But as the success of the dramatic adaptations of the first two Cromwell novels, Olivier- and Tony-award-winning *Wolf Hall* and *Bring Up the Bodies*, has perhaps already suggested, her novels are also profoundly theatrical. Meanwhile, in a rather different Tudor register, but also revealing a curious sense of both the theatricality and the immediacy of history, *SIX* reopened at the Lyric Theatre, London:

> It's a usual story ... the savvy, educated young princess
> Deemed repulsive by the wheezing, wrinkled, ulcerated man
> Twenty-four years her senior.
>
> <div align="right">Anna of Cleves, <i>SIX</i></div>

SIX, a musical about Tudor history written by a pair of Cambridge undergraduates for the 2017 Edinburgh Fringe, has become the perhaps rather surprising object of mass teenage adulation on both sides of the Atlantic. Taken up by talent scouts, it transferred, with a professional cast, to the Arts Theatre in the West End, and was due to open on Broadway just as the theatres closed for the COVID pandemic: its first Broadway performance was thus delayed until 17 September 2021. It imagines a pop contest among six queens, in which the role of lead singer will be awarded to whichever queen can prove she has suffered most at the hands of their common husband, Henry VIII. Each in turn has a song with which to make her case, until the last queen, Catherine Parr, questions whether it is right that they

---

[1] Mantel made this comment on the BBC Radio 4's *Today* Programme on 21 May 2021. The interview is covered at <www.bbc.co.uk/news/entertainment-arts-57157878>.

should all allow themselves to be defined in relation to their husband – they have spent 'too many years stuck in his-story'. The queens agree that they do not need Henry, and in a grand finale imagine their stories rewritten as musical successes: Catherine of Aragon joins a gospel choir; Anne Boleyn becomes a song-writer for Shakespeare; Jane Seymour has several more children and sets up a family rock group, 'The Royalling Stones', and so on …

SIX has some gloriously witty lyrics, drawing on true details of the queens' lives, and its music, in various modern genres, ranges from the soulful to the irresistibly joyful. Each queen tells her history in the music style of a different modern pop diva: Catherine of Aragon is partly modelled on J-Lo; Anne Boleyn on Miley Cyrus, Jane Seymour on Adele. Undoubtedly, *SIX*'s popularity is therefore indebted to the popularity of these stars and their musical styles. But I think there is something more that makes *SIX* 'the most uplifting new British musical I have ever had the privilege to watch' (Fiona Mountford, in the *Evening Standard*, 5 September 2018).[2] On YouTube you can watch a recording of a flashmob performance of the musical's theme song at the Tower of London: huge crowds are gathered to sing and dance; young girls in the audience are moved to hysterical tears when their idols, the *SIX* stars, arrive to join in.[3] Comments from YouTube viewers include 'Somewhere in heaven, the Queens are smiling and dancing along in joy'; furthermore, 'two of the queens were executed at the Tower, but in some way *SIX* the Musical kinda reclaimed the place in honor of all the queens', and 'this is a mass two-finger salute to Henry'.

The imaginative engagement with history that these comments reflect is extraordinary; that such an engagement is also deeply affective is as indisputable as it is bizarre – many comments on the flashmob and also on the stage musical mention people being moved to tears: 'I'm crying happy tears now', 'this made me cry so hard'. Perhaps this is connected in some way to the equally surprising fact that the flashmob and the musical are described repeatedly as 'wholesome' – 'one of the most wholesome and welcoming experiences of my life'. How did a history of marital violence and abuse become a 'wholesome' musical?

Explicitly, *SIX* celebrates the idea that a good life should not depend on the opinions of others. Little wonder that the first queen to recognize this is 'the Ugly one' – Anna of Cleves. Her story is prefaced by an ensemble

---

2 Used in *SIX*'s publicity handouts.
3 <www.youtube.com/watch?v=1zswkYhE8_0>.

number, 'The Haus of Holbein', which imagines a beauty parlour in which European princesses are prepared for their portraits by the German master painter: famously, Henry chose Anna after seeing her Holbein portrait, but then rejected her because she was not as pretty as her picture. 'The Haus of Holbein' parodies past and present obsessions with 'fixing' women's appearances: it advocates corsets and cinches, make-up containing poisonous lead, and heels so high that 'we cannot guarantee that you'll still walk at forty'; women who are reluctant to suffer to be beautiful are urged to ignore their fears in order to 'turn this *vier* into a *neun*'. But of course, women who have been painted or airbrushed are almost certain to disappoint in the flesh: as Anna's own song puts it, 'You say that I tricked ya, 'cos I didn't look like my profile picture'.

However, Anna's song, 'Get Down', cannot remain sad beyond its first line – 'sitting here all alone' – for she is 'on a throne' and 'in a palace that I happen to own'. Her marriage to Henry annulled, and a healthy settlement guaranteed ('check out my pre-nup') she is able to live as she wishes, with no man to tell her what to do: on her own terms she enjoys the dance floor, where she looks 'more rad than Lutheranism'; even with 'All eyes on me' there is 'no criticism' for the woman who 'Don't got no marriage'.

By contrast Catherine Howard's song, 'All You Wanna Do', exposes the powerlessness of the girl who is an object of desire: it presents its singer as a sexy rock chick while gradually revealing her history of abuse. *SIX*'s writers, Toby Marlow and Lucy Moss, acknowledge as their main sources Antonia Fraser's best-selling *Six Wives of Henry VIII*[4] and the BBC2 television series 'Six Wives with Lucy Worsley', itself strongly influenced by Fraser's book. Worsley offers a strikingly impassioned plea for a new understanding of Catherine Howard: Henry's fifth Queen was not a 'good time girl' but the victim of abuse that began when she was thirteen years old and in the care of the Duchess of Norfolk. The Duchess failed to protect Catherine from sexual exploitation by the Duchess's Secretary, Francis Dereham, and the girl's music teacher, Henry Mannox; Catherine was thus horrifically groomed – for her marriage to the much older Henry, but also for the rapist Thomas Culpepper, who became the teenage queen's predator: her response to him may have been that of the placatory victim (he was a violent man) and not the sincere lover, but it led in any case to her beheading. Marlow and Moss take up Worsley's account in a song that, although just as packed with witty

---

4   Antonia Fraser *The Six Wives of Henry VIII* (London: Weidenfeld and Nicolson, 1992).

puns as those of the other queens, nonetheless also portrays the psychology of the abused with a power that feels like a punch in the stomach. 'All You Wanna Do' is all the more disturbing for telling Catherine's story with a catchy tune: 'He just cares so much it feels legit', she sings, and 'I'm sure this time it's different', but eventually Culpepper is not 'the friend I need, just mates' and 'it's never ever different'.

Of course it is not Catherine's self-proclaimed status as 'the ten among these threes' but the sexualization of her childhood ('He was 23 and I was 13 going on 30') that is tragic. But the juxtaposition of Catherine's song with that of Anna of Cleves, liberated because un-desired, is particularly poignant. Anna actually decides to drop out of the competition because she discovers that according to her own judgement she is not really suffering at all. In the final number of the musical, with the re-imagined histories, she returns to Cleves triumphant and teaches Holbein's 'super arty' mates 'how to party'.

Responses to the queens vary with the age of the audience member. My own entirely unscientific study, conducted among friends and their children, suggests that eleven-year-olds like Anne Boleyn best, because she is 'cool', and 'she'd be my friend', and women with teenage daughters also enjoy Anne Boleyn because her ironically titled song, 'Don't lose your head', presents a marvellous parody of teen-speak. (To a boppy tune she proclaims that she is 'just trying to have some fun', texting Henry 'XO baby'; she is 'Sorry not sorry' for, among other things, causing Henry to break with Rome, which is 'totes God's will', but in the end her father's hideously punning advice that she should 'get a-head' puts her in a situation in which she must lose hers.) However, eighteen-year-old girls respond most strongly to Catherine Howard, because they identify with her unsuccessful attempts to find friendship through sexual attractiveness; these girls did not seem to find Catherine Howard as chillingly tragic as I did. Catherine of Aragon was praised as 'unapologetic', 'bold', and 'regal' for her song asserting that 'there's no no no no no no no way' that she can be replaced, but Jane Seymour's ballad about her 'perfect family', while 'a good song', presented an ideal that seemed inaccessible. Catherine Parr's 'calm confidence' was admired: her lyrical 'I don't need your love' wonderfully recalls that 'I wrote books and psalms and meditations | Fought for female education', and concludes: 'Why can't I tell that story?', leading to the musical's revisionist ending. But Anna of Cleves's song is the musical highlight, and Anna herself was characterized as 'unique'. To younger audiences, in an interesting reversal of 'Anne Boleyn would be my friend', she is 'someone you would want to hang out with' – she is aspirational rather than accessible. And older women love the wit of her rhymes.

SIX's Anna is the woman who defines herself, who revels in her independence, who does not care about how she looks to others – she is the feminist, the smart, sassy corrective to an image-obsessed age – hers, and ours. Paradoxical though it sounds, might Anna of Cleves's 'moment' be now?

Unfortunately, maybe not – or at least, not entirely. Indeed, recent attempts to re-imagine Anna seem in many cases to have taken giant steps backwards from the portrayal of her in *The Private Life of Henry VIII*, a film made in 1933. There, the free-thinking Anne plays cards with Henry on their wedding night, and claims her freedom from him as her prize. She wants a divorce so she can marry another man (although the historical Anna never did marry again). Much of the interest of this film lies in a complex case of reality mirroring fiction, for real-life husband and wife Charles Laughton and Elsa Lanchester played Henry and Anna; Laughton and Lanchester remained married, though Lanchester's autobiography claims that they were childless because Laughton was in fact gay. But the film itself is empowering to Anna, who deliberately makes herself unattractive to Henry – so although it is about her looks, at least she is in control of her image.

By contrast, in 2019 Alison Weir published the fourth volume of her 'Six Tudor Queens' series, *Anna of Kleve: Queen of Secrets*.[5] The book begins with Anna in Cleves secretly bearing a child to her lover, her charming illegitimate cousin, Otho, who then becomes part of her court after the annulment of her marriage with Henry, and brings their son to join her. If the author, with an eye to the modern reader, wants to show us a woman who has experienced real love, the story also of course justifies Henry's historical claims that his fourth wife's belly and breasts revealed her to be no virgin. Henry's preoccupations continue to drive the story.

More than seven decades earlier, Margaret Campbell Barnes's 1946 novel *My Lady of Cleves* also gave Anna a secret passion, but here it is Holbein himself – a man who bears a 'fortuitous resemblance' to Henry and at the same time grew up near Cleves and, like Anna, misses the 'vast skyscapes'.[6] The novel thus provides a rationale for Anna's response to Holbein, but the

---

5 Alison Weir *Anna of Kleve: Queen of Secrets* (London: Headline Review, 2019).
6 Margaret Campbell Barnes *My Lady of Cleves* (Philadelphia: Macrae Smith, 1946) 9.

entire narrative seems preoccupied with explaining the 'flattering' nature of Anna's portrait as presenting her through the eyes of her lover.

In Mavis Cheek's 2008 novel *Amenable Women*, Flora Chapman, a modern day widow whose house has been built on land that once belonged to Anna of Cleves, is rather relieved at the death of her husband, who constantly belittled her for her plainness (he called her 'Bun Face') and who had an affair with a younger woman; she finds an imaginative kinship with Henry's rejected fourth wife. We can well imagine that Anna, like Flora, is happier without her husband, because Cheek focuses on the husband's failings – or as Anne comments wryly in *SIX*: 'I didn't look as good | As I did in my pic. | Funny how we all discuss that | But never Henry's little —'.

Flora further identifies with Anna because Anna's allowance, like Flora's pension, was cut when her husband died, and because 'Anne sounded practical and sensible, at least'[7] – this is Anna, Queen of the WI, not *SIX*'s Queen of the dance floor. But most importantly, Flora identifies with Anna as a woman considered plain, so Anna disappointingly continues to be defined by other people's opinions of her looks, for all that Flora tries to make the best of things:

> One thing you could say about being plain in youth was that you remained at that level, approximately, well into your middle age. Suddenly you were ahead of the frightened beauties who began to crumble since you never had anything to boast about in the first place.[8]

In this novel, the Holbein portrait is imagined coming to life at night and chatting to other portraits in the Louvre. But, as Hilary Mantel complains, the effect is not empowering, because of the banal nature of her chatter which focuses once again on her appearance, and – rather clumsily – on explaining why novelists like Campbell Barnes are wrong about her. Mantel writes that it is part of the puzzle that the divorced Queen never, for the rest of her life, talked about what happened between her and Henry: Anna fascinates because she is silent.[9]

---

7   Mavis Cheek *Amenable Women* (London: Faber, 2008) 46.

8   Cheek *Amenable Women* 232. Flora also complains (232) that a common plainness was supposed to be the basis of Mary I's friendship with Anna.

9   See Hilary Mantel 'The Flanders Nightmare', *The Guardian*, 19th April 2008 <www.theguardian.com/books/2008/apr/19/featuresreviews.guardianreview18>.

Mantel's own presentation of Anna, in *The Mirror and the Light*, is always through the eyes of others – ambassadors, statesmen, ladies-in-waiting, and finally the novel's protagonist, Thomas Cromwell. Cromwell finds her on first view 'a pleasant-looking woman, who might be married to one of your friends; the city wife of a city merchant',[10] but then on seeing her dressed for her wedding observes that 'she no longer looks like a grocer's wife, but like what she is: a princess whose childhood was spent in a high castle on a crag, from where you can see for miles'.[11] She thus vindicates the assurances Cromwell repeatedly gives Henry that Anna's fashion and manners may be changed – and thus could adapt to suit the King's preferences; perhaps Mantel hints also at an idea that Cromwell as well as Henry sees in a woman what he wants for himself. But Cromwell seems also to recognize Anna's dignity by imagining her not as looked at, but as looking – from an exalted position (a high castle) – and seeing far. When he thinks of advising her to consider the opinions of others, particularly through the example of another queen, Katherine of Aragon, his own advice is exposed:

> If he were to counsel Anna, it would be to patience. The dowager Katherine won the admiration of all, when she sat smiling by the king she supposed her husband ... Never was she seen with tears on her cheeks, or an angry frown.
>
> 'Yes', Bess says, 'Katherine was a great pattern for womanhood. She died alone and friendless, did she not?'[12]

When he instead imagines Anna's own point of view, he seems to reach something more authentic:

> Call-Me says, 'You can work with the pre-contract, sir ... We would have to find a pension for the lady. And whatever the brother demands, by way of recompense. Though as she is still a maid, Cleves may find her another husband ...'
>
> He thinks, Anna may feel she has had enough of men.[13]

---

10   Hilary Mantel *The Mirror and the Light* (New York: Henry Holt, 2020) 732.
11   Mantel *The Mirror* 740.
12   Mantel *The Mirror* 788–9.
13   Mantel *The Mirror* 802.

In a novel that derives its power from an alignment of Cromwell's imaginings with those of the author, Mantel does not feel the need to give Anna another love interest. *The Mirror and the Light* hints at what *SIX* boldly raps out: Anna's good life does not depend on the admiration of others, or even of one man.

In the most brash, ebullient way, the musical *SIX* at once recognizes the victimhood of Henry's queens and challenges us to see them as more than victims, because the magic of theatre, which reanimates the dead, allows them to present themselves with all the energy of the subject. Of course, *SIX*, for all its witty allusions to historical details, is not concerned to tell historical 'truth', but rather to point out that the 'truths' we have are partial, lazy, and prejudiced. Theatre is the ideal form for such a message because in theatre each character may present themselves freed from the judgement of an external narrator, and there may be as many valid perspectives as there are characters onstage. In re-telling history, the theatre alone allows the revenant to speak their own point of view.

Mantel of course is writing novels, not plays, but her Cromwell trilogy is full of references to Tudor theatre – indeed *Wolf Hall* is prefaced by the cast list of *Magnyfycence*, a play by royal tutor John Skelton in which he offered warnings and advice to the young Henry VIII. Interludes and masques are frequently described in the novels: a play of 'Britannia Undefeated' is presented at Anna's wedding. Mantel is aware of the role such interludes played in the life of Henry's court, but her evocations of them are not merely for historical authenticity. She consciously draws on theatrical effects to allow the dead to perform. This is beautifully exemplified in her treatment of Anna's first meeting with Henry.

The known historical details of this meeting are distilled from contemporary papers by Antonia Fraser in her *The Six Wives of Henry VIII*, an important source for Cheek, Weir, and Mantel, as well as for the writers of *SIX*. Anna having travelled from Cleves and arrived at Rochester, the King became impatient to meet his fiancée, and in order to 'nourish love' disguised himself and surprised her as she was watching a New Year's Day bull-baiting. She, not recognizing him, paid him no attention, until he returned in his royal cloak and she 'humbled herself lowly' before him.[14]

---

14 Fraser *Six Wives* 373–4. Fraser draws on sources including the depositions of the Earl of Southampton, Sir Anthony Browne, and Charles Wriothesley as recorded in John Strype *Ecclesiastical Memorials ... of the Church of England under Henry VIII* 3 vols

ELISABETH DUTTON

Historical accounts of the meeting are fundamentally theatrical. Most obviously, perhaps, there is Henry's disguising: he comes to Anna in a cloak of 'marble colour' – multicoloured – and the gentlemen of the Privy Chamber who travel with him are all dressed in the same way. Then there is Henry's reappearance in the purple velvet cloak. Ideally this would be the removal of a disguise to reveal the true identity underneath, but in practice it is a costume change: not having met the man, Anna cannot recognize King Henry until he puts on royal robes. The meeting thus reveals the truth that 'the king is but a man, as I am', to quote another king in disguise.[15] But the meeting also stages spectatorship in intriguing – and, to Anna, confusing – ways. Anna is the spectator, watching a bull-baiting. Henry aspires to create an alternative spectacle for Anna to watch, but she does not recognize the performance as such, which disappoints its star. That this is so deeply problematic is of course because Henry wishes to be both actor *and* spectator, for he has come to inspect his new Queen. And Anna has no idea that the significance of the moment is not a scene of bull-baiting to which she is spectator, but rather a scene of royal courtship in which she must perform for a royal audience.

Our accounts of the meeting are those of spectators such as the Earl of Southampton, Master of the Horse Sir Anthony Browne, and officer at arms Charles Wriothesley – but of course it is the inaccessible feelings of the actors that make this moment historically significant, for it led Henry to comment 'I like her not', and quickly to annul his marriage. Alison Weir shows Anna's feelings by maintaining her position as spectator observing the king, 'a massively fat man with thinning hair' and 'a sour, sickly smell of sweat and something worse':[16] just as Henry is supposed to have found Anna wanting in relation to her portrait, so Weir imagines Anna disgusted by the contrast between Henry now and a portrait she has seen of him in his

(Oxford: Clarendon Press, 1822) *1:2* 454–63; 'Four Original Documents relating to the Marriage of Henry VIII and Anne of Cleves 1539–40' (Historical Reprints 12; 1886) 5–16, 22–4 in *A Collection of Eighteen Rare and Curious Historical Tracts and Pamphlets* edited E. Marsden and G. Goldsmid (Edinburgh: privately printed, 1884–6); and Charles Wriothesley's direct account in his *A Chronicle of England during the Reigns of the Tudors, from AD 1485 TO 1559* edited William Douglas Hamilton, 2 vols Camden Society NS 11 & 20 (1875, 1877) *1* 109–10.

15 William Shakespeare *Henry V* IV.1
16 Weir *Anna of Kleve* 124.

youth.[17] Barnes has Anna tricked by English ladies into trying on a blonde wig, so that, in another type of theatre, which Anna equates to prostitution, she can please the King by resembling Jane Seymour.[18] She is still wearing the unbecoming wig, and un-stayed and un-gowned, when Henry arrives: 'Never was woman taken at greater disadvantage'.[19] Although Barnes narrates the scene from Anna's point of view, what Anna observes is not Henry's grossness but his 'disappointment' in her, his 'cheerful, rubicund face' pained like that of 'a child deprived at the last minute of some promised treat'. Astonishingly, Barnes imagines that 'even in her humiliation' Anna feels a 'mothering instinct' to comfort the King.[20]

By contrast Mantel, brilliantly, focuses on the theatrical elements to tell her story, precisely because in theatre, with bodies to watch but no omniscient narrator, we infer characters' responses from their actions, expression, and the words they use. She uses a Messenger's speech: the account of Henry and Anna's meeting is relayed through Gregory, Thomas Cromwell's son. It is made a performance:

> He thinks of the scenes he used to stage with George Cavendish, the cardinal's man. He would say 'Show me how it was, George – who sat where, who spoke first.' And Cavendish would jump up and play the king.
>
> He can lay out this stage in his mind, where bride and groom meet: the old hall at Rochester, the great fireplace with its carved emblems: a fern, a heart, a Welsh dragon holding an orb. He can follow the king with his train of merry men; they hold their masks loosely, playfully, because they expect to be recognized in seconds. And indeed, as they pass, the new queen's servants kneel.
>
> 'Anna was warned?' he asks. 'She was ready?'
>
> 'She was warned, but she was not ready. The king billowed in, but she was looking out of the window – they were baiting a bull in the courtyard. She cast a glance over her shoulder, then she turned away to the sport.' ...

---

17   Weir *Anna of Kleve* 125.
18   Barnes *My Lady* 73.
19   Barnes *My Lady* 85.
20   Barnes *My Lady* 86.

'The king bowed low.' Gregory takes a gulp of wine. 'And addressed her, but she did not turn. I think she took him for – I do not know what – some Jolly Jankin dressed up for the festival. And so he stood, his hat in his hand – then her people swarmed in, and someone called out, "Madam," and a phrase to alert her …' Gregory falters. 'And then she turned. And she knew who he was. And as Christ is my Saviour, Father, the look in her eye! I will never forget it.' Gregory sits down, as if at the end of his strength. 'Nor will the king.'[21]

In order to understand the meeting, Cromwell must through his son's account re-stage it in his mind – the theatre here is like a police reconstruction of a crime. The reconstruction captures set (the old hall, the great fireplace, the attendant merry men) and actions (a glance, a bow, Henry's hat in hand) as well as lines, although interestingly two of these are not fully given but their places indicated: he addressed her, there was a phrase to alert her; the only actual scripted line is 'Madam', anonymously called out. There is only one moment of speculation about the characters' thoughts, and it is highly tentative: 'I think she took him for – I do not know what …' We are told nothing about how Anna looks: that she was 'not ready' might indicate something about her dress, but here seems to indicate something heavier, about her lack of inner preparedness for Henry.

We are told nothing either about how Henry looks, although Cromwell later comments that 'the king's looks tell the tale'. Suggestively, one's 'looks' are both one's physical attractiveness as perceived by others, and the expressions with which one regards others (as in the phrase 'he gave her a stern look'). The tale that the King's looks tell is about himself, not about Anna: performing for a full house, 'all the people who crowded into the room at Rochester, to see him nourish love', he is shocked by Anna's response into becoming his own spectator: 'he saw himself in the mirror of her eyes'.[22] For a moment, the play is interrupted, and it is this, not anything about Anna's person, that dooms their relationship.

However, the crowd in the room at Rochester is still spectating, and the show must go on. Anna has realized she is part of the scene, and begins to perform:

21   Mantel *The Mirror* 724–5.
22   Mantel *The Mirror* 752.

> 'Then she recovered herself. She dissimulated marvellous well. And so did he. She said in English, "My lord and my king, welcome."'
>
> It was for him to say, welcome. 'Go on.'

Although she mistakenly speaks Henry's line, she nonetheless makes an appropriate gesture, and the King is able to rescue the performance:

> 'She made a smooth curtsey, very low, as if nothing had occurred. And the king smiled and uplifted her. He said, "Welcome, sweetheart."' What it is to be royal, he thinks.[23]

Brilliantly, Mantel finishes her re-staging of the scene not with a comment on love or beauty, but with Cromwell's reflection – sympathetic? impressed? – on Henry and Anna's performance of royalty. Cheek has Anna's portrait describe the meeting to her modern admirer, Flora: Anna was watching the bull-baiting, and continued to do so not because she did not recognize the King but because she was in shock. 'Where was my golden prince, my noble paramour? Henry VIII was gross, red-faced, panting and sweating, old and virtually slavering. I was speechless with disgust and horror ... and I was not a coquette to act pleased.'[24] But of course it is not the coquette who must fake love, nor the prostitute of Barnes's blonde wig: it is for royalty to perform political alliances as if they were romantic plotlines.

It is not that royalty is a form of theatre, but rather that royalty is one consistent theatrical role by which individuals are constrained. The Duke and Duchess of Sussex may have discovered that this has not changed in centuries: their decision, in 2020, to step back from their royal positions, move to the US, and become financially independent was perhaps driven by the incompatibility of their private, personal aspirations with the inflexible model of public royal life. There is no real variety for royal performance.

Mantel's dramatic reconstruction of Anna's historically significant first meeting with the King avoids putting words into her head, and instead emphasizes the cataclysmic effect of Anna's momentary instinctive seeing, rather than performing being seen. A queen must always be the spectacle, rather than the spectator. The queens of *SIX* are spectacular, and of course

---

23 Mantel *The Mirror* 725.
24 Cheek *Amenable Women* 140.

though the West End theatre may give them a voice, we only remember them now because they were married to Henry. But if, as Katherine Parr argues, the queens should take their moment to define themselves independently of their husband, it is Anna of Cleves, the woman who was better at looking than being looked at, who shows them all the wholesome joy of liberation from 'his-story'.

University of Fribourg, Switzerland

Acknowledgements

Elisabeth Dutton gratefully acknowledges Harper Collins, for permission to quote from Hilary Mantel *The Mirror and the Light* (New York: Henry Holt, 2020), and the BBC for permission to quote from the interview with Mantel on BBC Radio 4's *Today* Programme on 21 May 2021, as covered on the BBC website <www.bbc.co.uk/news/entertainment-arts-57157878>.

EDITORIAL BOARD (2021)

Executive Editor:
   Meg Twycross (Lancaster University).
General Editors:
   Sarah Carpenter (University of Edinburgh),
   Elisabeth Dutton (Université de Fribourg),
   Gordon Kipling (UCLA).
Advisory Board:
   Phil Butterworth (University of Leeds),
   Garrett Epp (University of Alberta, Université Catholique de Lille)
   Richard Hillman (Université de Tours)
   Pamela M. King (University of Glasgow),
   Sally-Beth MacLean (University of Toronto),
   James McBain (Green Templeton College, Oxford),
   John J. McGavin (University of Southampton),
   John McKinnell (University of Durham),
   Peter Meredith (University of Leeds),
   Tom Pettitt (University of Southern Denmark, Odense),
   Matthew Sergi (University of Toronto),
   Greg Walker (University of Edinburgh).
Latin Consultant: Alison Samuels (Oxford)
Subscriptions Editor: Clare Egan (Lancaster University)

SUBMISSION OF ARTICLES

Contributions for consideration should be sent to one of the editors:

Meg Twycross, Department of English and Creative Writing, Lancaster University, LANCASTER LA1 4YD, United Kingdom
E-mail: m.twycross@lancaster.ac.uk

Sarah Carpenter, English Literature, School of Literatures, Languages and Cultures, University of Edinburgh, 50 George Square, EDINBURGH EH8 9LH, United Kingdom.
E-mail: Sarah.Carpenter@ed.ac.uk

Elisabeth Dutton, English Department, University of Fribourg, Ave. Europe 20, CH1700 FRIBOURG, Switzerland.
E-mail: elisabeth.dutton@unifr.ch

Gordon Kipling, 3428 Park Avenue, MINNEAPOLIS, MN 55407, USA
E-mail: kipling@humnet.ucla.edu

Articles should usually be sent as e-mail attachments, preferably in a recent version of 'Word'. See website for further information:
<www.medievalenglishtheatre.co.uk/submit.html>

Contributors are asked to follow the *METh* house-style (see website: address above). The language of publication is usually English, and translations should be supplied for quotations from all other languages, including French and Latin.

Printed in the United States
by Baker & Taylor Publisher Services